C000261683

'Welcoming church congregations are
can have a powerful, redemptive influ
of prison. I'm aware of wonderful ex:
around for good from this type of mir
Andrew Selous MP

'*Working with Released Prisoners* is a meticulous piece of work that is
a much-needed guide for anyone who seeks to work with ex-
prisoners.

'Having worked with the author of this book for fourteen years
within the chaplaincy department, I watched as he steadfastly
collated information and identified gaps in the system in order to
halt the "revolving gate" lifestyle that becomes the norm for many
prisoners. Working as I do with men in transition from
incarceration to freedom, I feel that this book has hit the nail on
the head, for forethought and wisdom. The clarity, which is the
pattern throughout the writing, offers a wealth of practical, tried
and tested methods that give an optimum outcome.

'This book is derived not only from personal experience, but
also from meticulously detailed research into a subject that has
haunted the writer throughout his years of working with, and caring
for, ex-prisoners. His heart is in the detail. The use of Scripture
throughout to illustrate the practicalities means that this is a
spiritual teaching as well as being informative for the reader.

'The author challenges us throughout not just to be concerned
for released prisoners, but to be moved to do the work the Bible
teaches in difficult and challenging circumstances.'
*Rev Sandie Hicks, Minister, Brightlingsea Baptist Church, Essex' former
Chaplain to HMP Dovegate*

WORKING WITH RELEASED PRISONERS

STEPHEN DAILLY

instant
apostle

First published in Great Britain in 2019

Instant Apostle
The Barn
1 Watford House Lane
Watford
Herts
WD17 1BJ

The views and opinions expressed in this work are those of the author and do not necessarily reflect the views and opinions of the publisher.

British Library Cataloguing-in-Publication Data

A catalogue record for this book is available from the British Library

This book and all other Instant Apostle books are available from Instant Apostle:

Website: www.instantapostle.com

E-mail: info@instantapostle.com

ISBN 978-1-909728-96-7

Printed in Great Britain

In memory of Helena Price

Contents

Acknowledgements

First, I must say 'Thank you' to Simon Edwards, without whose heart, pioneering vision and hard work there would be very little to write about. When I met him, I was a chaplaincy volunteer at Her Majesty's Prison (HMP) Dovegate and he was serving a type of life sentence. He's now my boss (I guess we crossed a few 'boundaries' there, bro!). In building Walk Ministries, we've walked far together, but I've seen him go into places that I couldn't and wouldn't dare go. I'm proud to call him my friend.

Thanks also to Karen, Simon's wife, who makes sure the lights stay on at Walk and generally keeps everything and everyone in order. She read an early draft of this text and made sensible suggestions.

Thanks to Wez Johnson, who contributed a couple of sections to the book. Wez is another man with a passion for Jesus and a desire to see prisoners set free. At the time of writing, he manages the accommodation at Walk.

Thanks to Ray Duckworth for his Foreword. Ray has had a long career in the Prison Service; when I first met him, he was head of security at Dovegate and had not long been a Christian (thereby hangs another long tale, but this is not the place to unfurl it). He later became director of the Therapeutic Prison at Dovegate and later of the whole establishment. Subsequently he moved to take over running another prison in the south-west, guiding it through a period of change, before retiring from the service. He has recently been engaged in research into desistance, particularly the role of faith-based rehabilitation.

Thanks also to Tony Davis, who helped with the chapter on 'Working with Those in Dependency and Addiction', and to Carol

Riley, who assisted with the chapter on 'Working with Women'. Both have significant expertise and experience.

Finally here, thanks to the men who have kindly allowed me to make use of their experiences. I have disguised their identities and changed some details, but I hope I haven't garbled them too much: Paul, Mick, James, Rob, Andy, Pete, Ant, Steven, Luke and John.

Beyond this particular book, I would like to acknowledge some of the Christian brothers and sisters who have inspired and guided me in working with prisoners and ex-prisoners over the years, many of whom are or have been chaplains in various prisons: Rev John Fagan; Rev Jo Honour, who led a lovely ministry at HMP Foston Hall; Rev Peter Douglas, who prayer-walked the site of Dovegate while it was still a large and muddy hole in the ground; Rev Sandie Hicks, whose open-hearted willingness to follow Jesus 'whatever' continues to inspire; Rev Tony Rigby, Dave Myers and the late Rev Richard Bailey. Between them, Sandie, Tony, Dave and Richard in their various capacities must have guided about a thousand prisoners to Christ during a period of eight years at Dovegate, among whom was Simon Edwards. Also part of this story are: Lasona Moore, Richard Wisdom, Di Cutler, Andrea Stafford and Jan Lovell.

The writer to the Hebrews says that we are surrounded by a great 'cloud of witnesses', the heroes of our Faith. These are some of my 'heroes'.

Thanks finally to the team at Instant Apostle who have brought this book to birth, particularly to Manoj, who saw the need for it, and Sheila, who is a super-efficient editor.

Foreword
Ray Duckworth

England and Wales has the biggest prison populations per capita in Western Europe.[1] In the last thirty years of my career as a director of private prisons, I have witnessed at first hand the challenges that prisoners face throughout their custodial lives, and when they are finally released out of the prison gates and back into our society. Regrettably, and all too often, they return to prison, either recalled under their licence conditions, or remanded in custody for additional crimes committed during the honeymoon days of their release.

For some individuals, their time in society can last hours; others manage longer. I have seen and been part of the Ministry of Justice resettlement agenda. It is woefully under-resourced and limited in its understanding of the challenges faced by ex-offenders on release; quite simply, when ex-offenders leave prison they become the responsibility of the National Probation Service (NPS) and Community Rehabilitation Companies (CRCs). They fall under another service provider and another budget. Those who are fortunate enough to have been provided with a resettlement course in prison have merely passed through a tick-box exercise that modern government managerialism uses to measure its key performance target to justify the financial spend. Too much focus is placed on service delivery and value for money; the system is compartmentalised and disjointed.

With a high recidivism rate for ex-offenders, it would be obvious to anyone that the current strategy for rehabilitation and

---

[1] Jones, 2017.

resettlement is failing the public purse, and society. The Payment by Results (PbR) agenda, where private prisons and CRCs are paid for their success in keeping prisoners out of prison, has fallen by the wayside because it is too expensive and difficult to do.

The NPS has been torn apart in favour of privatisation and the introduction of CRCs. The NPS is underfunded and disfranchised and the CRCs are working to a service contract that provides efficient systems of measurement, removing the individual from the service. Resettlement Prisons, introduced as a result of a recent strategic restructuring exercise, are proving inadequate and under-resourced and yet the resettlement boxes are being ticked and the statistics satisfy ministers.

Those individuals who have paid their dues to society, or are completing sentences in our communities, are left to fend for themselves, ill-equipped and ill-supported to deal with the challenges that modern society brings; try claiming benefits and you will see how difficult it is! Universal Credit (UC) may be sound in theory, but in practice I believe it almost encourages individuals to take the law into their own hands!

For many, very little has been done in custody to address the individual's practical deficits in the basic domestic planning and organisation that are necessary to manage a home. Very little support is provided in prison for basic skills such as money management, budgeting, problem-solving and building emotional resilience. All these deficits were clearly evident when they were first incarcerated; however, the emphasis is placed on education and key skills that are measurable and provide good educational abilities, and resources are focused on educational attainment and employment skills, not on the basic life skills required.

Prisons continue to turn out 'offending behaviour' courses as an answer to the reoffending and recidivism. I have spent a career delivering key performance targets for prison performance ratings. A simple understanding of 'cause and effect' would quickly highlight that the crimes committed by the majority of prisoners are the result of poor emotional resilience, poor problem-solving and poor judgement, stemming from the lack of basic moral fibre.

Prisons have become holding pens for men to simply bide their time until release. Of course, there are some fantastic examples of prisons that are getting it right; however, over the years, budget cuts have seen good, experienced prison staff paid off to save money and a great deal of good practice lost. Generally speaking, when you cut budgets, all the added value in services is stripped away and replaced by the basic delivery provision. This basic stripping away of services results in further institutionalisation of individuals.

Prison provides prisoners with a regime that is both reliable and predictable: food, clothing, utilities, washing, cooking, entertainment and relationships, both constructive and destructive, where planning, organisation and problem-solving is done for them. If a prisoner has a problem, they inform an officer, who will try to solve the problem for them, because time spent out of cells becomes limited. Years spent in prison has both a neurological and psychological impact on prisoners. If you 'don't use it you lose it'; the lack of activity over time causes prisoners to lose their ability to deal with simple everyday tasks such as problem-solving and decision-making. Our world is more technologically based than ever and so many people are becoming marginalised by their inability to understand and use new technology and the internet; prisoners have the same dilemma.

Leaving custody presents the thrill of release and freedom that very quickly turns into an unfamiliar and very unfair place. Prisoners are given their discharge grant and their belongings and told to report to their probation officer or CRC by a certain time, if they have a licence. The majority leave with an address for accommodation but no idea what they are walking into. Most head for the nearest pub for a few drinks; some return to the dealers to feed their habit that has been either maintained or developed in prison. It is generally accepted that moving home is one of the most stressful experiences that people have, yet the service fails to understand this basic concept.

All ex-offenders wear the invisible badge of ex-con for the rest of their lives; this is their psychological burden and a significant pain of imprisonment. When they do well, you hear the good news of someone who has changed their life; when people talk about that person they tend to prefix their name with 'the ex-prisoner' or 'ex-offender' John. The label will always go with them.

Businesses say that they are equal employers and welcome ex-offenders, but very few actually live by the rhetoric. Work is hard to come by for anyone who has served time. The ex-offender is immediately judged for any poor decision they make and is castigated accordingly. Depending on what they look like, they are categorised: if they are thin and small they are a drug addict; if they are old, overweight or odd-looking they are a sex offender. Most people want to naturally protect themselves from the bad element of society, so not surprisingly ex-offenders are reticent about disclosing their past. When the sentence for the crime committed has been paid and the ex-prisoner re-enters society, where can they turn to for help? Society, generally speaking, is unforgiving. People never forget. Once a con, always a con.

While we focus on the offender, we must never forget the victims whose lives are changed forever by the criminal actions of those people serving sentences. No matter what crime is committed, someone somewhere is affected by it. Criminal actions cause an immense amount of hurt, pain, suffering and fear in our society, which can last for a lifetime. As a society we must try to find a solution to the crime problem. With so many prisoners returning to prison, if we can start here we can make a difference to ex-offenders and potential future victims of crime.

The government is absolutely reliant on third sector providers to help ex-offenders when they are released from custody. There is no direct funding for the bespoke services that many faith-based organisations provide. There are many charities that are working tirelessly to help ex-offenders to resettle into communities, and all have their own methods of approach; they have learned from their mistakes and become better and better over the years. There are a number of charities that are truly making a difference to ex-offenders' lives and significantly improving the potential of ex-offenders to go 'straight' and become assets to society.

This book provides you, the reader, with a practical understanding of the challenges faced by those individuals who have paid their price, or are paying their price, for their past. The book provides an ethnographic view of the lives that have passed through Walk Ministries, providing an invaluable understanding of the thoughts and feelings of men who have been through the criminal justice system and been ejected into society. The poignant vignettes provide us with a true understanding of what it is like for someone when they are released from prison.

The honesty that the writer provides about the journey of Walk Ministries and the wisdom gleaned from many experiences are invaluable to any faith-based organisation seeking to do something to help offenders when they leave prison. Working with ex-offenders is not for the faint-hearted; ex-offenders present opportunities that undoubtedly challenge even the most eager Christians.

Walk Ministries, through their consistent approach and continuous love for the fallen, have shown us how it can be done. They have grown over the years into an organisation able and equipped to give hope and life to those who have nothing but Jesus to turn to. The path is narrow but the rewards are great!

Ray Duckworth has had a career in the Prison Service that culminated in being director of the Therapeutic Prison at HMP Dovegate, then the overall director of HMP Dovegate, and finally director of HMP Ashfield during its transition from a Young Offender Institution (YOI) to a 'sex offender' prison. He has recently completed a post-graduate degree examining the effectiveness of faith-based programmes post release.

About This Book

Five years ago, I was involved with others in building a project to support those being released from prison, who wished to pursue a Christian faith. At that time, we were venturing out on a limb; nothing like what we were trying to do existed. We had no resources and little experience. The project's leader, Simon Edwards, had just been released from prison himself, and others joined us from a similar background. We moved by faith, learning to trust God. We made mistakes and learned lessons as we picked our way through a landscape of addictions, manipulations, dangerous situations, sceptical statutory agencies, legal frameworks and impenetrable church politics.

This is the book we wish we'd had when we started.

In the quarter to March 2018, 17,904[2] prisoners were released in England and Wales. We might estimate that about 10 per cent of these have some kind of Christian faith (as opposed to the 45 per cent or so who put down 'RC' or 'C of E' on a form). That amounts to around 1,790 Christians. Or to put it another way, 138 people with some sort of Christian faith are released from prison in England and Wales each week.

Of course, these figures are speculative – a guesstimate – but the number looks about right. And it begs a question: *where do they go?* The sad fact is that many of them go back to prison.

Some may slip anonymously into a church. No questions asked, all well and good, potentially. Others, perhaps with more serious offences, will come under close supervisory arrangements, and may

---

[2] Ministry of Justice, 2018 (accessed 20th August 2018).

not be able to join themselves to a church without going through detailed risk assessments and a full disclosure of their past. In all likelihood, they will not put themselves through this and will stay out of church altogether.

Some will be rejected outright ('I'm sorry, but we can't accept people from the hostel down the road'); others will be treated with suspicion and perhaps even hostility by the church they enter, sometimes being shunned by their former Christian friends. Others will be greeted warmly by a church but find very little practical support; they may even be inadvertently put at risk by church members or leaders who don't fully understand their needs.

Overall, the likelihood of a released prisoner finding a supportive environment in a church through which they can re-enter the community is slim. In fact, the situation is worse than that. For men and women who have come to Christ in prison, the reception they find in some local churches may actually *increase* the likelihood that they will return to custody. I have no numbers to back that up, but having worked in the field in various voluntary and professional capacities for twenty years, it is my observation and firm belief. In many cases, this isn't because the churches released prisoners go to don't want to help them, but because they lack understanding.

Those who have an existing church connection may fare better because they have a level of established relationship within that community. Even where a church may not be able to provide much support, at some level there is a point of *belonging*, and this is very important. But many new believers returning to the community from prison are not 'cultural Christians'; they have no obvious point of contact. Even though they are Christians, the church seems like an alien environment to them.

Living in the real world

People coming out of prison have difficulties in their lives. That might seem obvious, but it has to be stated clearly. Those of us in the evangelical and charismatic parts of God's kingdom are apt to think – and we often assert – that Jesus is 'the answer'. By this we seem to mean that if you come to Christ and believe in Him for salvation, that that 'salvation' will fix everything. This is an example of 'magical thinking'; we're not sure how it's supposed to work, but we feel that somehow it should.

True, Jesus' sacrifice at Calvary cleanses us from sin. If we believe in Him, we can stand holy before God:

> The vilest offender who truly believes,
> That moment from Jesus a pardon receives.[3]

We are saved from God's wrath and share in the marvellous inheritance of Christ. Trust in Jesus Christ for salvation removes our guilt and our shame and restores our dignity. The Fall, in the sense of our isolation from God, is reversed. We are *saved*. We have eternal life. This is brilliant.

What salvation doesn't do (at least, not immediately) is remove the consequences of our evil or unwise actions. Consider David and his sin with Bathsheba in 2 Samuel 11–12. He committed adultery and murder, and lied and manipulated. When confronted with his sin by Nathan the prophet, he confessed it and repented before God (Psalm 51). Nevertheless, his actions seriously affected his and many other people's lives. There were far-reaching consequences that he had to live with.

A person who has come to Christ in prison might have made extraordinary steps in their faith. They might know the Bible well and have identifiable spiritual gifts and a defined ministry. They might be an able worship leader or a prolific evangelist. They may

---

[3] Fanny J Crosby, 'To God Be the Glory', 1820–1915.

have led more people to Christ than you have. But none of this means that they have addressed the attitudes, behaviours or core problems that took them to prison in the first place. And, as we said above, the fact that they have just come out of prison in itself means they are facing challenges.

Some of these challenges will be basic, to do with self-care and 'coping with life'; some will be more specialised, such as drug-dependency or mental illness. Or there may be issues connected with offending behaviour or a risk that the person poses to particular groups of people. In order to provide effective support to released prisoners, you have to be able and prepared to engage with these things. To admit that a person finds it hard to control their moods or to get ahead of their long-term drug habit is not to doubt their faith or to impugn the efficacy of Christ's sacrifice – it's just being realistic.

The Bible tells us that 'fervent love ... will cover a multitude of sins' (1 Peter 4:8), but it doesn't say anything about that love being blind.

On the other hand, if we shrink back in fear and hold our guests at arm's length or seek to put them in a 'safeguarding' box, we won't be showing love at all. We will leave them more hurt and alienated than they were to start with.

We must love wisely.

Churches typically fall into two equal and opposite errors when confronted with released prisoners. When hearing that a new attender is an 'ex-offender' on licence, they might be inclined to hit the big red panic button and reach for their safeguarding manual, leaving the ex-offender feeling even more isolated and stigmatised. A response motivated by fear. Alternatively, they might make them into some kind of celebrity, smothering them in love and attention, having them share their faith stories in the morning service. This is dangerous. It leaves the released prisoner disorientated because trust is something they find hard – and soon they are going to be let down again. The church can't deliver on the promises it seems

22

to be making. It's also dangerous because you really don't know who this person is or what they might do. What happens when they relapse into their heroin habit?

There should be a middle way, a way motivated by the gospel of Christ, but also informed by an understanding of what pressures released prisoners might face and how to provide support for them, and that understands that this is not someone else's problem.

The role of the Church

> The Spirit of the Lord GOD is upon Me,
> Because the LORD has anointed Me
> To preach good tidings to the poor;
> He has sent Me to heal the brokenhearted,
> To proclaim liberty to the captives,
> And the opening of the prison to those who are bound ...
> *Isaiah 61:1*

This is a scripture to which we will return often throughout the book; it is the verse that Jesus opened His ministry with in the synagogue at Nazareth. It stands as His manifesto and it should also be ours. It looms behind Christ's Commission to 'Go ... and make disciples' (Matthew 28:19).

I believe that the Church of Jesus Christ, in all its denominations and its various expressions, must be at the forefront of ministry to the poor, the broken-hearted, the marginalised, the homeless, the addicted, and those released from prison, who might be all of the above. And to be fair, much is being done in terms of food banks and night shelters in our cities, and organisations such as Betel and Teen Challenge are well-established routes out of addiction for many.

While there have always been a few projects working with released prisoners, it has never been a core activity of the Church in this country – yet two of the four clauses in the passage above are about releasing people from prisons:

He has sent Me …
To proclaim liberty to the captives,
And the opening of the prison to those who are bound.

Is Jesus speaking metaphorically? Is He referring to those who 'labor and are heavy laden' (Matthew 11:28), 'prisoners of their circumstances', so to speak? Or those who are bound by addictions or other kinds of oppression? Or perhaps a religious law?

Jesus, in quoting this, probably does mean these things too. But Barabbas, for one, found a very literal 'opening of the prison'. Jesus literally took his place on the cross while he walked free. I'm not trying to make a political point here. Obviously, there are people who need to be in prison for good reasons; what I am saying is that the Church should be at the forefront of receiving them when they are released and assisting their transition into the community. This is true whether or not they are believers, but it must be particularly true of our brothers and sisters in Christ.

At one level, this book will be an exploration of our response to Isaiah 61:1.

The purpose of this book

The purpose of this book is to explore some of the ways in which the Church as a body and we as Christian people can engage with men and women as they come out of prison. Along the way we will look at some pointers for receiving them into the fellowship of a local congregation in ways that are supportive and safe, but the main focus of the book will be on setting up and operating projects within the community geared toward rehabilitation and resettlement.

That might seem like a tall order. Even if you are a well-resourced church and have people available with relevant experience, you might think it feels like a big leap. You're right: it is. But hopefully, something in what follows will help to focus you on the steps you need to take in order to make a start.

Part 1 (chapters 1 and 2) examines your motivation for wanting to get involved in this field of ministry; the key chapter is 'Why We Should Care', which is followed by a study of the Walk Project in Stoke-on-Trent, the project I have been privileged to be involved with from its inception. Many of the lessons described in the book are gleaned from our experience in developing and operating this service.

Part 2 (chapters 3–5) is about understanding released prisoners. Chapter 3 looks at what prisons are for and how they operate, and briefly discusses some of the history of criminal justice. If we are going to work with men and women when they come out of prison, we need to understand at least a little of what their experience has been. This leads on to chapter 4, 'Understanding Released Prisoners', where we seek to look at the particular challenges and problems released prisoners face.

The last chapter in this section – 'Why People Stop Offending' – looks briefly at how the understanding of offending behaviour has changed over the last thirty years and how this has informed the way prisoners are treated and managed following their release.

Part 3 (chapters 6–10) looks at some considerations involved in setting up a project: 'The Role of the Local Church' (Chapter 6), 'Realising Your Vision' (7) and the selection and management of your staff and volunteers (8). These chapters refer to things that will be quite specific to you and your context: you know your own locality and your motivation to do this work, you have a vision and some able co-workers who are embarking on the journey with you, and so you will need to apply these thoughts to your own situation. The following two chapters, 'The "Strands"' and 'Managing Property', are more technical and seek to draw lessons specifically from what we have learned at the Walk Project.

The final and longest section of the book, **Part 4** (chapters 11–17), examines various aspects of 'best practice', as we and similar projects in other parts of the country have found them. Some parts of this are technical and may not be relevant to everyone.

Finally, a brief Appendix summarises the ways in which you, as an interested person or a group of people, who feel the call of God, can become involved in this ministry.

Our purpose in writing is to encourage you to pursue the vision for ministry or service that God has given you. It is essential that those embarking upon ministry projects of this or any other kind are following a genuine call of God and not attempting to fulfil some perceived need, either in themselves or in others. We work alongside prisons and the other statutory agencies who are responsible for upholding the law and ensuring the public's safety (including our own), who may not understand us and may be suspicious of our spiritual motivation. We also have to maintain an awareness that the people we work with are likely to be manipulative and difficult from time to time.

This book is written for those with a call to work primarily with adults. While much of what follows will also apply to juveniles and young offenders, these are not the focus of the book. Working with young offenders is a separate area of ministry.

Some people will find some of the things that I have to say about safeguarding and accountability within the church challenging or difficult. In short, my argument is that church congregations should be safe places; a mutual regard for one another's safety should be part of who we are, part of our culture. When people arrive in our midst having been recently released from prison, they should be able to be incorporated into that safe community. But for this to happen, the normal conduct of church life should demonstrate perhaps a greater level of openness and mutual accountability than we have been used to.

> Bear one another's burdens, and so fulfill the law of Christ.
> *Galatians 6:2*

True, some released prisoners do present issues of safeguarding, but in my experience, threats to vulnerable congregations come from many other places too.

Use of language

What we are saying in this book pertains to men and women; however, some 90 per cent of released prisoners are men. Most of my personal experience has been supporting men, either inside or outside prison, and the Walk Project, at the time of writing, is specifically a men's ministry. So, while I've tried to use gender-appropriate language where possible, there is a bias in most chapters towards working with a *male* client group. I have also tried to write in accessible English for a non-specialist readership.

Use of names

In general, where the people I refer to have been in contact with the criminal justice system, I have used aliases to disguise their identity. The exception to this is where the person is a member of Walk staff or has a separate public profile; this applies to Simon Edwards and Wez Johnson.

Citations and references

This is not an academic work or textbook; it is intended to be a useful manual for church leaders and anyone else who has an interest in supporting released prisoners from a Christian perspective. Nevertheless, I have tried not to make any unsupported assertions; where I have used statistics or other sources of information – conscious that these are susceptible to be misapplied – I have referred back to my source and, where appropriate, to the original research.

There is a full bibliography at the back of the book, along with a short selection of books and other resources that I have found particularly helpful.

Summer 2018

Part 1

1
Why We Should Care

I never knew Helena well. I met her in the chaplaincy of Her Majesty's Prison Foston Hall in September or October 2002, where I was part of a Prison Fellowship team helping with an Alpha course. She was sad to the point of desperation. Her husband and her young son had both tragically died and she had been left struggling to cope without any proper support, with a daughter of eighteen months. Her life had spiralled out of control: the wrong friends, drug use, shoplifting and eventually selling drugs. She bottomed out in prison, trying to deal with her grief and what had become of her life.

In the chaplaincy she found some solace in the support of staff and other prisoners who understood her and were able to get alongside. She wrote short poems to help express herself. Towards the end of the Alpha course, she let Jesus into her life. She began to open up a bit and even allowed herself to be a little hopeful again – a change of mood that was reflected in her poetry. She looked different; she had a whole new demeanour.

The chaplaincy was able to put her in touch with one of the larger churches in her hometown; they agreed to meet with her when she was released. This was just after Christmas, 2002.

We didn't hear any news for several months and assumed that Helena was now beginning to rebuild her life with her daughter, her new faith and a new supportive group of friends. It was impossible for us to maintain contact because at that time those supporting prisoners inside prison were forbidden from continuing contact outside – for sound and sensible reasons to do with security.

The next we heard of Helena was that she had died by her own hand at HMP Newhall.[4] She killed herself on 14th February 2003, St Valentine's Day. She was twenty-seven years old and left her young daughter.

People often ask me what I do for a living; this is usually followed by a supplementary question. I hear the same few questions, often repeated in slightly different forms.

- Should we not be more concerned with the victims of crime than with those who perpetrate it?

- Should we not spend our valuable time and resources on more deserving people – the poor, the homeless, or disadvantaged children?

- Why don't these people take responsibility for their lives and get a job?

- We pay taxes. Surely, it's the government's job to sort out these problems?

These questions come in various permutations. Sometimes they come with cynicism or bitterness from people whose lives have been disrupted by the offences of others. Sometimes people are genuinely bewildered – you do *what?*

In this chapter I will attempt to answer these questions seriously, but first I want to consider some facts and figures.

---

[4] *The Guardian*, 2004 and Gardner, 2005.

In England and Wales, we send 149 people to prison out of every 100,000 of the population, ahead of Scotland at 141;[5] the highest figures in Western Europe by some margin. In November 2017[6] the prison population stood at 86,185 while at the beginning of 1993 the figure was only 41,600; it's hard to explain the size of this increase over twenty-four years, but in part it is due to the passing of longer and open-ended sentences by courts.[7] At the time of writing, about a quarter of prisoners are serving sentences of four years or more. At the same time, slightly under half of prisoners are serving sentences of six months or less,[8] and of these about 60 per cent will reoffend within a year of release.

Overall, about half of all adults released from prison are reconvicted within a year.[9] On average, it costs £36,237 to keep one person in prison for one year.[10] Reoffending by those recently released from custody costs the UK economy between £9.5bn and £13bn a year[11] – this is more than is spent on mental health services.[12]

At a time when investment in mental health services is stagnating,[13] a quarter of women and one-sixth of men in prison report symptoms consistent with psychosis[14] (the rate among the general public is about 4 per cent). In the year to March 2017, there

[5] Institute for Criminal Policy Research (ICPR), 2016 (accessed 15th January 2016).

[6] Howard League for Penal Reform: *Prison Watch*, https://howardleague.org/prisons-information/prison-watch/ (accessed 13th November 2017).

[7] Ministry of Justice, 2013d.

[8] Ministry of Justice, 2015a. Table 1.9.

[9] Ministry of Justice, 2015b. Tables 16a, 16b and 17a.

[10] Ministry of Justice, 2014b, Table 1, and HM Prison Service, 1993.

[11] National Audit Office, 2010.

[12] Robinson, 2015.

[13] Harpin, 2015.

[14] Ministry of Justice, 2013a.

were 113 self-inflicted deaths in custody, the highest number on record.[15]

If these statistics paint a confusing and grim picture of the prison system, this description is accurate. The situation is messy and in a constant state of change. Perhaps this is always the case; the criminal justice system deals with the most difficult people in our society – in the words of one prison chaplain, 'the baddest, the maddest and the saddest'. The government is under a lot of pressure to reduce offending, to be 'tough on crime' and also to cut spending across the sector. Police, prison and probation staff, lawyers and many other professionals, along with volunteers from different organisations, struggle to make the system work as efficiently and humanely as they can. All this leads to difficult choices and uncomfortable compromises – and in the middle of it are many people like Helena, whose lives have come off the rails.

- **Should we not be more concerned with the victims of crime than with those who perpetrate it?**

This is a very emotive question and the answer is: 'Yes, of course we should.'

Every local newspaper and regional news programme regularly carries stories of offences committed against vulnerable people who are unable to defend themselves. An elderly lady is pulled off her feet as her handbag is snatched and she suffers a broken hip – a life-changing injury. A war veteran is robbed of his savings in his own home and left with severe bruising. These are deeds of unconscionable violence and a stunning disrespect for those who deserve to be treated with dignity. There can be no justification for things like this. Of course, we should concern ourselves with the welfare of these victims and all the others like them. They are our neighbours, friends and family members. Naturally, we must support the police and local authorities as they seek to prevent such

---

[15] Prison Reform Trust, 2017, p4.

things from taking place and bring offenders to book. Those who do things like this must be punished. Society – and any understanding of justice – demands that proper retribution should take place.

Our immediate emotional reaction is to want to see bad things happen to offenders. We want them to be in prison – banged up behind bars. We want them to be taught a lesson they won't forget; made to take responsibility; taught to mend their ways. But this is where things get less clear.

What do we want the punishment to achieve? Do we want it to stop the offender doing something like it again in the future? Or do we mainly want it to make us feel better, to give us the sense that 'justice has been done'? And this is the thing: the justice system has to do both of these.

When an offender is found guilty in court, the penalty has to reinforce a sense that the law is being upheld. We need to see and believe that justice has been done. On the other hand, if the person is going to come out of prison after six months or a year and do the same thing again, no good has been served. Another victim has been created; the offender is now more deeply entrenched in their offending; the community feels less safe; and the whole process has cost tens, if not hundreds, of thousands of pounds.

The first time someone offends, we might say that it was all down to them; it was their choice. But if they keep offending after coming out of prison, we must share that responsibility. We – or our representatives – had the opportunity to do something about it. In fact, one-third of male prisoners, and nearly two-thirds of females grew up in the state care system.[16] We, as responsible members of the wider community, have an interest in what happens to the people living in institutions.

Offences such as the examples above are never 'excused', but equally they are not 'random acts of mindless violence' either. They

---

[16] BBC, 2015 and Blades, Hart, Lee & Willmott, 2011.

come from somewhere; they are motivated. A proper concern for the victims of offences must also consider possible future victims of similar offences. This means that we have to consider carefully what happens to offenders after their conviction so that we don't make bad situations worse.

- **Should we not spend our valuable time and resources on more deserving people – the poor, the homeless, or disadvantaged children?**

This is another valid question. Of course we should concern ourselves with these vulnerable groups. However, in our communities, these are inextricably linked to both the victims and the perpetrators of crime.

Poverty does not cause crime. In fact, the suggestion that it might do is insulting to the millions of law-abiding people who happen to be financially disadvantaged. Nevertheless, those who live 'in poverty' (defined as below 60 per cent of median income – on 2016 figures, £12,600 per year) can find crime 'all pervasive in its influence on daily life'.[17]. They may find themselves surrounded by offending of different kinds that has a disproportionate effect on their communities and they are far more likely to become victims than other groups. A survey of headline statistics of 'poverty' against 'crimes' over the last thirty years shows a clear parallel, though not an exact relationship, between the numbers of people identified as 'in poverty' and the overall number of crimes reported.

People who are young (sixteen to twenty-four), unemployed, lone parents or living in inner cities are the most likely to be affected. If we are going to dedicate resources to helping those in poverty (for example, through operating food banks or debt counselling services) we are going to encounter those involved, one way or another, in criminal activity. We can't embrace the one issue without also addressing the other.

---

[17] Webster & Kingston, 2014.

Homelessness is another complex social issue. It includes rough sleeping, people and families in temporary or unsuitable accommodation and those 'sofa surfing' with friends. People can become homeless for many reasons, and the reasons for a person sleeping rough on the streets will be different from those for a family being forced to live in temporary bed and breakfast accommodation. However, 'leaving prison' is one of the top four reasons listed by the homelessness charity St Mungo's for people being on the streets.[18]

Prisons are under considerable pressure to find suitable accommodation for those being released, but even so, a significant number of people find themselves going out to 'no fixed abode'. In 2012-13, 12 per cent of prisoners released from custody had no settled accommodation;[19] in October 2010, one-third of rough sleepers in London reported having been in prison.[20]

When a person does not have suitable accommodation, they are susceptible to becoming a victim of crime and are also more likely to offend. In the autumn of 2014, it was estimated that 2,744 people were sleeping rough in England and Wales, an increase of 14 per cent over the previous year.[21] A recent briefing by the charity Crisis estimated that 34 per cent of homeless young people committed crimes in 2012, and 17 per cent committed imprisonable offences 'so they would receive a custodial sentence and accommodation'.[22] The old cliché about 'wanting to be inside for Christmas' is disturbingly accurate. According to a government report in 2012:

> More than three-quarters of prisoners (79%) who reported being homeless before custody were reconvicted in the first

---

[18] St Mungo's, 2013.

[19] Ministry of Justice, 2013b. Table 15.

[20] Hombs, 2011.

[21] Office for National Statistics.

[22] Crisis, 2012.

year after release, compared with less than half (47%) of those who did not report being homeless before custody.[23]

We tend to think of 'disadvantaged children' as being those in local authority care or perhaps the children of separated parents. However, a 2007 report found that children of prisoners are at risk of poorer outcomes than other children, and that:

> They represent a large vulnerable group (over 160,000 children affected each year, 2½ times the number of children in care) but they are invisible: most services who would be in contact with the child ... are unaware of the family circumstances unless informed directly by the family.[24]

Since that report the situation has changed a little – more information is now available to schools and local authorities, and many prisons now hold 'family days' where some prisoners can meet with their partners and children. Some prisons even have family support staff. However, the number of children affected has increased to 200,000.[25]

Children with a parent in prison are unlikely to reveal themselves to school staff for fear of social stigma and bullying, and so remain hidden from local services and from the pastoral systems of schools. They often feel isolated and ashamed. A volunteer in the play area of a prison visits room once asked a young lad what he wanted to do when he grew up: 'I want to be in prison like my dad.' Almost two-thirds of the sons of imprisoned fathers will themselves go on to offend.[26]

On the face of it, there are many vulnerable groups more deserving of support than those convicted of offences. However, when we look a little more closely we find that to support those

---

[23] Williams, Poyser & Hopkins, 2012.

[24] Ministry of Justice, 2009.

[25] Barnardo's, 2015.

[26] Murray & Farrington, 2008, quoted in Clewett & Glover, 2009.

who are poor or disadvantaged is inevitably to support offenders, those released from prison and others affected by the imprisonment of family members.

- **Why don't these people take responsibility for their lives and get a job?**

It's understandable that law-abiding and hard-working people might think like this. Many serving prisoners will often express a desire to 'do the right thing' when they are released; many will talk about 'giving something back'. Some will have been using their time well, completing courses in literacy or work skills. A common aspiration is to become self-employed – and this may be feasible for some.

The problem is that many, if not most, released prisoners are poorly equipped for the workplace. This isn't just a lack of work skills or education. Possibly they have never had legitimate employment, nor has anyone they know, including their parents. They have little work ethic, work culture or any role models to learn from. Agencies like the Jobcentre may seem to be speaking a different language and to be making unreasonable demands. Released prisoners possibly (probably) don't have good communication skills and present themselves poorly; they may be suspicious of people who appear to understand the rules of a game that they feel excluded from. They may express frustration at filling forms in or doing things online when they may not have easy access to the internet. They may have poor anger management and become impatient with Jobcentre staff and others who seem to be the gatekeepers to their finding work or accessing benefits. Starting with good intentions, they quickly become disillusioned and go back to what they understand and feel comfortable with.

This is not an insurmountable problem, but it takes time, patience and investment to bring many released prisoners to a point where they can become productive members of the workforce.

- **We pay taxes. Surely, it's the government's job to sort out these problems?**

Ultimately, it is the government's responsibility to ensure the safety and security of all its citizens. It is responsible for policing and preventing people from becoming the victims of crime. It is responsible for dealing safely and decently with those convicted, and minimising the risk that they will offend again. It is responsible for the supervision of offenders once they have been released until they complete the sentence given by the court.

Over the years, philosophies of justice and punishment have changed. At one time, it was mostly about 'retribution' – making offenders 'pay back' for their crimes. Sentences used to be imposed 'with hard labour', making people sweat out their years in prison completing meaningless tasks. More recently the emphasis has been on 'rehabilitation' – on trying to equip those who have offended to live in the wider community. This turns out to be a lot harder and more complex than it might first appear. In recent years, serious research has been undertaken as to how offenders can be turned away from offending. The model in place in the UK since the mid-1990s is based on assessing and managing the risk that a person represents. Particular factors contribute to this risk, and many of these can be addressed, reducing the risk that the offender will reoffend.

Wise people in university faculties and government departments work out what should be done; what interventions will be effective to reduce offenders' risks of reoffending and equip them for life in the 'real world'. Conscientious and motivated people in the police, prison and probation services apply these interventions. These frontline staff are under-resourced and overworked, and placed under pressure to get results. Consequently, when they are dealing with offenders, they tend to see a list of previous offences, risk factors and problems to be solved. 'Getting to know' their clients as real people is all but impossible – and carries its own risks. The effect of this is that people who have grown up alienated in dysfunctional communities, in care, young offender institutions and prisons, continue to be alienated by the very process that is supposed to reintegrate them into society.

The government – through the police and the other statutory agencies – does what it can with its limited resources to keep the community safe and secure, but it is ill-equipped to meet the needs of the people who find themselves in its care, all of whom are more or less vulnerable.

Why we should care

We should care because the fear of crime is a constant blight on our communities. If we are to be active in our communities, to make them better places to live and work, where the vulnerable are nurtured and not preyed upon, it makes sense to work with people coming out of prison, to make it less likely that they will offend in the future.

We should care because those being released from prison are themselves among the most vulnerable and poorly supported people in our midst. Having offended does not make them less vulnerable; often the offences they committed leave them stigmatised – sometimes the fact of having been in prison is a social stigma in itself.

Every person is unique and bears the image of God. They are capable of change – of redemption. Everyone is capable of creativity and achievement, and if not of fulfilling their whole potential, at least of living a worthwhile and satisfying life. Jesus in His ministry was often found among social outcasts – the 'unclean', the rough fishermen, the tax collectors, sex workers, sinners and the chronically sick. In his own words, he came 'to seek and save those who are lost' (Luke 19:10, NLT). All of us have a responsibility and as Christians in particular we have a mandate to be among people exactly like this. There is much work to do and it is difficult and messy. Those we seek to support are often suspicious or manipulative. They are often difficult to love.

A spiritual imperative

> For the love of Christ compels us …
> *2 Corinthians 5:14*

In the end, we care because God cares.

Sitting in my car not far from HMP Foston Hall after one of these Friday night Alpha sessions, I was struck with a godly thought that I believed to be from God – an epiphany, if you will. The women we met with didn't easily open up to strangers, especially to male strangers (all of them had problematic relationships with men). But on this occasion, some had shared their particular burdens and it had left me deeply moved and feeling helpless. What could I do? I had pulled the car over to compose myself before going home to my wife and children.

The thought was this: God loves each person who has ever drawn breath on this planet with the same intensity that He loves His own Son.

Jesus came for the lost ones, as well as those who are fine. Our mandate as followers of Christ is to do the same.

Challenge

We started this chapter with a young lady who took her own life in prison. In some way she had failed to connect with God's people, among whom – as a Christian – she should have been able to find support.

Consider the community where you live and where your church has its ministry:

- Are there people like Helena that you are aware of?

In our discussion, we also mentioned those who are 'poor', those who are homeless, those who are cared for by the state, disadvantaged children and those who are unemployable, as well as those who have offended and are imprisoned.

- In what ways can a person be 'lost'?

- Are there ways in which your community of believers can actively 'seek' and 'save' those who are lost?

A thought

This is a matter of life and death.

2
The Walk Project

Equipping released prisoners to develop tools for a new life through fellowship and unity in Christ.

Origins of the project

For several years I worked as a chaplaincy volunteer, first at HMP Foston Hall and later at HMP Dovegate, a high security men's prison. The work of the chaplaincy is essential to the humane operation of a prison; chaplains are concerned with the pastoral care of prisoners and prison staff, and this is a huge and demanding job.

Not all prisoners are gangsters, rapists or drug dealers. People finish up in prison for all sorts of reasons, but the fact that they are there means they are at the extremities of human experience. Prisons are difficult places; few would be there out of choice. They hold people behind high walls and razor wire, strongholds full of threat. And drugs are everywhere – if people can't escape physically, they will seek to escape in different ways – and with the drugs come corruption, intimidation and fear. In this context, the chaplains serve with grace and patience and bring a measure of healing and solace. To prison staff, a prisoner is a number, a name and a list of offences and risks. They can't afford to get closely involved. To the chaplains, each prisoner is a unique expression of the image of God, full of potential and hope.

It's not surprising, then, that chapel services are popular, especially if there are visitors from outside, and especially if the visitors are female! Some attend because it's something of a haven away from the wing or their cell; some will come to meet people they would not otherwise have contact with – perhaps to do some 'business' on the back row. Some go because they genuinely want to seek God and find some answers beyond themselves and the world they know.

Between 2005 and 2012, more than 700 men made a commitment to Jesus Christ at Dovegate prison. More than 100 of these were baptised. Some were long-serving prisoners, and we were able to watch them grow and mature in their faith over a period of months and years; others were only there for a short time.

The chaplains worked hard to ensure that those who were released into the community were referred to an appropriate church. The chaplaincy had links with many churches of different denominations in the local area; some of these would regularly send visitors into the prison to lead services or to support the chaplains in various ways. Nevertheless, a large number of these men returned to prison within months. Some of them were men who we had seen undergo deep and genuine changes to their motivation and way of thinking. Some became Bible students – a small number even attending Bible college after their release. They left prison with high hopes and a determination to 'do it right this time'. Often, they returned broken, disillusioned and angry. Sometimes they were suicidal.

The hard fact of the matter is that whatever we were doing with these men simply wasn't enough. There was a mismatch between what these mainly Christian prisoners were expecting on their release and what support was actually available to them on the outside. You would think (and we and they were thinking) that being a Christian would make a difference. That they would have brothers and sisters 'on the out' who were eager to support them. In prison, their experience of 'church' was a particular thing. The chaplains were visionary Christians and selfless ministers, who would weep with you and take your abuse, and stay with you long after they were supposed to go home, because you were going through a crisis. And then there were other prisoners on the same journey of faith, who understood where you were at, and who would be there – not always in a gentle way – to hold you accountable in your behaviour and attitudes. The church in Dovegate during those years was organic and embracing against the hard and often hostile background of a high security prison.

The Church on the outside is different. Even the liveliest and most engaged church in the area wasn't much like that. Often the men found churches to be shallow and insincere – an unfair judgement, but understandable in the circumstances. Churches in the community have very different roles from prison chaplaincies. They have elderly ladies and young families, and stressed people juggling jobs, families and ministry commitments. Very few churches were equipped to deal with men who were coming out of prison – as much as they might have wanted to.

It became clear to us that there needed to be a bridge between prison and the outside world. It would need to be a substantial bridge, with good resources, expertise and access to professional help. It would need to work in and with the prisons, churches and other supportive organisations, and alongside the statutory agencies. But more than this, crucially, it would need to get beside the men and nurture them – to *love* them – through their transition into 'normal' life.

No such organisation existed. Most of the necessary parts were there in some form, but they were not joined up. Some organisations offered supported accommodation, some offered support to help people find work, others offered drug and alcohol interventions, and so on. The probation service is good at managing risk but can lack compassion; many churches are compassionate but are open to being manipulated.

From the perspective of the prison chaplaincy, we knew what was needed; we had a good perspective of the problem over a number of years, and we had some expertise and some contacts, but we lacked a person with the necessary drive and charisma – the gifting – to make it happen.

Simon's story

In 2006, Simon Edwards had just been convicted for a string of robberies following a £250,000 binge on crack cocaine, and given a type of life sentence. In prison, separated from his partner and unable to contact his daughter, he suffered a breakdown and tried to take his own life.

Recovering from this, he was transferred to HMP Dovegate in 2009, where he met Darren. He knew Darren from a previous prison sentence – they had a lot in common and he was a friendly face. But Darren was different, there was a peace and grace about him that was new. He said he had become a Christian and, shortly afterwards, Simon also accepted Jesus Christ as his Saviour.

Simon became part of the church in Dovegate, eager to share the new hope and reality that he had found. His job for part of this time was working as an orderly in reception, where new prisoners were brought in. He noticed that many men who he knew had also come to Christ were returning to prison in the space of a few weeks or months. He cried out to God: 'What will happen to me when I get out?'

In response, God gave him a very clear picture of what was needed: a group of men who had successfully made the journey out of prison into the outside community and could walk alongside other men as they stepped out of the prison gate. This group would also provide safe accommodation and a route into employment through a building company. Simon had previously run a building company and knew the construction industry well.

After a few years, he was transferred to HMP Sudbury, an open prison, and started to make serious plans. Soon, he was able to get temporary release for home visits and voluntary work – he made good use of these opportunities to build a network of useful contacts among local churches and other organisations like the YMCA. During this period, I met with Simon several times in cafés and later in my home over bacon sandwiches and coffee to share his ideas and help him develop them. I had known Simon when he first came to Christ in Dovegate, and now, four years later, it was hard not to be impressed with the scope of his vision and the clarity with which he communicated it.

He was released from prison in June 2013 and almost immediately set about getting the Walk Project underway with a couple of houses run through a friendly letting agency and another owned by one of the original trustees.[27]

Five years later, Walk has kept and clarified its original mission, but has matured and developed. We now work with a group of social landlords and manage a range of supported accommodation across Stoke-on-Trent; we have well-developed programmes and policies, and growing relationships with local agencies such as the police, probation service and the Department for Work and Pensions (DWP).

How it works

The referral process

Typically, a serving prisoner who is drawing towards the end of his sentence fills in an application form, which he gets either from the chaplain or directly from us. On receiving the form, Walk will contact the prison chaplaincy and arrange an initial meeting with the candidate. Ideally, this will be an informal 'get to know you'

---

[27] Walk began as a project of another small charity, LifeKeys, but rapidly outgrew it.

session, where we talk a bit about who he is and why he wants to join Walk. We will also conduct a detailed needs assessment so that we can assess his suitability and start to build a plan for when he arrives. We need the candidate to take ownership of what he has done in the past, including the hurt he might have caused, and also the risks he might present now. This means trying to make an honest assessment of his use of drugs and alcohol, and any other needs that he might have, including an estimation of his physical and mental health. This puts quite a lot of pressure on the interview.

At this early stage, we might try to put him off. Walk isn't everybody's 'cup of tea'. For all that it provides accommodation and support for released prisoners, at its heart it is a Christian discipleship programme. It walks with men as they seek to become disciples of Jesus Christ – so although not everyone who joins would describe himself as a practising Christian, he has to be open to the spiritual content of the project.

Given an appropriate level of support, people can change, but only when and as much as they want to change. It is often clear at an early stage whether a man seriously wants a different life or if he just wants to put his past in a corner and be left to get on with it. Many people facing release from prison will say almost anything to get into a safe, comfortable, supported house managed by nice Christians. We will discuss this process in more detail in chapter 11, 'Assessing and Managing Risks and Needs'.

Release day

Release day is a big deal for a serving prisoner. Ever since he was sent down he has been waiting for this day. He might be dreading it; possibly he's waiting in anticipation. Some people talk about a 'golden hour' when a person first comes out of prison. Will he be met by one of his old mates? Will he head for the nearest pub? Will he be left to fend for himself? It's essential that we pin down in advance everything that will happen on the day he comes out, and manage it.

At nine in the morning, a couple of Walk staff will be waiting for him in the prison car park. Our man appears with his prison-issue holdall (until recently, prisons used to send men out with all their stuff in a bin liner stamped 'HM Prison Service'). The first thing on the agenda will be a meeting with probation, so we'll go there first. He'll meet his offender manager and they will explain his licence conditions. Nowadays everyone coming out of prison in England and Wales has either a licence or a Post-Sentence Supervision (PSS) order. Probation or the supervising agency will be a constant presence in his life for at least a year. If we're travelling a distance, we might stop on the way and get a coffee or a burger – our man has been dreaming of those yellow arches ...

After probation, we'll go to the Walk office and start the induction process, which will involve him signing some paperwork. We might take him round to sign up with a GP. Nearly all will be 'signed off' from work by the doctor on the grounds that they are 'in recovery' in a support project – and many come with a mental or physical health diagnosis, in any case.

One of the great things from the participant's point of view – and none of them quite get this at first – is that he doesn't have to worry about money. We'll help him with his benefits claims, and in the meantime, we will feed him, house him, give him a basic phone and some new clothes (he's probably wearing what he was arrested in). Finally, we'll show him his room and introduce him to his house leader, who will be his first line of support. Each of the shared houses is led by a participant who has been with the project for a while.

It's important that all of this has been explicitly agreed in advance. Our man will have been worrying about how he's going to get through the first few days, but his plans will probably involve some measure of 'picking up where he left off'. This is understandable; he has few friends and only his £46 release grant in his pocket (a bit more in Scotland) and this is not a good base from which to change your way of living. So, on the first day out we make sure that there are no surprises. If we deviate from the script, we are likely to lose him.

It's not always as smooth as this. Quite often, the man comes to us at short notice or post-release, sometimes in a difficult situation, or he may transfer to us from another project.

Moving on

After the first day, we'll give him a bit of space to find his feet and get to know people. He needs time to adjust. He'll be involved in the Walk activities: most of his time will be occupied in working, but there will also be times of worship and a discipleship programme (the Out Course), Walk's life skills programme, and various Bible study groups. All the lads will go to church on Sunday, and each house attends a different church; Walk is non-denominational.

We might put a paintbrush in his hand, but he won't be ready to have a job straight away. Over the first couple of weeks we'll ease him into voluntary work with a local business or charity. Most of the real work we do with the men happens in the context of a workplace. Parallel to the project, we also operate a building company as a separate enterprise. It mostly employs people who have been in trouble, some of whom are also in Walk. When our man's behaviours, attitudes and attempts to manipulate show up, he's among people who can support him and keep him accountable, because they have 'been there'. After six months or so, we'll expect him to be off benefits and earning a part-time wage. After about a year, he will either be offered a flat within Walk, and continue on low wages with a lower level of support, or he might be ready to 'move on' from the project and live independently.

During the first week, we will spend time with him. Some of this is in the context of essential paperwork, but mainly we want to reassure him and get to understand his hopes and fears; the things he struggles with; his relationships; his aspirations. We match all this against a detailed set of criteria that gives us a fair approximation – on paper – of the journey he needs to make and what milestones to look for. He might have his own goals, maybe to have contact with his children, or to become qualified in a trade. We'll be looking for these too, but we will also be looking to support him in a range of skills, from managing his money to gaining qualifications in numeracy and literacy. Over time we can chart his progress. It can take a long time to identify some of these milestones, and even longer to address them meaningfully.

We must remember why we are here and what we are doing. Our man has decided to change his life, to turn away from the way he was living, and embrace a new model. We provide the context in which this can happen, the stable and supportive environment in which he can go through a period of profound change. Walk is not an easy option. When Paul speaks of being 'transformed by the renewing of your mind' (Romans 12:2), this is what he is talking about. It isn't something a person can just decide to do. At the very least, this kind of change will require the active support of the staff and other participants of Walk. But becoming a disciple of Jesus Christ will require walking in repentance every day and this is only possible by the wise support and encouragement of Christian brothers and sisters, guided by the Holy Spirit.

Together we:

> work out [our] own salvation with fear and trembling; for it is God who works in [us] both to will and to do for His good pleasure.
> *Philippians 2:12-13*

People leave Walk for several reasons. Sometimes they 'crash' and return to some elements of their old life. This is disappointing, but as we discuss in chapter 14, 'Working with Those in Dependency and Addiction', recovery and rehabilitation is seldom a linear path and we might expect participants in a recovery programme to relapse a few times before becoming stable. Occasionally, this involves further periods in prison, but mostly not. Often, we welcome these men back after a few months, or perhaps, with their agreement, we refer them to another project elsewhere in the country that might better suit their needs or break them away from unhelpful local influences.

One of Walk's early participants did this and later went on to manage the men's recovery house at another ministry. He now runs his own building firm. Our aim for the men who follow Walk to its conclusion is to see them in full-time employment, living independently and planted in a supportive church. Another of our early participants now runs his own plumbing and heating business and is employing another participant. He now mentors several of the men through coaching them in the gym. Another, who has spent about half of his life in prison, is employed by a charity working with care leavers[28] and has recently been given a support position by the local Community Rehabilitation Company (CRC).

Discipleship

Walk is explicitly a Christian discipleship programme, and whether they share our faith or not, all candidates must understand that following Jesus is our passion. I have described in part the practical outworking of this discipleship in a renewed life; we also address these things specifically. Everyone in the project attends a local church on Sunday morning, and perhaps at other times too. Everybody in the supported houses meets regularly for worship and basic teaching. This introduces topics like 'Who is God?', 'How do I pray?', 'How do I read the Bible?', and core points of Christian doctrine.

The things we teach are explicitly worked out practically in the shared houses, in the office, in the workplace and in the relationships the men have with each other. Almost everything we hold 'in faith' finds a practical outworking at some point.

---

[28] Young people moving out of the 'care' system because they are eighteen.

Challenge

Walk came about through the passion of a few Christian brothers and sisters, seeing the acute need of people coming out of prison, and trusting God to meet it.

- What are you passionate about? What does your mind drift to in idle moments? What kind of a difference would you like to make to the world you see around you? Consider these things prayerfully.

Part 2

3
Prison Sentences

Depriving people of their liberty is not something that can be done lightly. Some voices, mainly on the political right, still insist, as Michael Howard famously did, that 'prison works'[29] and want to see more offenders locked away for longer. If they are locked up, the reasoning goes, they are not committing offences. Other more conciliatory voices want to see prisons used only in the most extreme cases, and then with an emphasis on rehabilitation. We have already noted that more than 100,000 people find themselves in prison each year – a number that has almost doubled since the early 1990s.

These are headlines. Later in this chapter, I will examine what it means when people are sent to prison. What kind of impact does it have on them? What particular issues do they face when they are released? Of the 86,000[30] or so people behind bars in the UK at any one time, all but a few will be released sooner or later. What will happen then?

---

[29] Howard, 1993.

[30] The prison population is fairly stable at about this number, but people come and go all the time.

But first I will look at how prison sentences work and the kind of experiences we might expect those released from prison to have been through.

Types of prison sentence

If a defendant is found guilty at trial, they may be sent to prison. Depending on the nature of their offence and previous record of offending, they may receive one of two types of sentence.

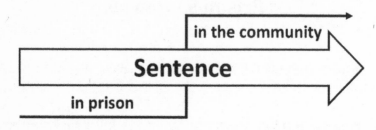

*Figure 1: **Longer fixed-term sentences** of two years or more are simple. Half is served in prison and half 'on licence' in the community.*

Most likely they will receive a determinate or fixed-term sentence that lasts for a specific period of time. Part of the sentence, usually half, will be served in custody; the rest will be in the community on licence, supervised by the National Probation Service (NPS), if the sentence is for two years or more (Figure 1). That will hopefully be the end of the matter; he or she will finish their licence and get on with their life.

Since March 2015, under a new law[31] in England and Wales, all released prisoners will receive at least a year's supervision, regardless of how long they have served or what their conviction was. So, if the offender is sentenced to six months in prison, they will serve three months in custody followed by three months on

---

[31] Offender Rehabilitation Act 2014.

licence (the six months), and then an additional nine months of supervision. This arrangement is supervised by an independently operated CRC, which has the responsibility for supervising those who present a medium-to-low risk of reoffending and who serve less than a year in prison (see Figure 2). Those deemed 'high risk' will have a similar arrangement, supervised by the NPS.

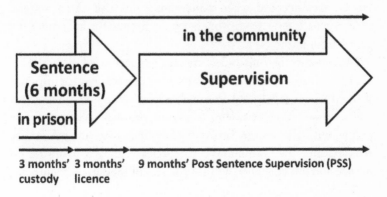

Figure 2: **Shorter fixed-term sentences** *are more complicated. Half is served in prison and half on licence, then the supervision period is topped up to one year.*

The CRCs were set up to work with offenders 'through the gate'. They work with the offender to identify and address their needs before release, and then continue afterwards.

Further reforms to Transforming Rehabilitation have recently been announced, to be introduced in 2020, including better funding for 'through the gate' services. Preliminary details can be found in Russell Webster's blog.[32]

In some circumstances – if the offender has committed murder or is thought to pose a serious threat to the public – they may receive an indeterminate sentence, that is, a sentence with no fixed

[32] Webster, R, 2018.

release date. Indeterminate sentences have a tariff or minimum term imposed by the court, after which the offender may be eligible for release subject to certain conditions. The Parole Board[33] is responsible for deciding whether a prisoner serving an indeterminate sentence is released. Their decisions are based on the level of risk the person is likely to present, and they will take many factors into account when determining this risk. After release, indeterminate sentence prisoners are on licence for life, under the supervision of the NPS.

At present, the only indeterminate sentence used in the UK is the life sentence. True to their name, life sentences last for life, even if the prisoner is released from custody at some point. The court will set a tariff, or 'minimum term'; the prisoner will then stay in prison until the Parole Board decides that they are safe to be released into the community. After release, they will still be on licence and under supervision for the rest of their lives (Figure 3).

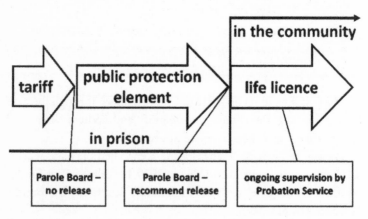

*Figure 3: **Indeterminate sentences** have a tariff but no fixed release date. Those released are on licence for life.*

---

[33] A useful information video about the Parole Board:
https://www.youtube.com/watch?v=n8X4gmEYy0I (accessed 2nd August 2018).

Life sentences are always given for murder (mandatory life sentences) and can also be given for other serious or repeat offences (discretionary life sentences).

Life sentences usually work in three stages:

- Stage 1 will be in a maximum security (Category A) prison and will last about three years.

- Stage 2 will be mostly in a high security (Category B) prison and will be 'as long as it takes', usually up to the prisoner's tariff.

- Stage 3 will usually last two to three years in standard security or 'open' (Category C or D) conditions and will focus on rehabilitation.

- The rest of the sentence – the 'life' bit – is served in the community under supervision.

For a period between 2005 and 2012 there was also the Indeterminate sentence for Public Protection (IPP). These sentences became notorious and have since been abolished after the High Court ruled that they were unlawful. IPP sentences worked in the same way as life sentences, but generally with shorter tariffs; it was not uncommon for an offender to receive a tariff of a few months or years but end up serving many years with no clear end in view. Five years after their abolition about 3,500 IPP prisoners – about two-thirds of all those sentenced – were still in custody. Since December 2012, IPP sentences have been replaced[34] by life sentences for serious second-time offenders; other serious offenders may receive Extended Determinate Sentences (EDS) of up to eight years, of which the offender will serve at least two-thirds.

---

[34] Legal Aid, Sentencing and Punishment of Offenders Act 2012.

In 2012, the average tariff for IPP was 4.7 years; for discretionary life, nine years and for mandatory life (ie murder), 20.2 years.

In certain cases, such as where a murderer has killed multiple times or there have been other aggravating factors, he (or more rarely she) will be given a whole-life tariff. Currently about sixty people in the UK have whole-life tariffs. They will never be eligible for parole.

Types of supervision

Everyone released from prison is supervised in the community. Those serving longer than two years, with indeterminate sentences are supervised on licence by the NPS; those with sentences of less than two years have some mix of a licence and Post Sentence Supervision (PSS), supervised by a CRC. Rarely, an individual serving a short sentence will be placed under supervision by the NPS if they are deemed to present a high risk of harm, should he or she reoffend, in which case the NPS will also supervise their PSS.

Being on licence means that the released prisoner has to abide by a set of rules under the supervision of a probation officer or offender manager; failure to do this will result in the offender being recalled to prison. In this sense, the probation service is a law enforcement agency first and foremost, as it supervises men and women who are still serving sentences passed by a court, albeit in the community. This is a significant change in emphasis from its original mandate in the Probation of Offenders Act 1907 to advise, assist and befriend those under supervision.

Those on licence are subject to seven basic conditions. They must:

- not behave in a way that undermines the licence;

- not commit an offence;

- keep in contact with their offender manager;

- allow their offender manager to visit, as arranged;

- live at an agreed suitable address and not stay overnight anywhere else without prior agreement;

- only do work subject to approval, and seek permission before taking a job;

- not travel outside the UK without prior approval.

They may also be given additional conditions, such as: having to attend certain courses or interventions; having restrictions on where they can live or go, or whom they can meet; having their access to computers or the internet restricted; having a curfew; or several other things. Rules can be adapted to individuals – for example, since January 2014 some sex offenders are required to take lie-detector tests. Over time these extra conditions may be eased off and the frequency of meetings may be reduced from weekly, to fortnightly, to monthly, etc.

PSS looks superficially similar to probation but works in a different way. It has the same seven basic rules as a licence, but there are no additional conditions. The most important difference is that it is a civil order, not a judicial requirement. Those on PSS have completed the sentence passed by the court and are technically 'ex-offenders'. Because of this they are usually not supervised by offender managers who work for the NPS but by enforcement officers who work for a CRC, though they may still refer to themselves as 'probation officers' or 'offender managers'. The difference between the two is not always apparent to the offender under supervision, and the whole arrangement is often referred to simply as 'probation' – a deliberate obfuscation.

A member of Walk staff recently rang the NPS office in a particular town by mistake, thinking it was the CRC. 'No,' said the person on the other end of the line, 'we're Sainsbury's, they're Lidl.'

Breaches

If an offender breaches their licence, they will be recalled to prison. An offender manager may issue up to three warnings before recalling someone – but the end result will be the same. If an offender breaches their licence, they will go back to prison.

Breaches of PSS orders are different. It is not part of the original sentence, so there is no automatic recall. A new judicial process is needed, so those who breach are referred to a magistrates' court, which has the power to give a fine, impose 'unpaid work' or sentence the person to up to fourteen days in prison, after which the judicial process will start again.

If you are feeling a bit perplexed by this, take heart. More than once, a couple of years after these changes came into force, I have sat in on meetings of clients with their supervising officers who were also confused.

Prison

A prison is a secure location where people are physically confined and deprived of their freedom. In England and Wales, convicted prisoners are assigned security categories, based on the likelihood that they will attempt to escape, and accommodated accordingly. For men and women aged above twenty-one, there are four categories:

- **Category A** (or for women: Restricted) prisoners are those whose escape would be very dangerous to the public or to national security.

- **Category B** (or for women: Closed) prisoners are those who do not require maximum security, but for whom escape needs to be made very difficult.

The physical environment of Category A and B prisons is similar, but the administration differs according to the requirements of supervising prisoners with differing levels of risk. Both of these establishments have high walls with inner fences and high levels of physical security.

- **Category C** (or for women: Closed or Semi-Open) prisoners are those who cannot be trusted in 'open' conditions but who are unlikely to try to escape.

More so than A and B, Category C prisons have an emphasis on preparing prisoners for release and will offer more skills-based courses with useful qualifications. Category C prisons tend to have high fences rather than walls.

- **Category D** (or for women: Open) prisoners are those who can be reasonably trusted not to try to escape and are given 'open' conditions. Such prisoners may be eligible for Release on Temporary Licence (ROTL) to work in the community or for home leave after a certain period.

'Open' prisons have little of the physical security apparatus apparent in the more secure prison types, though a prison regime still operates and it might be many months before prisoners are eligible for temporary release.

Typically, prisoners serving long sentences will progress through the categories, serving most of their sentences in Category B or C secure prisons and progressing to D to prepare them for release. Each year, a prisoner's security category is reviewed.

Prison life

Life in prison is strictly regimented. There is a set programme – the regime – with which all prisoners, staff and visitors must comply. This determines every aspect of prison life: unlocking and locking times, meal times, association times, the availability of work or education classes, etc. Nothing is left to chance. Prisons and regimes vary, but things like the availability of television or recreational equipment, or wearing own (ie non-uniform) clothes are usually earned privileges.

Prisons provide education programmes including literacy, numeracy, some GCSEs and other courses, including vocational qualifications; most also have factory workshops and other employment opportunities, often operated by outside companies. Prisoners cannot refuse work or education unless they are medically unfit; they are paid small amounts of money into their prison account, which they can use to purchase items such as toiletries, extra food and clothes from the prison shop.

Some prisoners are able to follow courses of Further and Higher Education, but these are subject to availability, funding and security considerations; some even complete degrees. Law is a popular subject.

If three officers are in charge of a wing of seventy prisoners during a shift, they need them to be compliant and to follow instructions. In order to work, a prison needs its inmates to be as obedient as possible – and there is a tension between this and the need for prisoners to be able to cope with life after they are released. One of the unspoken aims of secure prisons is therefore to depersonalise and institutionalise the prisoners. A prisoner is 'institutionalised' when he or she is completely acclimatised to prison life and 'loses interest in the outside world, views the prison as home, loses the ability to make independent decisions, and in general, defines himself [or herself] totally within the institutional context'.[35] The prisoner:

- becomes unable to take responsibility for his or her actions;

---

[35] Bartol & Bartol, 2014.

- loses confidence and the ability to make decisions; and

- becomes stressed and insecure outside the prison environment.

Prisoners serving longer sentences should go through a rehabilitation process that helps to address institutionalisation before they are released.

Prison accommodation

Accommodation – the actual cells that make up prisons – is the most valuable resource in the prison system apart from the staff; it needs to be used very efficiently, therefore it is basic. Strict regulations exist to make sure that it is fit for purpose.[36] In normal circumstances, there will be a bed, some sort of storage for belongings, a washbasin, a table and a toilet, which the prisoner must be able to use 'with some privacy' if the cell is shared. The practice of 'slopping out' – the humiliating morning ritual of emptying a 'soil bucket' – has now been abolished in most of the prison system, but still continues in a few places where facilities have yet to be upgraded.

In some prisons, cells will also be equipped with telephones from which the prisoner can contact a limited range of approved numbers (this removes the necessity of people competing for the use of a payphone on the wing and any legitimate reason for prisoners to possess a mobile phone). There is usually an alarm system so that prisoners can contact officers in an emergency.

Most prisoners will try to make their 'pad' as homely as they can – it is, after all, their home. There will be an Incentives and Earned Privileges (IEP) scheme to reward prisoners for good behaviour. Most prisoners are on 'Standard' regime; those on 'Enhanced' may have access to games consoles, their own clothes and extra visits; those on 'Basic' will lose everything except for the necessities.

---

[36] Ministry of Justice, 2012.

Wez Johnson: A day in the life

I often hear people say that prison is far too easy, and that prisoners are treated too well: that they have games consoles and the like. I have to say – from the point of view of a former prisoner – that these things are not accurate.

Being in prison is a constant monotony of routine. Everything is determined for you: the time you wake up, the time you take your medication, your mealtimes and the time to make phone calls etc. The only things that aren't determined are the time you actually go to sleep on an evening and your actual thoughts.

I wake up and open my eyes. I stare at the ceiling for a good five minutes, taking in my surroundings. I can hear keys jangling and footsteps coming up the landing. I can hear the clink, the unique sound that comes from unlocking a heavy, thick, steel door. I consider the day ahead. What will happen at work today? Have I got any appointments at healthcare, dentist, etc?

What happens next will depend on which prison you are in, but what follows is typical.

08:00: Doors open, breakfast and morning meds.

08:30 to 09:00: Morning work detail. Where I went in the prison would depend on what job I had been allocated. At my particular prison, the jobs available were working in the textiles workshop, being a wing cleaner or perhaps working in the library. For the most part I tried to get a job as a wing cleaner as you are out of your cell for most of the day. If you are well-acquainted with prison life you know which jobs to apply for and who to speak to in order to get the job you want.

A job in the kitchen is in most cases the most highly paid job in the prison but also one of the hardest. In the kitchen, prisoners might work longer hours and seven days a week, but the payoff is that you get to eat extra food, and also sneak items back to your cell – albeit unofficially!

12:00: Dinner would commence at around this time. We would be taken back to our cells where we would be locked up until the start of afternoon work detail at 14:00. The food consists of the lowest grade meat and it's not uncommon to see the hairs still on the chicken's legs.

16:30: Work detail would finish at around this time where we would then once again be locked behind our doors until Tea is served.

18:00: Tea is served from the hotplate on the wing and is normally something like a pasta bake or a pie and potatoes.

19:00: 'Association' is the time that most prisoners look forward to, where they are allowed about an hour to mix socially with other prisoners and perhaps play games like pool or table tennis. This is also an opportunity to make phone calls to friends and family and the one time you would have to take a shower.

It's best to plan your association time in advance to take into account how busy the phones will be at a particular time. For instance, when the phone credit goes on to your account on a Monday, that would involve queuing for most of your association, so perhaps you would use that evening to do other things and pick a different day to use the phone.

19.58: Association is about to come to an end, so there's just enough time to whip round and see if anyone has a TV guide to check the evening's listings in case there's a good programme or film on.

20.00: Association has come to an end and I'm now locked behind my door for the night. In a few seconds I have my evening mapped out [soaps], then I'll write a letter to my partner and be done before the film starts at ten, then it's off to bed.

I lay in my bed for a few minutes reflecting on the day's proceedings before falling asleep and starting the whole process again.

Challenge

> I was in prison and you came to Me.
> *Matthew 25:36*

We are not commanded to visit those in prison, but Jesus lists it as an example of the kind of thing that the righteous do, and unwittingly serve God in the process of serving the vulnerable. Perhaps you or your church has an established ministry to those in prison, either through the chaplaincy of your local prison or via a specialised ministry such as Prison Fellowship. If not, this is something you should consider.

• Test your calling and see if this is something God has for you.

Not all prisons welcome visitors from outside, but many do, particularly prisons with lower security categories or those 'local prisons' preparing prisoners for release back to their communities.

Find out

• Where are your local prisons?

Talk to the chaplain and ask how you can help.

• Where is your local Prison Fellowship group?

Check their website[37] for details.

---

[37] https://www.prisonfellowship.org.uk/ (accessed 2nd August 2018).

Prison Fellowship have set up prayer groups covering nearly every prison in the UK; they also support the work of prison chaplaincies in many other ways.

4

Understanding Released Prisoners

Imagine a young man in his late teens or early twenties who has committed a serious crime. It wasn't his intention, but through his recklessness, someone was killed. He is arrested and charged with a string of offences, including manslaughter. Maybe he knows that he's looking at a long time in prison and is aware of the hurt this is causing his family, as well as the guilt he perhaps feels for the thing he has done and the harm he has caused. In spite of the bravado he shows to the world, he finds it hard to sleep at night. Perhaps the case is well known, and his face is in the newspapers and on the TV each evening. For a week or two, he is 'public enemy number one', until the media find another villain.

If he decides to contest the case and plead 'not guilty', there will be a trial. Every sordid detail will come out in public; it will be debated and argued over in the theatre of the court and then chewed over once again by the press. The legal professionals will play their well-rehearsed and polished roles, as they cajole and challenge witnesses. In the middle of it, with his head in his hands, sits our man.

When the guilty verdict is passed, it isn't telling him anything he doesn't know. He's told that he's going to spend the next ten years in prison; he knows it's what he deserves, but that doesn't make him feel better, as the reality of the situation begins to sink in. He's strip-searched, given a threadbare uniform and banged up in a ten-by-six-foot room that he will probably share with another prisoner. 'Banged up' is an appropriate term; the most characteristic sounds of a prison are keys and chains rattling and heavy steel doors banging. This will be his life for the next ten years.

Prisons are designed to depersonalise; prisoners are reduced by the system to a number and a set of risk factors – this must be so, or they wouldn't be able to operate. A wing might have three or four officers and eighty prisoners – though at the time of writing, the ratio in many prisons is much lower, possibly one wing officer to fifty prisoners. The men must be trained to obey the requirements of the regime without challenge or the prison simply cannot function. Prisoners are institutionalised by design.

So, after ten years have passed, our man has spent more than a third of his life in prison (and this wasn't his first sentence). During the crucial period when he should have been leaving home, beginning work, forming a relationship and starting a family, he has been taught to be a prisoner. His life has been entirely defined by a series of decisions that he made on one evening ten years earlier. The local media might catch wind of his release – and for a moment, he will be notorious again, reducing any chance of his quietly slipping back into life.

You might say, 'Fair enough, he deserves it.' Perhaps that's true. He will come out of prison under close supervision, but how can we, the community, reduce the likelihood that he will do something like it again?

The common expectation is that prisoners nearing release are counting down the days and hours until they are escorted out through the gate and into freedom. For some, this is undoubtedly true, but for many, release comes with apprehension – even fear. And it isn't only long-serving prisoners who feel this way. Most people leaving prison have few useable skills; they don't have healthy relationships; they have little or no employability and little real understanding of how the world works. Furthermore, in many cases, they are released into the same circumstances and peer group in which they offended in the first place.

In practical terms, there are two categories of problems that people face when they are released. There are:

- the unresolved problems that they had before they went to prison; and

- the new problems that result from their imprisonment.

The previously existing problems

Our man offended in the first place because he had a disturbed understanding of the world and how to relate to people in it. It's hard to cite accurate figures, but the large majority of prisoners suffer from at least one diagnosed mental health condition. One in four women and one in six men said they had received treatment for a mental health problem in the year before they went to prison; a similar proportion of women and men in prison reported symptoms consistent with psychosis (the rate among the general public is about 4 per cent).[38] This is further complicated by long-term alcohol and drug misuse, and other problematic cycles of behaviour, like gambling or co-dependent relationships. Dame Anne Owers, former HM Chief Inspector of Prisons writes:

> Prison has become, to far too large an extent, the default setting for those with a wide range of mental and emotional disorders.[39]

Mental health

Some of the mental health issues mentioned above are the direct result of drug taking (in most cases, when a person has stopped taking drugs for a while, the symptoms lessen) and the stress and anxiety often suffered in the process of release from prison. These can be greatly reduced over time by providing safe and secure living

---

[38] Prison Reform Trust, 2017, p13.
[39] Owers, 2007.

conditions with a strong and supportive social network, which our man may or may not have had before he went to prison. Love is a healer. This may involve the support staff 'being there' for the person as a source of stability and as people who can be trusted; this may also mean getting 'in his face' from time to time and challenging him; holding him accountable for his decisions and behaviours. It requires a large investment of time and patience. I've made this sound quite clear-cut, but in reality, it's messy.

However, the majority of mental illness will need intervention by professionals. In these cases, our focus should be to support the individuals in managing their condition and any treatment regime they are under.

Many people feel uneasy with the thought of mental illness. We might feel uncomfortable around people whose behaviour is unpredictable and possibly challenging, or who are demanding of our time and attention. But at a deeper level, encountering mental ill health in others makes us aware of our own vulnerability. There is a stigma attached to illness of the mind, which is very different from physical illness – and we need to be aware of our own reactions in this respect. What is it that makes us uncomfortable?

Those we support may feel overwhelmed as they face uncertainty and leave the close boundaries of the prison environment, particularly if they are struggling with poor mental health. Prisons typically medicate these illnesses, and people should either be released with a supply of their medication or, more likely, a prescription to be fulfilled at a particular pharmacy when they get out; this doesn't always happen, especially if the person is being released from some distance away. The person may not think to check this, so, part of our support will be to make sure that this kind of thing goes smoothly without causing the person undue stress. Someone with a prescription for antidepressants may be OK for a day or two without their medication, but this is not the case with some other medicines.

Through this, where possible, we should try to create a *therapeutic partnership* with those we support, based on mutual trust and respect, within which the client can begin to take ownership of their situation and move towards definable goals. Any mental health professional working with the client will also be trying to achieve this, so ideally, we should work together to support the client. This is not something that will necessarily happen quickly, and it will require a sustained relationship of at least some months to achieve.

This is hard to do, and leaves scope for those we support to behave badly or to be manipulative, particularly where different parties are working with them. In later chapters, we will discuss 'Good Communication', 'Safe Working' and how to manage boundaries around the support we offer.

Furthermore, we should be aware of our clients' symptoms and their treatment plan, if they have one. If the client is engaging with the community mental health services, it can be helpful if we have input into their treatment plan.[40] In reality, this is unlikely to happen; however, as far as possible, we should be aware of what the treatment plan is so that we can support the person in following it.

It is essential that we know what medication they are on. Our experience is that people on antipsychotic medication or mood stabilisers will often try to reduce their dose or may save their pills and then binge on them later. We need to know what the client's current prescription is so that we can monitor the way the medication is taken. This requires liaison with the client's GP and/or mental health team, which will also need explicit consent from the client. Within a project such as Walk, all medicines must be carefully controlled, securely stored, logged and taken under supervision.

---

[40] Center for Substance Abuse Treatment, 2005.

Risk of suicide

People leaving prison have a risk of suicide ten times that of the general population. If we are working with those who are depressed or sad, we should be diligent in following up missed appointments, unusual behaviour, etc. Sometimes this can be a large time commitment.

Ask each person directly about their mood and any associated suicidal thoughts, especially if they have a known history of suicide attempts.

Drugs

We might think that people leaving custody should be 'clean' and not be actively abusing any substances, but this is often not the case. Drug abuse within prisons is rife, and if they have had a very short sentence, they may still be in touch with the local drug culture, which, regardless of any physical dependency, can in itself be hard to break away from.

Those addicted to opiates such as heroin are likely to be on a drug replacement therapy such as methadone or Subutex® (buprenorphine). These are supposed to remove the need for street heroin while the user scales his or her use down to zero; in reality, they are often given as 'maintenance' treatment, and no serious attempt is made to reduce the dose. These drugs, too, are open to abuse, and are often shared and traded like street drugs. While long-term methadone use may be regarded as 'safer' than street heroin, it is itself highly addictive and a lot harder to withdraw from. Our clients' default behaviour may be to seek out drugs or alcohol when they are lonely, angry or stressed, or if they just happen to bump into an old friend.

Work readiness

The young man in the example above has had no experience of employment. He may have few conventional work skills and little work ethic. Someone who has lived in criminality may be quite resourceful and enterprising, but have little concept of how the job market works or what would be expected of them as an employee.

Of course, everyone's experience is different, so it's impossible to generalise about these things. But consider someone growing up as a kid on a large city estate. His parents may not have worked regularly; his grandparents may have been made redundant from a large employer in the 1980s. As a child, he aspires to a lifestyle that he sees in the media which – even if he were to find employment – cannot be supported by the local economy. The only real money is in crime, most likely in drug dealing or vehicle theft.

To survive in that kind of world, they will have gained skills which might be transferable to the workplace. For example, to survive as a drug dealer, a person has to apply all the principles of market economics; they will understand cash flow, supply and demand, customer relations and the importance of paying suppliers on time. They will have worked quite hard and have something resembling a career path – but there are none of the usual safeguards. If you owe money to the bank, they are not likely to shoot you to get it back. Some ex-offenders have been members of lucrative criminal enterprises; they have skills – and these can be reapplied.

But most of these men and women will not have a conventional work ethic. Introducing them to a settled and disciplined lifestyle can be challenging, as will the prospect of being employed and 'going out to work' at 7.30 every morning.

Living skills

Related to this, many prisoners' life skills are very poor. They may have a poor concept of themselves as a person in society; they might have poor cognitive or decision-making skills (few people find themselves in prison after making good decisions), and linked to this, they may have poor emotional management.

Prisoners and ex-prisoners are unlikely to be in stable relationships, even if they were before imprisonment. Many relationships will have involved some level of manipulation or co-dependency and may have been violent or abusive. In some cases, the person you're supporting will have been the abuser.

The problems that result from imprisonment

Most people who go to prison take a lot of issues with them. In the strictly controlled environment of the prison, these are likely to have been suppressed, and where some attempt has been made to address them, the circumstances mean that interventions have limited effectiveness. Prison itself, and the fact of the person's isolation from their family and community, also causes difficulties when it comes to reintegration.

Damaged social networks

In cases where a person was in a good relationship before being sent to prison, there is a strong chance that they will lose touch with their partner while they are inside. This is recognised as a problem, and some prisons make steps to help prisoners stay in touch with their families through family days, parenting classes and other initiatives such as Storybook Dads.[41] These schemes, though popular and proven to be effective in reducing reoffending among some offenders, can only operate on a relatively small scale.

According to the Prison Reform Trust,[42] 40 per cent of sentenced prisoners said that they had lost contact with their families since entering prison. It's hard to concentrate family life – or even much of a relationship – into brief phone calls or a one- or two-hour visit once a month. Some prisoners are held many miles away from their families, who face a long journey every time they

---

[41] www.storybookdads.org.uk (accessed 2nd August 2018).
[42] Prison Reform Trust, 2014.

visit. As a result, the incarcerated partner becomes estranged, and the remaining partner, left with all the pressures of home and children, 'moves on'. About a quarter of those married before entering prison become divorced or separated.

Some released prisoners cannot return to their families because of the nature of their offence and are faced with having to start again from scratch and build a new life, possibly with the social stigma associated with that offence.

Accommodation

It almost goes without saying that people leaving prison need somewhere to live. Prisons are not supposed to release people into a state of homelessness, and can be fined substantial amounts when they do; nevertheless, it is common for prisoners to be released to 'no fixed abode' or issued with a tent and a sleeping bag. This is hard to credit, but true. A team from Walk once went to a northern town to interview a candidate who had been referred by a local agency. We met him at a drop-in centre and conducted the interview. He had been released from prison the previous week and probation had curfewed him to a tent in the woods. Alternatively, the prison might provide bed and breakfast or a hotel room for a night. These men and women are being released into a position of great vulnerability.

People enter prison from all sorts of backgrounds. Some were in inadequate accommodation to begin with; others were renting, and some were settled in a family home. Whatever the background is, any spell in prison of more than a few weeks is likely to compromise it – and may leave the person with a burden of debt from unpaid rent, etc.

Work

In the same way, those who had legitimate employment before they went to prison (a minority) will almost certainly have lost it by the time they come out. Depending on what the person's offence was, they may not be able to return to their previous employment or profession, and some employers automatically exclude people with any prison record. Not all historical offences need to be declared to prospective employers (if they are 'spent'[43]), but it is a legal requirement to declare 'unspent' convictions. Understandably, this acts as a deterrent for those seeking work after leaving prison. There is a temptation to lie about the past, or simply not to mention it. Some employers are happy to employ ex-prisoners, but a failure to 'disclose' will almost always result in immediate dismissal if it is discovered, and is an offence in itself.

In reality, regardless of how difficult it is to find a job, if a person has spent any length of time in prison, they will not be in a proper psychological state to enter employment for at least a few weeks, even if they can find it.

These problems are exacerbated for women leaving custody, who may have the additional responsibility of young children to care for.

Money problems

Prisoners in England and Wales are typically released with a grant of £46. This is the same as it was in the 1990s. They may have managed to save a little money from their prison wages; in some cases, they will receive a travel grant (in the form of a voucher) if they need to travel home by train. Many prisoners are released with only their release grant, the clothes they were wearing when they were arrested and a mobile phone, if they have one, which probably won't have credit on it.

For a person to get set up in rented accommodation from scratch, with food and clothing to cover them until their benefits start to kick in, will cost in the order of £500. In some parts of the country, it will be substantially more than that. We have already mentioned that many released prisoners carry a burden of historical

---

43 Unlock, 2017.

debt. This may not be a large amount of money in absolute terms, but it is likely to be a disincentive for the person to 'settle down' into regular employment and accommodation.

Christians released from prison

> I look forward to worshipping with my brothers and sisters
> in normal circumstances.
> *Prisoner at HMP Dovegate*

What can local churches do? Maybe you don't have the skills or the confidence, or even the calling from God, to create a specialised project. That's fine, but all of us have a part to play: 'the love of Christ compels us', as Paul says in 2 Corinthians 5:14. How can our local churches help the gentleman above to worship 'in normal circumstances'?

In some respects, Christians coming out of prison are even more vulnerable than other released prisoners. They have their fair share of the challenges we've already discussed, but also the reasonable expectation that they will find a welcome among their brothers and sisters in the local church. Too often, this welcome is misdirected, inadequate or entirely absent. Usually they are misunderstood; sometimes they are met with suspicion and hostility, and this can lead to disillusionment. Sometimes they feel that the prison chaplains have set them up to fail by linking them with an inappropriate church.

We believe that local churches should be a key element in resettling released prisoners back into the community. This is especially true where they have a relationship with Christ, but even where they haven't come to Christ yet, we should be able to have a role. Of course, this mandate extends beyond the specific area of released prisoners; there are many people in our communities who are 'lost' in addiction or homelessness or various other kinds of isolation. You might look at the scale of the problem and feel that you have little or nothing to offer, but just because you can't do everything, doesn't mean that you can't do anything.

What can local churches bring to the table?

They should bring a lot.

One notable risk factor for ex-prisoners' reoffending is the lack of positive social networks and the dominance of their past criminal associations, particularly if they are in their local area. A church is (or should be) a ready-made positive social network with a firm ethical basis and good pastoral support. It is a place where, we hope, sad and lonely people can be comforted and where people stand shoulder to shoulder and face the same way (more or less literally) without judgement. It is a place where 'good living' is modelled and can be shared.

Maybe it isn't quite as simple as that, but apart from any spiritual imperative to 'Go into all the world' (Mark 16:15), the local church is ideally placed to fill this role, and there is nothing else – no other 'institution' – in our society that can do it in the same way.

The problems with the Church

So, churches are excellent places to send ex-prisoners.

Unfortunately, not. One of the reasons Walk came about was the number of genuinely born-again Christian men who were leaving HMP Dovegate with high hopes and great motivation, only to return – broken – weeks or months later, after failing to engage with the church that, in most cases, the chaplaincy had introduced them to.

Most churches are not well equipped to support people with complex needs, and sometimes they are not well connected to their communities. Whereas they should be places where men and women can find healing for their hurts and a haven from their fears, too often they become artificial environments where special people meet on special occasions to do special things in a special language.

Looking to Jesus

A person who is sufficiently motivated and well supported can change their behaviour, and if they are in Christ, the Holy Spirit will form His character in them as they submit to Him. Our role in the local church initially is only to hold the door open, and maybe to hold our guests' hands as they walk through it. In other words, the basic role of the church is to create a place where the Holy Spirit can work in the lives of those we welcome. And this is what we all want.

Unfortunately, it is never this simple. Hosts and guests alike have unrealistic expectations, both sometimes lack understanding, and miscommunications are common. Additionally, many church people have a particular cultural background. We might expect those we welcome to start to look and sound like us – to adopt our cultural clothes. That won't happen, nor should it. We will probably find this challenging, and that's not a bad thing. People can't wash off their tattoos and battle scars, nor will they start drinking tea from a cup and saucer. And if they do start doing these things, we must wonder why.

In Luke 18, a rich young ruler comes to Jesus, and quickly 'became very sorrowful, for he was very rich' (Luke 18:23). He was already satisfied with what he had, and Jesus went onto explain the hardships and hazards of being 'rich'. When, in the next chapter, Zacchaeus, the hated tax collector, met Jesus, the story ended very differently as Jesus restored his lost identity:

> Today salvation has come to this house, because he also is
> a son of Abraham; for the Son of Man has come to seek
> and to save that which was lost.
> *Luke 19:9-10*

Perceptions

Things in churches are rarely what they seem to be. Even in 'non-liturgical' churches, proceedings play out in particular ways. What might at first appear informal and ad hoc to a casual observer is in fact a highly coded drama. There are particular ways to behave 'in church' which are quite alien to outsiders – and what really disturbs our guests is that *we* respond differently in church from how we do outside. Churches – like prisons – are institutions.

Is it OK to stand here? Can I talk? Can I use my phone? Can I sit where I like? Can I get a drink? What's happening now? Can I say something? Are those chairs special?

Please don't touch me.

But those things aren't the real issue. If you go into a different place, it will be unfamiliar; that is to be expected. The block our guests have is the fear of judgement and isolation – just as everyone else does – and an apparent cultural divide.

If I have a secret drink problem, if I'm hooked on pornography or if I'm sleeping with prostitutes, will I feel able to talk to someone about these things, maybe to ask for prayer or help? Or what if I'm in a same-sex relationship? Will I still find a welcome and compassion if I let the cracks show?

If most of us 'cultural Christians' have a bad day, we might swear a bit, break some crockery and kick the cat; but if our friends just out of prison have a bad day, it's often *really* bad. And they are going to tell the truth about it if you ask them how they are: 'I slept with a lad's missus last night after we all did coke together. He had a go at me, so I gave him a slap. I feel really bad now. Will you pray for me?'

Splits

One of the biggest disincentives for non-Christians looking towards Christ or for new Christians looking for a church is the behaviour of the Church towards itself. Maybe this evangelical church won't talk to the URC down the road because they're perceived as liberal. Perhaps I'm suspicious of the people who sit on the other side of the aisle because they might be charismatic. We claim to believe in a single Church, yet our behaviour does not support this. As 'cultural Christians' we might barely notice these things; after all, there are deep historical reasons for our denominational strains. But those looking from the outside will see our inconsistencies and challenge us on them.

A person who has come to Christ in prison is likely to have an idealised view of the Church, where Catholics, Anglicans, members of the Salvation Army, free church people and everyone else worship and attend Bible Study together. They don't all agree on everything, but they respect each other and can worship in unity.

Jesus said: 'By this all will know that you are My disciples, if you have love for one another' (John 13:35).

Expectations

Although we believe the Scriptures and genuinely want to serve God in our world, our expectations of what is possible are limited by our experience of the Church and the teaching we have received.

The people we are aiming to support, if they are serious about following Christ, have no such limitations. They tend to take the Bible and the teaching they receive at face value, apply it directly to their lives and get immediate results. There is some danger that we who have been around the Church for years become cast as the 'elder brothers' in this scenario (see Luke 15).

I'm going to close this chapter with another account from Wez, this time about his experience of release from prison.

Wez Johnson: Being released – twice

I have spent a significant amount of time in prison over the years for such things as supplying heroin, commercial burglary and fraud. My last sentence was six years for robbery. Being released from prison is a familiar experience for me.

As my release approaches, I have spent time visualising every detail of the day. I have been locked up for the past three years and I tell myself that I am now ready for release. The truth is, though, that I am far from ready. I have served three years, and nothing has changed; I have no intention of 'going straight'.

I saw a CARAT (drug support) worker before my release and I told her straight, that upon release I planned to have a 'blowout' on drugs. The worker expressed her concern.

When my release day arrived, this was pretty much the only thing on my mind. I wanted to get as 'wasted' as possible. Soon, the formalities of being strip-searched and given my civilian clothes were done, I was handed my release grant, the gates were opened, and I was free!

I headed straight to the nearest shop to buy four cans of lager, and jumped on a bus. Once in the city centre, I tried to spot anyone who would sell me some heroin. Incredibly, looking back, I justified my behaviour by the amount of time I had just spent in prison. I believed that the world 'owed me one'.

I soon came across a couple who I suspected from their appearance were 'using'; it turned out that they not only used but also sold heroin.

I was mindful that I had an appointment with my probation officer at two that afternoon and so I shouldn't become so drunk as to arouse suspicion. But that is not an exact science. Often drug users believe that they look perfectly fine when in fact the opposite is true. I was also aware that I had to check into the probation hostel before six that evening.

I attended my appointment on time and spoke with my probation officer, who asked me quite directly if I had had a drink that day. I replied that I had only had a couple of cans of lager. A lie!

She also asked if I had taken heroin; again, I lied. As a career criminal, I was in the habit of minimising or denying everything. She didn't investigate the matter any further and very soon I was on my way.

I used the remainder of the time left before I had to be at the hostel to drink more alcohol and take more heroin. My only goal was to get wasted.

I quickly lost track of time and realised I had missed my six o'clock deadline at the hostel, but I thought it worth the chance of turning up anyway in the hope that they would be gracious and let me in.

I arrived in quite a state. The fact that I knew I was in a state meant I was probably on the verge of collapse and in danger of overdose. My tolerance to heroin was very low after my time in prison.

I rang the intercom and two staff came out to greet me. In no uncertain terms they told me that I would not be allowed entrance as I was under the influence and this was against hostel rules, and that I should ring my probation officer. However, she was not in the office by then. I asked if it would be OK to come back tomorrow when I was not under the influence and the reply came back once again to speak to my probation officer.

I didn't much care that I had not been let into the hostel as I was not short of money. I tracked down an old girlfriend and we decided to go for drinks around town and get even more drunk. We booked into a hotel and spent the remainder of the evening there together.

Next morning, I vaguely recalled the events of the previous day, but was still not concerned. I decided to continue in the way I had begun, and so went out and bought more alcohol and more heroin.

We went to the house where we were going to consume our drink and drugs. As we were outside, I noticed a police van drive past the end of the street. I didn't think much of it other than that I was carrying drugs, so I set about hiding them more effectively about my person. About thirty seconds later, the police jumped out of the van and arrested me. They told me that my licence had been revoked and that I was being recalled to prison.

I was gutted. I wasn't even sure what I had done wrong and I had only been out for twenty-four hours.

The following day I was in a prison cell, not even sure when I would be eligible for release again. My sentence didn't expire for another three years.

When you are released, you are not really a free man. You are released at the halfway point of your sentence under the proviso of good behaviour. If any of your licence conditions are broken, you can be recalled back to prison.

I can't quite put into words how broken I was inside. I felt numb. I had lost hope. As far as I was concerned, at that point, I would have been quite happy to rot in jail and not have them open my door again until the full three years were up.

The next months were one of the lowest points in my life. While I could still put a good face on, I was self-medicating my feelings of depression with other prisoners' prescribed meds, which alleviated my depression to some extent; I was also still on the antipsychotic drug from my previous spell in prison.

About this time, I was caught in two positive drug tests. My need to reduce my feelings of anxiety and depression were greater than any consideration of the consequences. But then, out of the blue, I found out I had a parole hearing coming up. With the positive tests, the prospects of parole did not look promising.

In spite of pretty good reports from the prison staff, and the fact that I had completed the courses I was supposed to do, my continuing drug use would be the deciding factor. I told everyone that I was certain I would be denied parole.

My solicitor told me that I would receive their decision the following Wednesday, but on the Monday, I heard my name called out on the tannoy. When I went to the office they told me that I had been granted parole and was being released immediately. Only God knows how on earth they reached that decision! But I wasn't about to complain!

Nobody knew I was being released. I had only found out myself twenty minutes before and so here I was, walking out of the same prison that I had done ten months earlier. However, this time was different. I had a strong persuasion that I could no longer continue going through the same revolving door.

I went into the very same shop I had done ten months previously, only this time I didn't buy alcohol but tobacco and some chocolate. Although I had not yet come to Christ, I truly had a repentant heart and no longer desired to continue in my old ways.

I telephoned my girlfriend to let her know I had been released, and that I would be seeing her soon. I travelled to see my family and didn't even entertain the idea of having any drugs or alcohol. When I saw my probation officer, I was sober as a judge. These were all new experiences for me. I had never done any of these things sober before.

Nevertheless, a few days after release, I found that the thought of leaving the house was quite daunting. After a couple of weeks, my partner started to have a major issue with it. I had heard the term 'institutionalised' thrown around in prison, but never thought it was something that would affect me.

However, I felt anxious and nervous whenever I had to go out, so I would do my best to make the trip as short as possible. It wasn't long before this put so much strain on my partner that we split up.

I stayed in a hotel for a while and would venture out each day to the library to read and stay there until it closed. This went on for a few months. I kept myself to myself and isolated myself from the people that I knew, who were part of my old lifestyle.

I was beginning to lead a life that didn't impact society in a negative way. My probation officer even told me that the police were asking if I really was doing as well as I appeared to be.

After a while I was feeling better, and my partner and I got back together. I started volunteering for a drug and alcohol support agency, and became a mentor, helping others with their addiction. This gave me a feeling of worth and a much-needed boost to my self-esteem. It started to empower me to make decisions about my future.

In the midst of all this, I had started reading the Bible and asking questions about my faith in God. Not long afterwards I invited Christ into my life.

The journey from then to the present day has been amazing! I now have a full-time job in a Christian ministry, helping to equip men from a similar background to myself lead more fulfilling lives and turn from a way that can only leave them empty.

Challenge

People coming out of prison are individuals, each with their own challenges and their own story. They may come to us as Christians, or perhaps not, but the fact that they have been in prison means that they definitely face challenges and will benefit from support. The local church, with its positive social network, is ideally situated to provide this support.

Wez reports that when he first attended a church, some months after he came out of prison, he found exactly this: a safe and supportive environment where he was nurtured, encouraged and welcomed into fellowship, even though he was still on methadone and must have presented some challenges. His swift and sure progress in the faith is testimony to this.

Our experience from a prison chaplaincy perspective was that relatively few released prisoners found this kind of welcome.

I want to take two specific challenges out of this chapter.

Jesus opened His ministry with the dramatic quotation from Isaiah 61 that we have already mentioned, and which is one of the themes of this book. We must find ways to incorporate this purpose into the ministry of our local churches.

- In what way can we 'proclaim liberty to the captives, and the opening of the prison to those who are bound'?

As we saw in Wez's account, the ultimate success of people in changing their lives stems from their own motivation. They certainly can't be forced or coerced into it, but this is often a delicate process. However good a person's intentions are, if they are released from prison with £46 in their pocket, the clothes they stand in and their old friends' numbers in their phone, they are extremely vulnerable, particularly if their accommodation is unsuitable.

A supplementary question to the one above is this:

- How can we, as the local church, support those who come out of prison wanting to change their lives?

5

Why People Stop Offending

Over the years, a lot of thought has gone into why people *start* offending. Is it to do with poverty or a poor social environment? Is it related to mental health? Is it the product of poor parenting or a lack of education? Is it the result of some trauma in early life? Is it a spiritual problem caused by original sin? Or is it down to a person's individual choice in a particular moment? Are some people just evil?

Experts disagree, sometimes vehemently. Crime and offending are rich soil for political positioning, and prisons and the delivery of criminal justice are often seen as thankless money sinks; unpopular causes by comparison with other public spending commitments. The goal of making offence-free communities remains elusive.

In this chapter, I will consider the things that might help or encourage those who offend to stop; to *change*. If we want to support people as they return to the community from prison, we should have an idea of what is likely to be helpful and what won't. But first, what is a system of 'criminal justice' setting out to achieve?

Criminal justice

Any system of criminal justice needs to do several different things:[44]

---

[44] Andrews & Bonta, 1994 (paraphrase).

- It should punish wrongdoers, and usually there will be some sense of 'making the punishment fit the crime' so that the penalty for murder will be much more serious than that for shoplifting.

- It should prevent offenders from reoffending, at least for a period of time. If an offender is in prison, they have temporarily stopped causing a nuisance to the community.

- It should have the effect of making other potential offenders reconsider their actions. Potential offenders choose not to offend through fear of the consequences if they are caught.

- It should seek, in some way, to correct aberrant behaviour, either by conditioning a response or by seeking to address areas of need. In other words, people will stop offending because whatever 'need' was causing them to offend has now been met, or because they are better able to process that need.

- A criminal justice system should seek to help offenders re-enter the community as law-abiding citizens; and

- It may seek to restore or ameliorate the damage and hurt caused by the offence to its victims and to the host community.

Above everything else, it must be seen to be just; it must be fair. Almost all developed cultures subscribe to the rule of law where everyone without exception, including monarchs, judges, generals and government ministers, are subject to the same laws and penalties as the humblest citizens. Justice is administered with an even hand on the basis of clearly stated laws. If the administration of justice is believed to be arbitrary, favourable to certain groups, or corrupt, it will lose respect and ultimately become unworkable.

No criminal justice system can ever deliver all these things adequately, and indeed, some of these objectives may be in tension with others. A strongly retributive system may not be very good at rehabilitating offenders once their sentence is completed; a restorative justice model may have the effect of not incapacitating offenders while they are under sentence.

An important feature of the system is the manner with which it deals with the people who pass through its doors. Those who offend are often caught in a kind of trap and, having served their sentence, they are often ill-equipped to resume their lives. Sometimes they are prevented from doing so, either by the nature of their offence or simply because of the fact that they have a conviction. 'Going straight' is rarely a simple matter.

Those who are given the task of supervising or supporting offenders as they complete their sentences and re-enter the community must have a sense of what they are trying to achieve and how they are going to achieve it.

In the late 1960s, New York sociologist Robert Martinson reviewed a large number of rehabilitation project evaluations. His results and commentary were published in an article entitled 'What Works?', which was widely regarded as debunking the idea that it is possible to rehabilitate offenders at all. Martinson wrote:[45]

> ... with few and isolated exceptions, the rehabilitative efforts that have been reported so far have had no appreciable effect on recidivism.

and

> our present strategies ... cannot overcome, or even appreciably reduce, the powerful tendencies of offenders to continue in criminal behavior.

Martinson had assisted in a survey of 231 American studies on offender rehabilitation between 1945 and 1967; his article was extremely influential for thirty years or so, and effectively destroyed the idea that rehabilitative interventions were capable of reforming offenders. The article was nicknamed 'Nothing Works!' and his

---

[45] Martinson, 1974.

sceptical conclusions were treated as fact. This is the background against which the British Home Secretary (1993-97) Michael Howard (along with many other people at the time) declared that 'prison works'.[46]

The first consciously 'scientific', evidence-based approaches to rehabilitating offenders in the UK emerged in the 1990s, following the work of D A Andrews and James Bonta,[47] who examined offending behaviour from a psychological perspective. In 1995, James McGuire[48] and his colleagues, in a book also titled *What Works*, set out what is known as the 'Risk-Need-Responsivity' (RNR) model, which remains the foundation of most, if not all, of the work done with offenders by the prison and probation services. This views criminal behaviour as a psychological problem within individuals that can be treated and rectified.

The model first examines the *risk* that an offender will reoffend. This risk is calculated for a range of factors, some of which are fixed by a person's history and cannot be changed, and some of which are circumstantial and can be changed, given the correct treatment. The fixed or *static* risk factors include things like whether the offender has a family history of offending, the age at which the person first offended and whether their offending has increased in severity over time. These cannot be changed – and give a fairly accurate indication of the likelihood that the offender will continue to offend. The changeable or *dynamic* risk factors include issues like their ability to read and write, their substance dependency and their network of friends and associates. These are also known as 'criminogenic needs' because they are needs the person experiences that might lead them into offending. They are discussed in more detail in the chapter on 'Assessing and Managing Risks and Needs'.

Offenders are assessed when they first enter the system and then constantly reassessed. The criminal justice system views offenders

---

[46] Howard, 1993.

[47] Andrews & Bonta, 1994.

[48] McGuire, 1995.

primarily as bearers of risk – so the main aim of agencies like the National Probation Service (NPS) is to reduce this risk.

In 2005 the government produced a review of what has become known as the 'What Works' agenda,[49] in which they set out in detail how offenders should be assessed and treated in order to reduce reoffending. The model drew lessons from medicine, where new treatments are introduced on the basis of evidence produced by large-scale trials. Treatment programmes and interventions were painstakingly designed, often in accordance with the principles of Cognitive Behavioural Therapy (CBT), and long-term studies were set up to evaluate their effectiveness. In a trial for a new medical treatment, possibly tens or even hundreds of thousands of people will participate; some will be given the new drug, others a placebo. This isn't feasible with offenders in the criminal justice system; the numbers aren't that large, and it can take a long time – a decade or more – to see how effective the intervention is.

In this way, offending behaviour is treated like an illness. The *Risk* of an offender reoffending is calculated according to their established static risk factors and the criminogenic *Need* (the 'deficit' the offender is trying to make up in their offending). The *Responsivity* part of the model is in the treatment of this 'illness', which is through carefully designed interventions that take the form of courses or programmes, and (rarely) one-to-one sessions with a therapist. In theory, the higher the risk, the greater the 'need', and the more intense the therapy should be – and the interventions are especially developed to address particular criminogenic needs. There are 'Thinking Skills' programmes designed to address poor decision-making; other interventions designed to address anger and emotional management, and alcohol and substance misuse; and others to help participants to build healthy relationships. The model is quite elegant.

---

[49] Goldblatt & Lewis, 1998; Harper & Chitty, 2005.

Is this effective?

The assumption in all this is that offenders offend because they are 'deficient' in some sense, because of addiction or a lack of cognitive skills, or because of some other criminogenic 'need'. In this it is reductive; it harks back to the idea that people offend because of 'poverty' or some other extrinsic cause (exactly the thing that Andrews and Bonta were arguing against[50]), albeit that the model appears more sophisticated than that. It doesn't consider the fact that some people offend because they make a rational choice to do so.

In the third decade of 'What Works', it is fair to say that the RNR model is somewhat effective. Many individual offenders have found these programmes helpful and a few will have found them transformative. This was the intention. But, of course, their effectiveness depends on how they are delivered, to whom they are delivered and their availability. For logistical and administrative reasons, most of these interventions are only available to those more 'serious' offenders with longer sentences; however, a substantial number of offenders serve multiple short sentences of only a few weeks. These people are seldom included (they get a lower risk score), though perhaps they would stand to benefit more. Often their lives are chaotic, with dysfunctional relationships, problems caused by drink and drugs, and unsuitable or unstable accommodation – they really need an intervention.

Additionally, it's hard to count offences that are not committed. All you can say is that the person was likely *to* reoffend, and that they didn't. Did they stop offending because they completed a course? People's lives are complex. The course may have helped, but some other factor in his life might have been more influential. There are also scare stories. One cognitive skills course was

[50] Andrews & Bonta, 1994 – '… the socioeconomic context makes at best a minor contribution to variation in crime, relative to a host of other … variables' (p44).

suddenly dropped before the results of its full trial were published because it was found that it actually *increased* the likelihood of its participants reoffending in some circumstances. (It is the case that interventions of all kinds sometimes have the undesirable effect of increasing a person's offending unless they are administered and delivered carefully. The process of selecting suitable candidates is critical.)

Of course, it's not a bad thing to invest time and resources into helping people improve their lives, and alongside the therapeutic interventions, prisons have also expanded their education and work skills programmes so that, in addition to addressing their offending behaviour, prisoners often leave custody with useable work skills and some level of literacy and numeracy. But again, in order to access these things, the prisoner needs to be serving a substantial sentence.

The whole RNR model of intervention has been compromised since the 2008 financial crisis, which has greatly affected funding across the entire criminal justice sector, including the availability of courses, prison regime hours and the staff to deliver them.

Additionally, criticism of the RNR model revolves around its failure to motivate and engage many offenders in the process. Apart from the ethical and philosophical considerations of treating offenders as 'patients' (is 'offending' really an illness?), it can't rely on the collaboration of the 'therapist' and the 'patient' in the way that CBT must in order to be effective and to have integrity. CBT requires a therapeutic collaboration between the patient and the therapist; they mutually agree the goals of the treatment and, sometimes, its length and intensity. In the criminal justice context, however, the treatment goal (generically, to reduce the risk of the person's reoffending) is enforced upon the offender. He is given no choice in the matter; offenders are disempowered and robbed of agency. Maybe that is appropriate, but it undermines any therapeutic intention and probably any therapeutic effectiveness.

Interventions are almost always designed to enable participants to avoid the situations, thought processes and actions that might lead to an offence. This, in turn, teaches them to be hyper-vigilant to threats. There is little sense of promoting a positive outcome, only of avoiding negative ones. Interventions rarely engage with other important elements in participants' lives, such as the stress, trauma or poor self-esteem often suffered by prisoners, and these may be overlooked by a criminal justice system that does not regard these as 'criminogenic' factors. Indeed, participation in the criminal justice system is likely to *cause* these things or make them worse.

A more productive approach to therapy might be to embrace protective measures, such as building relationships and embracing hobbies, etc, rather than concentrating exclusively on minimising risk. Representing the purpose of the intervention in these terms might encourage each participant to 'become someone who lives a satisfying life that is … respectful of others'.[51] Recent theoretical developments have included working with offenders to embrace change in more holistic ways.

Local churches should be ideally placed in the community to work with released prisoners holistically, to help them build 'good' lives.

The idea of change

It seems obvious that a person with a long history of drug- or alcohol-related violence and repeated imprisonment needs to change. But let us consider what this means. We may be familiar with the phrase near the beginning of the twelfth chapter of Paul's epistle to the Romans:

> Do not be conformed to this world, but be transformed by
> the renewing of your mind.
> *Romans 12:2*

---

[51] Mann, 2000.

It might seem straightforward enough. 'Don't be like that ... be different. Be transformed.' But the difficulty is in the text itself: 'Do not be conformed to this world ...' Paul writes in the context of the distinction between the 'flesh', or human nature, and the 'Spirit' of God, the power for transformation. He is describing a spiritual journey. You can't just tell someone not to be 'conformed to this world'.

To be 'conformed to this world' means that your life experiences have formed you. They are your frame of reference. If every adult you know is involved in criminal activity, it will be hard for you to avoid normalising that behaviour and perhaps adopting it yourself. You may not have a moral problem with it, or at least, your moral landscape – your sense of right and wrong – will be differently calibrated from that of a person raised in a more benign environment. The same will apply to alcohol and drugs; they will be a familiar part of life.

Two generations ago, the expectation of young men growing up on big council estates in cities was that they would follow their fathers, uncles, cousins and grandparents into stable employment; this expectation no longer exists. It might be possible to find work, but it probably won't be well paid or secure, and it may not be seen as advantageous. The legacy of the social changes in the 1980s is that there is no 'generational expectation' of employment – no sense that sons will follow their fathers into a trade. In the short term at least, the way to earn money, to gain acceptance from your peer group, to impress the girls and generally to feel good about yourself is to engage in some sort of illegal activity.

It may be that at the age of thirty, the person sees that this is an unsatisfactory course and that their few contemporaries who studied at school and went to college, etc, are now doing quite well. But they can't just decide to change and be like them – or they can only do so with great difficulty. They have no study skills and their experience of education might not have been a happy one. Possibly, they have no clear sense of how their life could be different.

I'm generalising to make a point, but among the residents of Her Majesty's prisons, these elements are familiar.

Furthermore, to challenge someone in that position with 'you need to change your life', though it might appear obvious – and they might privately agree – is to undermine who they are as a person. Unless we are careful, we can come across as judgemental and dismissive of what has become a cultural norm in some parts of our society. We can't gain someone's confidence by disrespecting them, their family and their friends. What they hear is: 'You must change to become more acceptable to me.'

So 'change' itself is not an easy concept.

A person stuck in a cycle of substance dependency, offending and imprisonment may be well aware that they need to change, but may not have a clear idea of what they need to change into, or how. While the messages they get from the media tell them that they can have whatever they want quickly and easily, they know that isn't really true. They dream of a life where they can be a 'good' father (or mother) to their children, a provider and a positive role model – but they have no clear idea what these things look like or how to get them. It remains a dream.

In the heart of our society, local churches have a unique position. They are benign communities, ethically centred and pastorally supported, where this model of personal change can be modelled and taught.

Effective rehabilitation

The 'criminogenic needs' identified in the RNR model are real, and offenders can be supported into safe, stable and satisfying lives through addressing them. But these are not the whole story. A person must be motivated to change for a better life. They need a good sense of why they should step out of their cultural norm, then they need some sense of direction (change into what?); they need to believe that change is desirable and achievable. Although the RNR model has merit, it cannot provide these things.

In 2010, the Scottish Centre for Crime and Justice Research produced some guiding principles[52] for such a holistic approach. They were originally applied to criminal justice policy generally, but I've recast them to inform working practice in the community:

- Be **realistic** about the time it takes for a person to change deeply embedded attitudes and behaviour.

- Role model 'change' and build **positive relationships** with the people you're working with.

- Respect each person's **individuality**. Everybody's journey will be different; try to avoid one-size-fits-all approaches that actually fit no one.

- People's **social contexts** are important. 'Offending' can't be addressed in isolation from the local community.

- The **language** we use when speaking to and about offenders reinforces their (and our) perceptions. Labelling a young person as 'dangerous' or 'hopeless' does nothing to help them change.

- We **promote redemption**, and encourage and confirm positive change. There should be a clear end to 'punishment' so that effective rehabilitation can take place.

Among these recent approaches is the 'Good Lives Model' (GLM), first proposed by Tony Ward and C A Stewart in 2003.[53] It is a 'strengths-based' approach to rehabilitation that seeks to

---

52 McNeill & Weaver, 2010.
53 Ward & Stewart, 2003; Willis & Ward, 2010.

develop offenders' own particular interests, abilities, and aspirations – that is, their 'strengths'.

This model, which seeks to be complementary to RNR theory,[54] builds protective measures rather than only managing risk. It recognises that everyone has broadly similar goals in life, and that offending comes from misplaced attempts to meet these goals; it helps people to identify meaningful and valuable goals, and then work to achieve them. Such goals may involve good health and stable accommodation, satisfying relationships and a positive social network, outlets for creativity, etc.

These things don't come easily or quickly – it can be tough for a man or woman with no qualifications, experience or any real achievements to enter the labour market or education, or even to identify interests and aspirations. 'Recognising strengths' can be problematic for some people. The temptation to take shortcuts or just to give up will be hard to break.

Important to this focus on valuable goals is the understanding that the offender must have 'agency'; in other words, like everyone else, they will try to realise their goals through whatever means are available to them. In the past, they have not always been able to identify valuable goals, and even where they have, they have not been able to reach for them. There needs to be a robust and coordinated support network around them.

Challenge

> In heavenly love abiding,
> no change my heart shall fear;
> and safe is such confiding,
> for nothing changes here.[55]

There is, or seems to be, a natural conservatism about Christianity. The words we celebrate have been unchanged for millennia and are

---

[54] Ward & Maruna, 2007.

[55] Anna Letitia Waring, 'In Heavenly Love Abiding', 1823–1910.

to us the very Word of God. There is comfort in this. Moreover, many of our communities have grown up around buildings and centres of worship that have been there for a significant proportion of that time. The idea of 'change' doesn't come easy to us.

Yet personal, radical transformation is at the heart of the gospel. We are sinners, saved by God's grace, and the apostles write at length about the state of change we are all in, for example in Ephesians 4:17-32, where Paul teaches that the early Christians should:

> ... put on the new man which was created according to God, in true righteousness and holiness.
> *Ephesians 4:24*

And to the Romans:

> ... if ye live after the flesh, ye shall die: but if ye through the Spirit do mortify the deeds of the body, ye shall live.
> *Romans 8:13 (KJV)*

In Christ, we are in a constant state of transformation – of transition. We see it very clearly in some spectacular 'conversion' stories, but this is necessarily true of all of us. The first challenge I want to lay out is this:

- In what ways are you personally being transformed?

The second challenge in this chapter stems from the first:

- How can we make our church communities centres of transformation?

Part 3

6

The Role of the Local Church

The purpose of this book is firstly to highlight a major problem – an apparent blind spot in Christian ministry. Secondly, it is to challenge Christian brothers and sisters to address this need, and thirdly, to give some technical understanding and practical solutions to the question of how to go about this. Those who have been involved in Christian ministry to any extent will be aware of the acute lack of effective support services when people leave prison. This extends across the board from mentoring and supported accommodation to routes into training and employment; from substance dependency interventions to mental health provision. It is a matter of Christian compassion and a matter of social concern (not least when people reoffend); in some cases, as we have already seen, it is a matter of life and death.

While there has long been a strand of ministry, indeed a rich tradition in its way, going back as far as John Howard and Elizabeth Fry, mostly it has been a very thin strand. As a whole, the Church's response in this country has been insufficient. We have not identified the need. Where we have identified the need, we have not responded to it; and where we have responded to it, we have done so, too often, inappropriately.

There has been little confidence that pointing a released prisoner to a local church for support is a helpful thing to do, and what we sometimes interpret as a problem of 'safeguarding' in most cases is an indication of our unwillingness to engage with problems (ie 'people') that we find too difficult.

Scriptural precedent

> The Spirit of the Lord GOD is upon Me,
> Because the LORD has anointed Me
> To preach good tidings to the poor;
> He has sent Me to heal the brokenhearted,
> To proclaim liberty to the captives,
> And the opening of the prison to those who are bound ...
> *Isaiah 61:1*

This is Jesus' commission, and therefore ours too. He quotes the passage right at the beginning of His ministry as He sets out His stall, as it were, in Luke 4:18. He continues:

> Today this Scripture is fulfilled in your hearing.
> *Luke 4:21*

In this case, the Spirit of the Lord gives an anointing or empowering to 'preach good tidings to the poor ... to heal the brokenhearted, To proclaim liberty to the captives, And [to proclaim] the opening of the prison ... ' We can interpret the prison metaphorically as referring to spiritual bondage to things such as addictions, and captivity within the kinds of stronghold mentioned by Paul in 2 Corinthians 10. These interpretations are certainly valid – but the Bible is full of people actually incarcerated in real prisons, from Joseph imprisoned by Potiphar, to John exiled on the Isle of Patmos.

Jesus also said, in a passage that differentiates His faithful from His unfaithful would-be followers:

> Come, you blessed of My Father, inherit the kingdom prepared for you from the foundation of the world: for ...
> I was in prison and you came to Me.
> *Matthew 25:34-36*

The pitch of Jesus' ministry is towards the poor, the broken-hearted, the spiritually and physically hungry, the stranger and the sick, but nobody was able to visit Him during His brief and brutal imprisonment. He embraced captivity and death in order to break its power. Paul says of Jesus, quoting Psalm 68:18:

> 'When He ascended on high,
> He led captivity captive,
> And gave gifts to men.'
> *Ephesians 4:8*

... an idiom that begins with Deborah and Barak's victory song in Judges 5; a powerful image of liberation. Throughout Scripture, God's people suffer imprisonment, dispossession and exile, often for their godly testimony. God's heart is towards captives. Something vital has been taken from them and He wants to restore it.

Barabbas was a lawful captive, held in chains (Mark 15:7) and expecting death for his murderous insurrection. Jesus took his chains and died his death and Barabbas was freed. Through Jesus, his liberty was proclaimed, and his prison opened. In no way did Barabbas *deserve* to walk free that day.

The gospel is framed in terms of prisoners being released, and Jesus, in innocently suffering imprisonment, opens a path for the gospel in these darkest of places. It follows, therefore, that churches should reach into prisons and support prisoners; it also follows that churches should be part of the story for those coming out of prison, especially for those with a Christian faith, but also for those like Barabbas who, as yet, show no signs of repentance.

For many Christians, there appears to be a large cultural gap between the 'us', who feel secure in our faith and are happy to be 'saved', and the 'them', coming out of prison having served time for offending against the law. Perhaps we find 'them' personally offensive too. Perhaps some of 'them' have caused actual harm to some of 'us'. 'They' may have done things and gone to places that 'we' would not countenance. 'They' may transgress 'our' boundaries, and this makes 'us' existentially uncomfortable.

It's worth mentioning in addressing this that Christians are – by definition – ex-offenders. We have *all* sinned and fallen short of God's standard (Romans 3:23); we are redeemed and justified by Jesus Christ, and:

> the wages of sin is death, but the gift of God is eternal life
> in Christ Jesus our Lord.
> *Romans 6:23*

The starting point for considering the ministry of the local church towards those who have offended is that we have all offended. We can have no judgement or condemnation for those who have offended differently or more conspicuously than we have, or who have been apprehended and convicted of a criminal offence, whereas we have not.

> If we say that we have no sin, we deceive ourselves, and the
> truth is not in us.
> *1 John 1:8*

As Jesus said to the crowd who were about to stone the woman taken in adultery, whose guilt was not in doubt:

> He who is without sin among you, let him throw a stone at
> her first.
> *John 8:7*

It's important to understand this. If we work with people within the criminal justice system, we will find ourselves meeting some of the most damaged and vulnerable people in society. While they may have been the perpetrators of terrible offences, often they will have been offended against in equal measure. And many, probably most, find themselves stuck in a loop between prison, homelessness and addiction, which may have lasted for decades and can seem impossible to break. Many will find it hard, for example, to form relationships that are not manipulative. People like this can be hard to help.

Our prayer should be that God will enable us to see the men and women we work with in the same way that He sees them; indeed, in the same way that He sees us. So, armed with the 'love, joy, peace, patience, kindness, goodness, faithfulness, gentleness, and self-control' (Galatians 5:22-23, NLT) of Christ, the Church has an important role to play in supporting prisoners both before and after their release.

First contact

If you feel that God might be calling you into this area of ministry, where do you start?

Be a prison chaplaincy volunteer

All prisons have chaplaincies, and chaplains fulfil a vital role within the prison. It can be a lonely, stressful and isolating job, and most chaplaincies will be delighted if you offer to volunteer. The kind of things you might be invited to do may include leading worship, leading study groups, or simply participating in worship services. Some chaplaincies have schemes for visiting or writing to prisoners, or they may need help with administrative tasks. What you finish up doing will depend on your skills, your availability and your spiritual gifting. These activities will probably take place during the working day – at the time of writing, most prisons don't have 'regime time' after 6pm.

But it won't be as simple as turning up one Sunday and hoping to join the chapel worship service. There will be hoops to jump through before you are allowed to enter a prison. In many cases, the best way to achieve this will be through joining an organisation like Prison Fellowship.

Prison Fellowship

Thirty years ago, it would have been almost impossible to volunteer in a prison, but, largely through the work of Prison Fellowship (PF)[56] there is now an established network of prayer groups that are committed to praying specifically for prisons, prisoners and their families. They are linked to almost every prison in the country. Often, PF volunteers will go inside to support the work of the chaplains.

Some chaplaincies also start their own support groups, drawing volunteers from local churches. As a member of a PF or a chaplaincy support group, your primary task will be to pray; the chaplaincy may produce a prayer bulletin for this purpose. This is the single most important service that anyone can undertake, and is the foundation for all other ministries of this kind.

Visiting a prison

In order to go into a prison, volunteers will need to be cleared by security. If you're visiting irregularly by invitation of a chaplain, this will be a fairly informal affair. However, if you become more involved and are entering the prison more than a few times a year, you will need full security clearance, which is a detailed application involving references and historical vetting. The prison may also require you to complete their 'non-custodial staff' training – usually a week's full-time course. If you have unspent criminal convictions, you will usually be allowed to enter the prison only at the discretion of a senior governor or director.

Although this can seem quite an imposition, outside volunteers can have a huge impact on the effectiveness of the prison chaplaincy.

---

[56] http://www.prisonfellowship.org.uk/ (accessed 3rd August 2018).

Prison ministry

The key role of the prison chaplain is to provide faith observance and pastoral services to those who live and work in prisons. Chaplaincies are multifaith teams with ministers from different faith groups appointed in proportion to the need among the prison population. So, alongside Christian ministers from the main denominations, there will almost always be a full-time imam, along with visiting ministers from many other faiths as they are needed. Their responsibilities will include conducting regular worship services and study, prayer and meditation groups.

However, the primary job of all the chaplains is to provide pastoral support. This is an essential service within the prison, especially when prisoners suffer bereavement or a family illness, or simply need a shoulder to cry on.

As we have discussed at some length, criminal justice professionals regard prisoners primarily as loci of risk: the risk of reoffending and the risk of harm to others or themselves. Almost all interactions and relationships within the system are within the context of risk management. It has to be this way in order to run establishments safely and to minimise the danger, for example, of staff becoming compromised.

Against this, chaplains relate to prisoners as people. In particular, Christian chaplains see prisoners as people made in the image of God, and therefore innately worthy of respect and dignity and having the potential to do good things. The prison system evaluates people in relation to their past; chaplains see people in relation to their potential future. This is a critical difference, especially if we want prisoners' futures to be different from their pasts. Therefore, chaplaincy volunteers entering a prison, for example, to assist with a worship service, are trained not to ask after prisoners' offences or sentences. These things are irrelevant to that ministry and will cloud their ability to be 'non-judgmental'. (This is not the case when working with prisoners in the community, once they are released.)

There is much more to say about Christian ministry in prisons, but it goes beyond the scope of this book.

Community chaplaincy

'Community chaplaincy' is a diverse network of mostly small, 'faith-based' organisations that work within a locality to support released prisoners as they reintegrate into the community; such organisations may also work with other vulnerable people where need directs, such as those in substance dependency or homelessness – many of whom will also have been in prison at some time. They provide a wide range of services that typically include mentoring, drop-in centres and supported accommodation. Some groups also operate social enterprises to assist participants into work or to provide an income stream. Community chaplaincies may work with specific prisons or groups of prisons within a geographical area, while others have a wider scope; some have contractual arrangements to provide services with a local CRC, and a proportion of their funding will therefore fall under this model. Since 2010, the Community Chaplaincy Association (CCA)[57] has existed to support the development of a wide network of local community chaplaincy groups, of which there are currently twenty-four in the UK.

In many locations these are of central importance as they can coordinate the efforts of different smaller groups and agencies into the care and resettlement of men and women when they are released from custody, and also provide a context where experiences and 'best practice' can be shared. A local community chaplaincy may present opportunities for new projects to find their niche – for example, if you are running a drop-in centre that provides signposting to other organisations, a community chaplaincy may be the ideal platform to build the necessary network of contacts.

---

[57] Community Chaplaincy Association, n.d.

But, as small charities, these projects have not always fared well under the recent reforms to rehabilitation services. Some previously available and relatively generous funding streams such as the National Lottery have been strategically redirected towards larger partners within the funding model, and access to clients is sometimes only granted through tightly controlled contracts. A recent report observes:[58]

> The funding position is fragile. Community chaplaincies expand, shrink, or close as income fluctuates, and much staff and trustee time is taken up with fund-raising and bid-writing.

It continues:

> Understanding and negotiating the new world of bids and contracts [is] time-consuming, funding streams [are] uncertain and insufficient, and the introduction of market competition turned other voluntary sector agencies from partners to rivals.

At the time of writing, I am aware of several projects that have either closed or have lost key staff because of disrupted funding streams. A report by the Lloyds Bank Foundation[59] in 2016 found that a very poorly designed commissioning process was crippling some small charities, and this particularly affects community chaplaincy groups because they tend to work within the Transforming Rehabilitation agenda and are subject to its commissioning and funding structures.

If operating outside these official channels, organisations run the risk of being sidelined altogether and denied access to potential clients. However, our experience is that if you are offering a valuable service, this doesn't happen, and operational independence is a precious thing.

---

[58] Dominey & Lowson, 2017.
[59] Lloyds Bank Foundation, England and Wales, 2016.

Within prisons, chaplaincy departments are necessarily 'multifaith', and the CCA seeks to bring this into its community operation. This multifaith aspect means that community chaplaincies are able to attract funding from sources where diversity is an issue, and in these contexts may be able to build bridges between communities that are sometimes in tension. Although some evangelical Christian groups are part of the CCA, others may find it difficult to work within this loosely 'faith-based' environment. While it is quite feasible to have friendly relations, and sometimes pool resources or share expertise with organisations whose aims broadly align with our own but whose theology or world view may be inimical, it seems to me unnecessary to sign up to a shared Statement of Faith.[60] One wonders what would happen should an organisation with an atheistic basis want to join. Would they be denied membership? Or would the Statement become further expanded to include 'No Faith'?

For me, this is a much deeper issue than a label. It is my belief that since all people, whatever their cultural background or religious affiliation, are made in the divine image, their fulfilment can only be realised in pursuing a relationship with God; this in turn is realised through discipleship to Jesus Christ. People coming from different cultural contexts will see this differently, of course. Their 'journey of faith' may not make sense to me, nor mine to them, but these positions all have integrity within themselves. We afford one another greater respect by not pretending that we all believe the same thing.

Community chaplaincy is a very important part of the picture for those coming out of prison and provides essential services, but in the present economic and policy climate, many groups are facing severe challenges. Also, some may find the multifaith stance of the CCA problematic.

---

[60] Community Chaplaincy Association, 2011.

Things that can be done by a local church

While it's true to say that everyone coming out of prison needs help of some sort, not everyone will need the same type or level of support. While some people will need intervention in almost every aspect of their lives, others will be fine knowing that there's someone who understands on the end of a phone if they need it – and maybe they won't. The local church can get involved in all sorts of ways and at different levels – and all types of intervention will be necessary at one time or another.

Welcome to worship

Almost every time you hear 'ex-offenders' mentioned in a church context, it is in relation to 'safeguarding'. Protecting those who are vulnerable among us is clearly important, and may, in fact, be a legal requirement,[61] but this is never the whole story. We must remember who we are.

The most basic thing we can do in local churches is to provide a welcome for those coming out of prison and, amazingly, this is something that a lot of us get wrong. Is your church the kind of place where a stranger without much 'religious' background can walk in on a Sunday morning and be made to feel special? What about the other days of the week?

Quite a common response to a Sunday service will be, 'That was great! What's happening tomorrow?' Almost everyone coming out of prison will experience disorientation, loneliness, boredom and isolation in the first few weeks. Can you help?

You need to be aware of how 'user friendly' your church is (this is not to say that you should change the way you do things, but to be aware). Even informal services can sometimes be mystifying to people who aren't familiar with the language, etc.

---

[61] Pocklington, 2014.

Of course, you should be aware of potential safeguarding issues and have a particular person responsible for this; but also, be aware that *most* of the people who come through your doors on a Sunday morning don't present a particular safeguarding risk – even the ones who have been in prison. Some churches hit the panic button as soon as a visitor mentions the 'p' word. Avoid this: it will leave the person feeling isolated and even more vulnerable.

'Adam' was visiting his hometown on a weekend leave from an 'open prison' 100 miles or so away. He had a deep and mature Christian faith and long experience of ministering to others. One Saturday night he was looking for a place to find fellowship; a possible spiritual home for when he returned from prison. The lights were on in one of the town churches because they were training some staff and volunteers. Adam stepped into the lobby and was greeted by two young ladies, students at the university. They were on a break from what they were doing, so they made him welcome and asked him about himself. He told them the truth, that he was a prisoner on home leave, looking for a place to worship when he returned to the town. Adam gave them his contact details, including his prison number; they said they would keep in touch. Hearing the word 'prison', one of the leaders intervened, sent the girls away and told Adam that one of the male staff would contact him.

Walking around the town afterwards, Adam felt that he had been left vulnerable. He had given his private information to two strangers on the grounds that they had established a friendly rapport with him; this had now been more or less confiscated by the church leader, who presumably was following a policy to protect the girls from him. He almost returned and asked for his information back, but didn't. No one subsequently contacted him.

Several things went wrong. Firstly, a random man walking into a church building on a Saturday evening should not be approached by two girls. Secondly, the leader correctly intervened to take over from the girls, but entirely failed to recognise Adam's need. There might have been more serious consequences, if, for example, Adam had come looking for urgent help. Thirdly, Adam's mistake was in mentioning 'prison'. If he hadn't, doubtless he would have been treated to a cup of coffee, given some information about forthcoming events, and sent happily on his way.

And finally, if you said you're going to contact the person, then contact them! Have integrity.

Whether or not a visitor to your church has been in prison is certainly not the most important or interesting fact about them.

It's important for a church to have a safeguarding policy in place and a person with specific responsibility for it, but if you greet all newcomers on the basis of their potential risk, you will present a distorted image of the body of Christ and make few friends. Risk is the opposite of faith. If 'faith is the substance of things hoped for' (Hebrews 11:1), then risk is the 'substance of things most feared'. The risk-centred approach of the probation service to offenders may stop them reoffending, but it won't give them hope for a better future. We should be all about hope.

So, while we must be aware of risk and manage it, we also believe in change, and through all this, the love of Christ must be evident. It was appropriate for the church in the example above to treat Adam with some caution, but he shouldn't have been sent away in that manner.

It costs nothing to be kind.

Dedicated team

Welcoming released prisoners and those with similar challenges isn't the responsibility of the entire congregation, at least, not directly. There should be a dedicated team of people to handle this, possibly the 'prison ministry' team, or an outreach group who are in contact with outside agencies. It might be their role to stand alongside your guests, befriend them and manage their relationship with the wider church, at least for a time. Possibly, they might also coordinate discipleship and mentoring with all newcomers – not exclusively those coming from prison.

Mentoring

One of the services a local church, or a group of churches, might be able to offer is a mentoring scheme. Within the Church, this works as an aspect of discipleship, to reinforce and 'edify' the body of Christ.

Jesus mentored His disciples. He called His Twelve to follow Him in Mark 3, and in Mark 6 He sent them out on their first mission. In the intervening period, He involved them in His teaching and His work, instructing them, directing them, being a model for them and challenging their preconceptions and prejudices; the Greek word for 'disciple' in the New Testament can also mean 'student'. Jesus' instruction between Mark chapters 3 and 6 includes the following:

- teaching in theology and ethics (Mark 3:20-30; 4:1-34);

- relationship guidance (3:33-35);

- demonstrations of spiritual authority and power (4:35-41; 5:1-13);

- lessons in faith (5:1-20);

- lessons in compassion (5:21-43); and finally

- a lesson in perseverance (6:1-6).

After the disciples had returned from their first mission, he took them aside for some much-needed R and R and a debrief … that turned into the feeding of the 5,000, where they themselves were the means of delivery for Jesus' grace.

In the case of ex-prisoners, the issues are rather different from those of Jesus' disciples 2,000 years ago. We work with men and women who may have a history of offending and who have been imprisoned because they were judged to be dangerous in some way, and while this is not at the forefront of our minds, we cannot lose sight of it. Often, they are institutionalised. That means that they have lost the ability to take responsibility and make effective decisions. In most cases, before they went to prison they had serious life issues, possibly problems with drug and alcohol dependency that may have continued inside.

They may have been in prison many times; they might even regard it as 'home'. Perhaps they have little experience of what we might call 'normal' family relationships; possibly their home life was chaotic or abusive.

Jesus loves them. He came to seek and to save people exactly like these.

Think of the twelve disciples again. Thomas had trust issues; Peter appeared to have problems with self-discipline and was impulsive; Simon was a Zealot, a political radical possibly involved in an insurgency, while Matthew was a tax collector – a Roman collaborator; Philip was a slow learner; James and John were not called the 'Sons of Thunder' because they played the drums; and Judas Iscariot was a thief and a traitor. If Jesus had been anyone other than the Lord of life, His 'mentoring relationship' with these men would have ended on the cross – in blood, tears and broken dreams.

So, we have to think carefully about what we're doing.

On the other hand, there are people coming through prison chaplaincies who are wonderfully saved and whose lives have been transformed. They may have completed Bible college courses and be able to share their faith, lead worship and preach with a profound understanding of Scripture. For others, of course, their Christian faith is an adjunct to a flawed and problematic lifestyle.

The experience of sending these men out to local churches is mixed. Often, they struggle to accept the authority of leaders who aren't familiar with their issues and may not be sympathetic – or who may even find them threatening.

The need for mentoring – for *discipleship* – is clear. When Jesus promised to make Peter and his friends 'fishers of men' (Mark 1:17), this required patient and deliberate work on his part. If we are to 'make disciples' (Matthew 28:19), it will require no less from us. There is a need for mentoring in our churches, both informally and through structured programmes. Mentoring should be the norm among us.

Contracts

In a few cases it may be appropriate for released prisoners joining a local church to be given a contract to monitor their behaviour and ensure accountability. This is discussed in the chapter on 'Working with Sexual and Other High-Risk Offenders'.

Getting ready

These are a few of the ways in which people in local churches can make a real difference to the lives of those leaving prison. There may be other opportunities too, depending upon your local situation. But first, you need to check yourself.

What is your attitude to those who are on the margins of society – the modern-day 'lepers': the homeless, the abused, the addicted? Those who have offended? Those who are vulnerable and those who are potentially dangerous? Is your attitude the same as that of Jesus, who came to 'seek and to save' those who are lost (Luke 19:10)?

• Be aware of what is going on in your locality.

What are the local needs? Don't duplicate the project the church in the next street is running. Join it – or help to raise funds for it. Find out what services are available in your area for vulnerable people.

- Have a safeguarding policy and a named safeguarding officer.[62]

You can definitely go overboard on safeguarding and only see danger everywhere, but you must be realistic. If you have elderly, young or mentally unwell or other vulnerable people in your congregation, they need protecting from those who might cause them harm. (Most of these have never been to prison.)

- At least 83 per cent of ex-offenders are not 'sex-offenders'.[63]

Many people are frightened by stories of predatory paedophiles and rapists – but these are a small minority of offenders, who are only released subject to close supervision.

- Get training.

There are people who have experience in doing what you want to do, or something like it. Go and talk to them.

- Network.

If you can't help the person who turns up at your church, find out who can.

Challenge

> The Spirit of the Lord is upon me, for he has anointed me to bring Good News to the poor. He has sent me to proclaim that captives will be released, that the blind will see, that the oppressed will be set free …
> *Luke 4:18 (NLT)*
>
> The Son of Man came to seek and save those who are lost.
> *Luke 19:10 (NLT)*

---

[62] The Methodist Church, 2010.
[63] Barrett, 2017.

> ... go and make disciples of all the nations, baptizing them in the name of the Father and the Son and the Holy Spirit. Teach these new disciples to obey all the commands I have given you.
>
> *Matthew 28:19-20 (NLT)*

We noted earlier that about 86,000 people were in prison in England and Wales. Let's estimate that about the same number again are engaged in a similar offending lifestyle and have either been in prison previously or will be detained at some point in the future. All these people have partners, children, parents and other family members who are affected by their imprisonment. It is probably not unreasonable to suggest that this amounts to about half a million people, many of whom will have a lifestyle that accommodates offending. That is quite a large number, but (by comparison) it's about half the number of people who regularly attend the Church of England.[64] They have a disproportionate effect on our communities – from a feeling of insecurity to a significant drain on public resources. Some (we suggested about 10 per cent) may have some sort of Christian faith, but this is not well directed.

A thought: What if we in the churches of the UK were to make it our priority to reach that putative half million within the next ten years and bring them into the discipleship of Christ? They also have a spiritual heritage – a right to be participators in the grace of Christ – that no one is telling them about. What if we were to invest our time and treasure into engaging with them in fresh and intelligent ways?

It would be a difficult undertaking that not all of us are equipped for, but all of us are able to support those who are equipped – and who may already be doing this work.

Over time, we might expect to see significant changes in our communities.

---

[64] Research and Statistics, 2016.

- If a substantial proportion of those who are responsible for offending and criminal behaviour in our communities turn to Christ (and embrace more positive social attitudes), what social changes might we expect to see?

- Jesus gave a Great Commission to His first apostles (Matthew 28:18-19). What commission is He giving you?

7

Realising Your Vision

The Challenge at the close of the last chapter was about identifying what 'commission' you might have from the Lord, as opposed to the Great Commission, which is for everyone. Another way of looking at this is 'Vision'.

• Do you have a vision or a sense of calling from God?

This is not in the sense of an actual prophetic 'vision', but in the sense of 'the ability to think about or plan the future with imagination or wisdom'.[65]

How do you know if you are called?

Part Seven of the Alpha course[66] is 'How Does God Guide Us?' Nicky Gumbel sets out five ways, which, in delightfully Anglican style, all begin with the initials 'C S'. These are Commanding Scripture, Compelling Spirit, Common Sense, Counsel of the Saints and Circumstantial Signs. It is very helpful teaching on the subject of God's guidance. Sometimes, as we read the Bible, God will point a verse or passage out to us individually; this is one way that God commonly communicates with us, His children. There are certain scriptures, however, that contain explicit commands which pertain to all of us, for all time. These include, 'Believe on the Lord Jesus

---

[65] https://en.oxforddictionaries.com/definition/vision (accessed 7th July 2018)
[66] https://alpha.org/watch/alpha-at-htb#episode-56fb8b91d51cd416dc3f8096; Gumbel, 2001, p97 (accessed 10th August 2018).

Christ' (Acts 16:31), or 'if you have anything against anyone, forgive him' (Mark 11:25) and 'Go ... and make disciples of all the nations' (Matthew 28:19). There are others too, involving things like communion, baptism and preaching the good news; things which are not negotiable for practising Christians. There is no question about whether we ought to do these things, but of how we go about them.

As we read these scriptures prayerfully, God, the Author of these words, will surely show us. He wants His gospel to go into all the dark and obscure corners of the world, so that no one is lost.

> This is good and acceptable in the sight of God our Savior, who desires all men to be saved and to come to the knowledge of the truth.
> *1 Timothy 2:3-4*

> The Lord ... is longsuffering toward us, not willing that any should perish but that all should come to repentance.
> *2 Peter 3: 9*

God calls all of us who believe to live differently; to be light and salt in this world (see Matthew 5) and to share the good news about Jesus. Additionally, He calls particular people into particular areas of service. Some people are called to work with prisoners and those released from prison. Is He calling you?

If you feel a call from God, it's a powerful thing ... you know you've got to do something about it. Perhaps you have a strong motivation to 'Make the most of every opportunity in these evil days' (Ephesians 5:16, NLT). You have a sense of urgency: there is not a moment to lose. But also consider the previous verse (NKJV):

> See then that you walk circumspectly, not as fools but as wise ...

or the following verse:

> Therefore do not be unwise, but understand what the will of the Lord is.

As God opens doors for you – and He certainly will – you must move through them carefully. *Circumspectly*. And where God moves, Satan inevitably moves too. The last thing you want is for all your hard work, undertaken in faith, to fail or come apart, and this could happen in many different ways. All these examples have either happened to us at Walk or to people we know:

- Valued team members leave because you disagree over key points of strategy or Christian teaching.

- A tragedy happens through a team member's unprofessional conduct or through the lack of a clear policy.

- You compromise your core values in order to pursue funding; the funding is subsequently withdrawn.

- The core ethos of your project becomes diluted over time because staff members you brought in did not share your values or your fundamental mission.

- The core ethos of your project becomes diluted over time because responding to emergencies gives you 'mission drift'.

These are all familiar scenarios and there are many other possibilities. How do you avoid the prospect of other people picking over the bones of your hard work in five or ten years' time?

You must move forward with caution.

Vision test

Setting up a project to support released prisoners is not something you just decide to do one day. There is a very serious need for such projects, but identifying a need does not necessarily mean that you are the person to fulfil it, or that you can do it on your own. You must challenge your thinking to establish, for example, that your urge to do something is really a God-given conviction and not merely an urge to do something.

Research the areas of need you are seeking to address. Understand what you are setting out to achieve. The common issues among released prisoners are discussed elsewhere in this book – but what is your local situation? What services already exist? Are they effective? Where are the gaps? What do the police, and the prison and probation staff say? Can you link or partner with an existing organisation? Christian groups and churches are – or ought to be – well placed to address some or all of these factors, but are notoriously bad at networking.

What is your particular solution? What unique thing are you bringing? How do you propose to be an agent for positive change?

Then consider: what will your particular role be? Are you a do-er or a leader? Or are you an 'ideas' person or a problem-solver? Do you see yourself as a trustee with overall responsibility for a project, or as an executive or project manager, making connections and driving the vision forward? Maybe your role will be to support and facilitate rather than to lead. Take this away and pray about it with like-minded people. Ask for specific guidance.

Then, having established together that you do indeed have a God-given vision, you must ask yourselves:

- What are you trying to achieve?

- Why do you want to do this?

- Whom are you trying to reach?

- Who is going to run the project?

- Where will the project operate?

- How will the project operate?

These are serious questions that you and your colleagues must have the right answers to. Try to set some timed goals, or at least try to get a sense of how long it will take. Out of the answers to those questions, you should be able to create a business plan. (You should do this even if you are not going to seek external finances, because it will clarify your thinking and show up obvious flaws in your idea.)

Why do you want to do this?

Working in any capacity with those who have offended is demanding and sometimes difficult. You need to have a clear idea of the task you are taking on and why you want to do it. Each of the people in your group should answer this for themselves, but the vision should be shared.

> Write the vision
> And make it plain on tablets,
> That he may run who reads it.
> *Habakkuk 2:2*

Inspire those who are with you to share your vision. It may be that they have their own vision too, but you must be united in a common goal. Build your team into the vision; build the vision into your team.

For me, hearing of the death of Helena Price was a life-changing moment and was followed by another ten years or so of work in prisons in different voluntary and professional capacities. I became acutely aware of the need for projects to run outside prison to provide a bridge between the prison and the community and to carry on the good work the chaplaincy was doing inside. Nevertheless, while there were things I knew I could contribute to such a project, I knew that I was not the person to lead it.

For Simon Edwards, as a new Christian in prison, watching others he respected being released and then quickly returning to prison caused him earnestly to seek God: 'What's going to happen to me?' In response, God gave him a pastor's heart and a prophetic vision for the Walk Project as part of Christ's body in Stoke-on-Trent. In addition, his history and skills made him able to engage easily with the project's client group. In leading the Walk Project, he also models it.

As with all Christian service, what we do (our 'works') must flow directly and naturally from who we are and from our unique relationship with our Saviour (in other words, our 'faith').

So, ask yourself: what is your motivation?

Who is going to run the project?

Following on from motivation, any project operating at the cutting edge of Christian ministry and social enterprise needs leaders who are properly qualified. Your core team must share your vision and your values – this is essential; you must not be 'unequally yoked' (2 Corinthians 6:14) – so when you face challenging decisions, you will have a firm basis of trust in those around you. They must be spiritually motivated in the way described above; they each must have a very clear and God-given vision that will stand scrutiny and testing. There is a real danger that if wrongly motivated people become attached to the project at an early stage they will be hard to dislodge later and may cause damage.

Some examples of wrongly motivated people:

- Unaccountable team members. Leaders need to be accountable within the group and also beyond it to the leadership of their local church, though this may take a different form. Trustees play an important role in holding leaders accountable. It is essential that there is openness, transparency and trust between the core team because clients will try to play people against one another. It's also important that God can speak into your life through your colleagues without you being offended.

- Tourists. Some people are attracted to volunteer for projects like yours because they seem glamorous. In reality, far from being glamorous, they are messy and difficult. Tourists will embrace responsibilities within the team and then drop them when the real nature of the work becomes clear, or when another more attractive prospect comes along. This is unsettling both for the team and for those you work with. You need people who will be there for the long haul.

- Poachers. There are people who will attempt to hitch-hike on the back of your ministry or seek to become associated with it for reasons of their own. They may try to take credit for your work or perhaps steal your clients for their own projects. This always does harm and causes confusion to the people you're working with. It can undermine the integrity of your project and put the 'poachers' themselves at risk. They may find themselves drawn into inappropriate relationships with clients whose issues they do not fully understand. Poachers are often:

- Injured people. This might sound strange because often it's our understanding of pain that makes us able to engage with other people's brokenness. But if a person is carrying unhealed hurts, they can sometimes try to assuage them by trying to 'fix' others. They may believe that they can help themselves by helping that person; while meaning no harm, they can become predators. This might include men or women who have unresolved trauma from childhood, failed relationships, or even illness. Those who have been injured need to receive healing and exercise forgiveness before they can minister to others, and they must always be part of a supportive and accountable team. Just because a person is an ex-prisoner or a recovering addict doesn't necessarily mean that they 'have something to offer' other ex-prisoners and recovering addicts.

To keep the analogy going, your leaders must be gamekeepers, ready to work patiently and maintain secure boundaries over a long period of time. They must have integrity and be well grounded and stable.

In addition to this, they must:

- Be filled with the Holy Spirit, able to follow the prompting of God and gifted as pastors. And as pastors, they must:

o   Be able to serve people who are sometimes needy, manipulative and ungrateful.

o   Be able to lead. To motivate staff and volunteers, and to galvanise support from a sometimes moribund Christian community that mostly doesn't see working with released prisoners as something that they could or should be doing.

o   Have prophetic insight. Leaders should be able to hear from God and speak His life into whatever work they are doing. This will give your ministry the uniqueness and freshness that belongs to God's kingdom.

• Be ex-prisoners. There might be people on your team from a variety of backgrounds – social workers, teachers, drugs experts, counsellors and people with probation experience – but to have proper traction with men who have just come out of prison, you must have people in positions of responsibility who come from 'the lifestyle' and have served substantial prison time.

Jesus can comfort 'those who mourn' because he is 'a Man of sorrows and acquainted with grief' (Matthew 5:4; Isaiah 53:3). You might think that you need credibility with your trustees, with the local CRC, with the police or with funders, but the first place you absolutely *must* be credible is among your potential clients.

• Be accountable. Leaders (of any organisation) need people around them who will stand in front of them and say 'no' from time to time.

What are you trying to achieve?

Before you start, you must work out prayerfully and in detail what you want to do. This must be drawn from your vision:

- What has God put on your heart?

    This book assumes that your project is about supporting released prisoners in some way. How, specifically, are you going to do that? There are many areas of need and you probably won't try to meet them all, so:

- What needs are you setting out to meet?

    Don't be limited by what you perceive your resources to be – in God's economy, He will match the resource to the level of your need.

Walk's mission is:

> To equip released prisoners to develop tools for a new life through fellowship and unity in Christ.

Yours will be different, but you need a statement that will succinctly express your objectives to you and your staff. Every decision you make should be made in the light of this statement. You may derive a separate shorter statement or a 'strapline' for the benefit of people outside the project, but this also needs to communicate your basic purpose. How do you arrive at statements such as these?

Workshop the vision

Draw together your core team and spend at least a whole day clarifying your vision into a single statement. It should be:

- motivational, in that it states why you are doing what you are doing;

- inspirational, in communicating your goals to others; and

- aspirational, in that it leads people to reach forward and seek better things.

It should also be short – no more than two sentences – so that you can have it in front of you and reproduce it on paperwork. Aim to produce a memorable statement that describes your reason for existence as an organisation.

Your vision statement should be based on your shared values and carried through all your project's activities; it will show what you are trying to achieve so that other organisations will understand you. It should also act as a limiter to rule out certain activities that may not ultimately contribute to your project.

Imprecise statements are unhelpful:

> We aim to do the best we can to satisfy our clients.

This is meaningless. How are you going to help clients, to 'satisfy' them? A vision statement should be a compact expression of what you do and aspire to do.

Having formulated a precise statement of your vision, try to map out what you consider your journey will be over one year, three years and up to ten years. You have no idea what you'll be doing in ten years' time (or even one), but it's essential to have an idea of what your destination is, and make sure that your core team agrees. A plan like this will also be helpful when it comes to the business and financial planning that will follow.

Where will you operate?

What will be your 'catchment area'?

There are some obvious limiting factors. If you need to maintain close relationships with prison chaplaincies and visit them to see potential candidates, this probably gives you a realistic 100-mile radius. A long-standing and respected project offering mentoring and other support to released prisoners offered a nationwide service initially, but later revised this, and now offers support only within London. Locality is very important when you need to rely on face-to-face meetings.

It is also important to know what is going on elsewhere, so that you can make and receive referrals from projects in other places, if need be.

Operational base

You probably already have a community or location that you are passionate about serving – within that, you need a base. If you are going to work directly with clients, consider not being based in a church building. Depending on your clients, they may find a church off-putting; also, you might not want to overwhelm a local congregation with a project full of lovely but dysfunctional people. It may not be wise to base clients with unpredictable behaviour in close proximity to other vulnerable people.

At Walk, we find it helpful not to work through any one church or denomination. Through our experience in prison chaplaincies, we have an image of the body of Christ in which there is diversity in unity. Part of our mission statement – 'fellowship and unity in Christ' – expresses the way we seek to work with a network of different churches, denominations and ministries, and to be a catalyst for them to come together around the transforming power of Jesus. One result of this is that our men are 'planted' in several different congregations where they can grow as part of a church without unbalancing it. This requires a lot of patient groundwork.

How will you operate? Money ...

The Bible tells us repeatedly to trust God and not to worry about our provision. That's easy to say; harder to do. There are plenty of agencies who will invite you to apply for funding pots of various kinds: some Christian, some secular. We found four important things.

- When the apostle Paul writes: ' ... my God shall supply all your need according to His riches in glory by Christ Jesus'

(Philippians 4:19), he isn't being metaphorical; he means it literally.

- 'He who pays the piper calls the tune.' Almost all funding comes with strings attached. At the very least you will need to provide detailed monitoring of outcomes so that the funding body can see if its money is being well spent. This is reasonable from the funder's point of view, but possibly a distraction for you. If the funding is coming from a secular agency like the National Lottery, they may not like an overtly Christian ethos, particularly if you are 'faith-promoting' or 'proselytising'. There may also be problems with 'diversity', if you only work with men or women, for example.

This is not to say that all external or secular funding is 'bad' or in some way contaminated. After all, if you are causing ex-prisoners not to return to prison, you are saving the country very large amounts of money; it's only reasonable for that to be recognised. Nevertheless, you need to be careful what you apply for and how you apply for it.

- The moment you rely on external funding to pay staff, you create a monster. When you begin your project, your main concern is for the people you serve. As soon as you are in the position of needing to fund an essential staff position from an external source, the focus of your project switches from the clients to fundraising, and then the project exists primarily to support itself. This is obviously wrong. Furthermore, your funding could be withdrawn for reasons beyond your control.

- 'Payment by Results' (PbR), the government's preferred way of funding the various agencies working with released prisoners under the Transforming Rehabilitation initiative, is to be treated with caution. The 'Results' in question are not readily measured. If someone doesn't go back to prison within a year, whose intervention proved effective? His offender manager's? His drugs support worker's? The housing association's? His girlfriend's? Or did he just decide that it was

133

time to change? The concept of PbR is flawed and sometimes leads to unhelpful clinical decisions.

In a blog post in October 2017,[67] Russell Webster reviewed the government's published evaluation of eight pilot PbR-funded drug and alcohol recovery programmes. The schemes in the pilot saw an increase in the cost of treatment per client without improving their outcomes. He concluded:

> Unfortunately, this evaluation has confirmed my original assessment of these pilots as being fundamentally flawed... the design of the pilots effectively disrupted a critical element of treatment and recovery systems. Most new treatment entrants were not greeted by a skilled practitioner aiming to build motivation and engage them in a recovery journey but by a bureaucrat wishing to decide what payment tariff should be applied in their case.

That said, the flagship for all PbR projects – the resettlement scheme at HMP Peterborough, launched in 2010 and led by St Giles Trust – is still operating and in August 2017 announced a 9 per cent reduction in offending.[68] This scheme introduced the Social Impact Bond (SIB) as a new funding model to repay investors for achieving outcomes on a PbR basis.

At the beginning of 2018, nineteen out of twenty-one regional CRCs were facing a cut in their budgets under PbR because they had failed to meet their targets for reducing re-offending.[69]

What's that in your hand?

God asked Moses what he had in his hand (Exodus 4:2). By the means of his staff, God demonstrated His power to Moses and to those who were with him. God is well able to provide funding for

---

[67] Webster, 2017a.

[68] Webster, 2017.

[69] Savage, 2018.

your project. He is God: all the resource is at His disposal. He could do it supernaturally by means of fishing (Matthew 17:27) or by giving you a generous benefactor, but it's more likely that alongside your project, He'll show you a way to provide income for it that will also benefit your participants. If God is driving your project, He will resource it one way or another so, while a diversity of income streams is good, there should be no need to pursue financial support as a matter of priority: 'seek first the kingdom of God' (Matthew 6:33).

This is not to say that you shouldn't claim money to which you are legitimately entitled. If you are looking to provide supported accommodation, for example, you can claim Housing Benefit on behalf of your residents at a significantly enhanced rate. (This system may change as Universal Credit rolls out.)

This principle applies to the project as a whole and also to you as individuals. Walk has an ethos of voluntary work. When we first started Walk, no one was paid anything but minimal expenses; as we have grown, our expectation is that staff are paid for a number of hours but give at least the same again unpaid. We need staff who are disciples of Jesus Christ and who share our passion for the work. We build the same ethic into the programme, so that the men we work with learn to give their time freely before they are paid.

In God's economy, to be a leader, you must serve; to be first, you must make yourself last, and to be rich, you must become poor.

Charitable status

Some of the same considerations apply to registering as a charity. It confers certain advantages, but the administrative burden is considerable. You need the input of a lawyer[70] as you put your charitable articles together and decide what sort of charity you are going to be.

---

[70] Consider www.lawworks.org.uk, who provide free legal advice (accessed 3rd August 2018).

If your organisation will be trading, or will have a trading aspect, consider being a Community Interest Company or a Social Enterprise rather than a standard charity.

A charity must conform to the regulations set out in charity law, must adhere to at least one of the charitable purposes described in the law, and must have an income exceeding £5,000. The Charity Commission website sets these charitable purposes out at length, but these are the headings:[71]

- The prevention or relief of poverty

- The advancement of education

- The advancement of religion

- The advancement of health or the saving of lives

- The advancement of citizenship or community development

- The advancement of the arts, culture, heritage or science

- The advancement of amateur sport

- The advancement of human rights, conflict resolution or reconciliation or the promotion of religious or racial harmony or equality and diversity

- The advancement of environmental protection or improvement

- The relief of those in need, by reason of youth, age, ill-health, disability, financial hardship or other disadvantage

---

[71] See: https://www.gov.uk/government/publications/charitable-purposes/charitable-purposes#descriptions-of-purposes (accessed 10th August 2018).

- The advancement of animal welfare

- The promotion of the efficiency of the armed forces of the Crown, or of the efficiency of the police, fire and rescue services or ambulance services

If your income is under £5,000, provided you adhere to charity law, your organisation may still operate as a charity as long as you do not use the words 'registered charity' or 'charity status' to describe it. Registering as a charity may bring your organisation under scrutiny from the Charity Commission and the HMRC.

Consider partnering with an existing organisation

It may be that there is already a group in your area doing something similar, but not quite the same as you. You could learn from their experience and pool resources; a partnership might be mutually beneficial. You might be able to launch more quickly, and an established organisation may give you access to a developed professional network.

Challenge

Bring everyone who shares aspects of your vision together for a day. This might include those who are going to operate the project, along with any other stakeholders. Consider inviting someone who might be a potential client, and local church leaders, if they are on board (but be careful that they don't hijack your agenda or subordinate you in some way). A diverse group of people with different experience and different priorities is good. Don't invite leaders of other projects, even if you think they might bring useful contributions: this is about your vision, not theirs.

The aims of the day will be to clarify what your 'vision' is and, from that, what your 'mission' will be. You may also begin to identify some key personnel and their roles.

Your 'vision' in this sense is the broad brush of your passion. It's the engine that drives you; your call of God. Your 'mission' is what you are going to deliver on the ground, and how. It's helpful to write both down, but of the two, the 'mission' statement is the more important, because it will guide your activity.

- Assemble your team (including yourself!) into groups of three or four, each with a flip chart, and ask them to write down the things that they are most passionate about in Christian service. (Or, you could narrow it down: What do you think this project is about?)

- Bring the groups together into a plenary session and ask the group to prioritise the points identified.

- In small groups again, ask participants to think of ways to deliver these vision points practically.

- In plenary again, prioritise these into specific action points. These will hopefully form the mission of your project. You can take two or three of the action points to create a sharp focus. It is important that these are agreed by the group.

- You can develop this in two ways, time permitting:

  o Derive a mission statement from the points you have identified, of the type shown earlier in this chapter.

  o Try to identify some actionable targets: 'By next February, we will have achieved X. Y will oversee this.'

8
The Team

Whatever your project is going to do, you need a good team of people around you; people who share your vision and passion for Christ and who bring necessary attributes with them. Our experience at Walk has been that God sends the right people at the right time.

The servant's heart

> Let this mind be in you which was also in Christ Jesus, who, being in the form of God, did not consider it robbery to be equal with God, but made Himself of no reputation, taking the form of a bondservant, and coming in the likeness of men. And being found in appearance as a man, He humbled Himself and became obedient to the point of death, even the death of the cross.
> *Philippians 2:5-8*

The moment money becomes your motivation, you are immediately not as good as someone who is stimulated by passion and internal will.[72]

Following in the footsteps of Christ, we are here to serve. We serve one another; we serve those we are called to support, and in doing this we serve Him. It has to start with our attitude, regardless of whether we are paid for what we do. If you are thinking of starting a project of any scale, it will almost certainly be someone's

---

[72] Accredited to Sebastian Vettel.

main employment; if you're providing supported accommodation, you will need people to be 'on call' 24/7, if not living on site. If things are going to fall apart, it will be at three in the morning.

Money is a sensitive subject for many people; an almost universal source of friction. It breaks fellowship apart and is a powerful tool in the enemy's hands, but it is one of the ways in which the world is mediated and one of the ways in which we understand how the world works. It's a powerful thing because it seems so big and so real, and it can't be avoided. For most of us, our dependence on the world is like an addiction to money. But this isn't what Jesus teaches.

> Therefore I say to you, do not worry about your life, what you will eat or what you will drink; nor about your body, what you will put on. Is not life more than food and the body more than clothing? Look at the birds of the air, for they neither sow nor reap nor gather into barns; yet your heavenly Father feeds them. Are you not of more value than they?
> *Matthew 6:25-26*

These words are very familiar to us, yet somehow, we often lack the life of them. Jesus is saying, 'Your Father loves you, so trust Him.' If you are going to launch out into this particular deep, you will need to exercise faith and trust God. There is no other way to do it. This is not to say that you don't need to be savvy and know how the various financial systems work, but that if God is calling you to undertake a journey, He will provide the fuel.

At Walk, everyone volunteers. Participants are given voluntary placements as part of a route into paid employment; some staff are salaried, but no one is paid full-time. We cannot reasonably expect men coming out of prison into the community to work for nothing if we are not prepared to do it ourselves. When we started the project, everyone gave their time freely – fifty, sixty, seventy hours a week – and no one was paid for the first year or so. Now, most staff are paid part-time, but also give voluntary hours. We want to keep ourselves in the position of needing to trust God – and it's also the right thing to do.

So, the first point in this chapter is: everyone's a volunteer; some people are paid a bit too. We want to teach servanthood as an aspect of discipleship, and we must model it. If our funding ceased next week it would be painful, but we would continue to work: 'God shall supply all [our] need according to His riches in glory by Christ Jesus' (Philippians 4:19).

Contracts

Staff who do both paid and voluntary hours must have this formalised into separate contracts. Otherwise it will appear to onlookers (including the HMRC) that you are exploiting people by not paying the minimum wage. This includes project staff and any other people you have who work voluntary hours. At some point, someone will leave your project and accuse you of exploitation – a serious accusation. You must 'have your ducks in a row', so to speak.

The right people

In the light of this, it's essential that you have the right people on your team. We mentioned previously that there are tourists, poachers and gamekeepers. We'll develop this thought a little further.

Tourists

Some people like the idea of working with released prisoners. Maybe 'frontline' ministry appeals to them, or perhaps they are genuinely testing what might be a call of God. Or perhaps they are attracted by the 'romance' of working with people who have done 'bad' things. For Christians who have lived rather sheltered lives, the idea of getting to know people who have lived radically different lifestyles has a kind of frisson. I remember being directly challenged by a female prisoner at one of the prisons I visited: 'Why are you here?' In other words, 'Have you just stepped out of your comfortable middle-class life for an hour to look at us?' Or worse, 'Are you "getting off" on this?' The emphasis was definitely on the 'you' rather than on the 'why'.

Tourists will not stay for the long haul or when things get difficult or demanding. As servants, we need to check our own motivation. I could have been offended by that question, but I chose to take up the challenge; I had been asking myself the same thing.

Poachers

Poachers will join your group saying all the right things but will have an agenda of their own. While tourists are mainly a danger to themselves, poachers can damage your project and hurt the people you are working with. Poachers (to get creative with the metaphor) are wolves in sheep's clothing.

For example: George, a former volunteer, who left after a disagreement, is married with young children and lives a short distance away from your project. He and his wife start to invite participants to their house to eat with them, though this is against your policy.

- Various participants share their grievances about the project with George, who then shares them as 'prayer points' in his church.

- A couple of the people he invites to his house are recovering addicts on the verge of lapsing back into drug use and pose a danger to him and his family. He is not aware of this.

Poachers can be hard to spot, but they have some common characteristics:

- They have a problem recognising and submitting to authority. Often, they are people who find it hard to settle in a church.

- Consistent with this, they will fail to recognise boundaries and resist accountability structures – specifically the protocols you place around your ministry, but sometimes even things that might seem like common sense like, 'don't invite a heroin addict for tea'.

- They will tend to have a divisive effect on your team.

Often, people who turn out to be poachers have deep spiritual or psychological needs that are unidentified or unresolved. Looking into their background a bit will often show that they have had many jobs, many volunteering positions, many churches and even many marriages in a relatively short space of time. They may join your group in order to 'belong' and to gain self-esteem. This is not to denigrate anyone, or to question whether a person is really called by God. They may be, but their issues need to be identified and addressed before they can safely support others. Possibly they need to be participants before they can be colleagues.

Gamekeepers

Your core team is composed of gamekeepers. These are the people to whom God has given the vision and the ability to carry out His work. They walk out the gospel in a consistent way. We find that God sends them along as and when they are required – and they will fit in seamlessly.

These are the people who will step out in faith and work without pay; who will turn out at 3.30am to sort out a crisis and not be fazed by whatever mess they find, who will drop what they are doing and pursue a man into some crack den to pull him out, if that is what the Holy Spirit said or, alternatively, let him go without a word.

Usually, the gamekeepers have been in prison themselves, or have a colourful history of some kind; they know what is at stake, and they understand what needs to happen for a person to change. Gamekeepers have a deep knowledge of the Word of God and live it out practically.

In short, because someone expresses an interest in being part of your ministry, it doesn't mean that they should be. You must have the clear prompting of the Holy Spirit about who is in your team.

Compassion

A prison chaplain, working in a Young Offender Institution in the south of England, was feeling overwhelmed by the level of need she encountered from day to day. In the end, she prayed that God would enable her to see the people she was working with through His eyes. This made the difference.

Several years later, I worked with her in a different prison. At the end of a study session, twenty or so burly, tattooed and shaven-headed lads emerged from the chapel followed by the diminutive figure of the chaplain. 'My babies!' she exclaimed, as she headed towards the office. She genuinely loved them and, to them, she was a kind of surrogate mother, nursing and nurturing them in their first steps of faith. She was there when bad news came, or in the midst of their depression. She arranged self-esteem workshops for victims of bullying and prolific self-harmers. She fought their corner when they became stuck in the faceless system. And they were the loveless ones, the pariahs – the robbers, rapists, murderers and thieves that few others would go near.

This is the model of Christ, who goes out in search of the lost sheep. 'Feed My lambs', said Jesus to Peter (John 21:15), and we must too: 'Imitate me, just as I also imitate Christ', said Paul (1 Corinthians 11:1).

This work is never about you; it can only ever be about those you support and the One you serve. If, at any point, you become the focus, you are likely to become a poacher of one kind or another. You need to be well grounded in yourself, spiritually mature and psychologically resilient. You must also keep perspective; a participant might think you're a saint or a hero as you rescue them from an impossible situation, and two weeks later you'll be the devil incarnate when you won't let them have their smartphone back.

How?

You can only do this as God empowers you through His Spirit. Also, you need a clear moment of godly direction, like the chaplain above: 'Help me to be You to these men!'

Biblical qualification: a challenge

Read 1 Timothy 3:1-13, where the apostle Paul instructs Timothy on the criteria for selecting church leaders.

How well do you measure up?

When we work with offenders we often need to ask ourselves and each other searching questions and require truthful answers. We cannot and must not do this in condemnation; in fact, we must often hold a mirror up to ourselves. The question is, 'Can the enemy (or a very manipulative person) get a hook into you?' Are you:

- … above reproach;

- … faithful to your spouse (do you view sexually explicit material?);

- … self-disciplined in the use of intoxicants (alcohol, prescription opiates);

- … self-disciplined in the use of money;

- … self-disciplined in the use of time (including work–life balance);

- … living wisely (for example, obeying speed limits);

- … of good reputation;

- ... hospitable;

- ... able to teach (and able to be take correction);

- ... violent;

- ... argumentative;

- ... motivated by money;

- ... managing your family well?

And also:

- How long have you been a Christian (are you a 'novice'?)?

- Are you committed to Christ?

- Do you have a clear conscience?

If you didn't do very well, remember that 'If we confess our sins, He is faithful and just to forgive us our sins and to cleanse us from all unrighteousness' (1 John 1:9).

Credibility

At one level, God can and will call anyone to work with released prisoners. He called me, the ultimate church boy, and there are numerous more notable examples: David Wilkerson and Jackie Pullinger, among others, who had little idea of what they were getting into, but just went and God moved mightily. However, these are exceptions.

In general, your frontline staff – those who deal with participants from day to day – need to have similar life experiences to them. If you're working with homeless people or drug users, your staff should have been there; if you are working with released prisoners, your staff should have been there. There is no sensible alternative to this. If an addict who has been clean for a while starts to lapse, they will be able to disguise it from most people, but not from someone who has been in their shoes.

The same applies when participants are aggressive or offer violence. You need people there who will not be fazed by this – who will stand in the way and close it down.

Challenge

- Use the passage from Timothy to help you draw up a profile of the kind of person you want on your team.

   o   What character attributes should they exhibit?

   o   Which attributes are the most important?

   o   How can you cultivate these in a busy and stressful workplace?

You are going to call on people to change the way they are living their lives. Perhaps they will need to make radical changes. As Gandhi is alleged to have said, you must be the change you want to see in the world.

- How can you hold your team to the highest standard of behaviour without seeming heavy-handed?

- In your estimation, how important is 'lived experience' in peer mentors?

9
The 'Strands'

The chapter on 'Why People Stop Offending' gave an analysis of the current theories about how to support those who have offended to reintegrate with the community. The argument was quite technical and possibly alienating for some people. This chapter looks at how the problems facing released prisoners can be broken down and approached practically.

We want our projects to be successful, of course. We want our participants to be helped in significant ways; we also want them to have a positive experience of working and walking with us. We are inclined to claim that what we are doing is 'effective' because it feels good, even though we don't know this for sure. There has been at least one example of an officially accredited programme designed to decrease prisoners' likelihood of reoffending that had precisely the opposite effect.[73] As Christians, we are not immune from this kind of thing, and it is easy to convince ourselves that we are being effective and making a difference, when the opposite is in fact true.

We may also think that if our participants are in a Christian project, living in proximity with other Christians, going to church and 'under the sound of the gospel', that this will benefit them in some way, as if by osmosis.

We must be able to measure what we do; this is especially true if we are taking money from the council or from a charitable fund, who will normally ask for some sort of care plan or some evidence that we have a structured and purposeful approach. To be honest,

---

[73] Rose, 2017.

we need this anyway. We want to do a good job, so we need to have some way to measure and evaluate what we do.

When someone with complex needs comes out of prison, they may be given an 80 per cent probability of reoffending within the next two years. This is not untypical. They may have substance dependency and mental health problems, few skills and unstable accommodation; in addition to this, everyone they know is in a similar position. Their prospects are not great. A few people manage to pull themselves out of situations like that, but most will need the help of a lot of different people and agencies: the health service, drug and alcohol counsellors, probation officers, their friends and possibly a church as well. If they succeed, it can be hard to see who made the critical difference.

Then again, there are a number of people who will stay in the support system for years, moving from project to project without making any real progress. Local councils and other funders, needing to use their funds in the most efficient way, will be aware of this and will ask you to report on the level of support you provide and to whom.

Defining areas of need

In 2005, the National Offender Management Service (NOMS, replaced by Her Majesty's Prison and Probation Service, HMPPS, since April 2017) identified seven Pathways to Resettlement which contribute to reducing the likelihood of released prisoners reoffending.[74] Each indicates an area of need or deficit experienced by an offender that is likely to lead them to reoffend. These are known as 'criminogenic needs'.

---

[74] See http://www.recoop.org.uk/pages/pathways/ (accessed 16th August 2018).

1. Accommodation

This provides the foundation for all other support. Compared with a lack of safe and suitable accommodation, all the client's other problems appear relatively small.

2. Education, training and employment

Having a job can reduce the risk of reoffending by between one-third and one-half.

That makes it sound as if everyone coming out of prison needs a job, but it's not as simple as that. Very few recently released prisoners can move straight into the labour market.

3. Health

Offenders are disproportionately more likely to suffer from mental and physical health problems than the general population, and also have high rates of alcohol misuse. Not surprisingly, about a third of adult prisoners have emotional well-being issues linked to their offending behaviour.

4. Drugs and alcohol

The large majority of offenders admit that drug or alcohol use was either directly or indirectly involved in their offending. They may also have health problems related to drug use, such as Hepatitis C or thromboses.

5. Finance, benefits and debt

Ensuring that released prisoners have sufficient lawfully obtained money to live on is vital to their rehabilitation. About half of prisoners report a history of debt. Most prisoners will claim benefits on release; it can be difficult to negotiate a benefits system that can seem obtuse and even hostile. The new Universal Credit system, at the time of writing, sees applicants often waiting six weeks for their initial payment.

6. Children and families

Maintaining strong relationships with families and children plays a major role in helping some prisoners to make and sustain changes that help them to avoid reoffending. Prison will have placed additional strains on these relationships.

On the other hand, the very last thing that some released prisoners need is close contact with their families, who may present a significant risk for them in reoffending.

7. Attitudes, thinking and behaviour

Prisoners are more likely than the general population to have negative social attitudes and poor self-control.

NOMS later added two more Pathways for female prisoners:

8. Abuse

Women with histories of violence and abuse are over-represented in the criminal justice system and can often be described as victims as well as offenders; coercion by men can form a route into offending for some women.

9. Prostitution

A significant number of women in prison have been sex workers. Often prostitution is closely linked with crimes of exploitation, such as human trafficking and slavery.

These should not be thought of as sealed boxes, but as areas of focus. In many cases, if a person's accommodation and money are sorted out, they 'have a leg to stand on', as it were, and some of the other things, like employment, will start to look more positive. Similarly, if their dependency on alcohol is being addressed, it is possible to work with them on their mental health difficulties or their relationship with their family.

The areas are generic but form a useful guide to the kind of things that are going to help keep people out of prison and enable them to integrate with wider society. It's very unlikely that you will be able to address all these Pathways, at least not all at once, and it may be that you find yourself reinterpreting some of them.

For example, at Walk we don't find that 'Children and families' is a useful category. We like the men we work with to have good relationships with their families, but in most cases, it comes some way down the list, and there have been several instances where uncontrolled contact with his family has led almost directly to a participant's reoffending. Often these relationships need careful qualification and management.

However, we created a category called 'Social networks and relationships'. We want to see those we support breaking away from their former associates, who may be linked with drug taking, homelessness and offending, and forming new networks that are positive and 'pro-social'. Initially, these may be based on the Project itself and the local church. For this reason, we prefer to work with people from outside their immediate area. This deviates somewhat from HMPPS' policy of keeping people in their localities.

If a client has begun to build good-quality relationships within the law-abiding community, when things go wrong (which they will, at some point), his default response might be to seek those people out rather than his former associates.

How the Walk Project works

From the outset, we understood that we needed a systematic approach. We started to build the Project within the original seven Pathways. Those were a good starting point, but they didn't exactly describe what we were trying to achieve. Eventually, we settled on nine 'Strands'. These define in some detail everything that we seek to achieve with our participants.

The Strands are:

- Accommodation

- Dependency

- Social networks and relationships

- Physical and mental health

- Self-care and living skills

- Money and debt management

- Attitude, thinking and behaviour

- Education, training and employment

- Spiritual growth

These headings are subdivided into specific statements through which we can assess and monitor the candidate's type and level of need before he joins the Project; the type of support that we will be able to provide; any referrals to other agencies for the things that we can't provide; the participant's ongoing level of engagement; and his level of outstanding need. Every contact a member of staff has with him is recorded against these criteria.

This is a big undertaking, and there is a danger that the whole thing could degenerate into a 'box-ticking' exercise; we have to be vigilant against this.

Accommodation

This divides into:

- Accommodation
    Before the person comes to us we carry out a detailed structured interview in which, among other things, we look at what his other options will be if he doesn't join us. We will

also make a decision, if we accept him, as to what the best housing option will be for him within Walk.

- Utilities

    Initially, we ensure that his electricity, gas, etc are paid for. Later, these will be his responsibility.

- Housing and other support

    We make sure at an early stage that he has the necessary support elements in place. Some of these will be specialists, such as a drug and alcohol counsellor; others may be local volunteers, such as a peer mentor.

Dependency

The Pathways look at 'alcohol and illegal drugs' but we pitch this a little wider. If a person is going to become a disciple of Jesus Christ, he cannot remain dependent on anything else. This, of course, is a lifelong journey for all who call themselves Christians, as we learn to depend on God. In practice, we narrow it down to: alcohol, street drugs and recreational substances, abuse of prescription drugs, unhelpful or unhealthy relationships and pornography.

Some of these we approach directly through intervention or therapy; some are approached more indirectly through ethos and spiritual guidance. In practice, though, we divide the Strand up into three areas:

- Alcohol and illegal drugs

    If a candidate is an active drug user or is on a maintenance medication, we direct him to Liberty Farm, Walk's high dependency unit, where he can get clean and stable.

- Lapse and relapse

    Lapse is a constant danger for those who have been in addiction. If a resident should return to drug use, he may be able to hide this from staff for a while, but within a short space of time, he will take his whole house down with him. Staff and participants need to be constantly vigilant and try to pick up the changes in attitude and thinking that usually precede a lapse. Residents must also be closely supported through times of stress, when their default response will often be to use drugs.

- Prescribed opioid and other addictive meds
    Problems can arise when doctors legitimately prescribe opiate-based analgesics. Their effects are similar or identical to the street drugs the person has been addicted to, and their use will almost certainly lead to a relapse.

We have had several incidents where former addicts, who have been clean for many years, relapse after being prescribed opiates for illness or an injury.

Other aspects of Dependency are supported informally.

Social networks and relationships

This is a crucial category, and one that has often been overlooked by those working with released prisoners. A large part of identity is who a person identifies himself with: if he sees himself as an offender among other offenders, he will probably continue to offend.

We divide this section into:

- Understanding personal relationships
    Some people only have experience of relationships that are problematic in some way. Maybe they come from a dysfunctional background of some kind and find it hard to base relationships on trust. Sometimes they will favour an identification or an emotional tie over a relationship built on mutual respect. It can be hard to break through these things, and good relationships as they start to form are sometimes brittle. It's easy to say the wrong thing without knowing it.

If there is a single key to the successful rehabilitation of released prisoners, it is probably social integration. When someone feels that they have a place in the community – a 'stake', that they have something to offer and that they are valued – it takes away the need to look for meaning and identity elsewhere.

- Family and children

    Part of this process may be the person's rejoining his family. Sometimes he will see this as a priority, particularly if he has children that he wants to maintain contact with. But this usually has to be managed carefully – we have seen several men relapse and slip back into their old lives after regaining contact with family members.

    We normally leave it several months before this kind of meeting is even considered, and then we arrange it carefully and gradually. Where children are concerned, the arrangement is mediated by a social worker.

- Romance and marriage

    Originally, we did not intend to include any particular guidance or teaching on this topic, but it became apparent that it was necessary. In fact, several participants who were mature in their Christian faith had very little idea of what Christian marriage looks like. As part of the Out Course – Walk's classroom-based life skills programme – we provide detailed teaching on this topic.

Physical and mental health

We divide the category into four sections:

- Medical practitioners

    When a participant first joins Walk, we take him to the local medical centre to sign up with the GP. We give him a letter from the Walk Project explaining that he is on the programme.

We expect the GP to sign him off, at least for the short term, so that he can begin to settle back into life with the stability of Employment Support Allowance (ESA).

To begin with, we monitor appointment times, etc, but after a while, we expect participants to manage their own.

- Physical health

    At their initial interview, candidates are asked about various aspects of their health. We need to know if they have a food allergy, for example, or if they have a communicable disease, like Hepatitis C, or one that has the potential to be life-limiting, like diabetes or hypertension.

- Mental health

    Most people leaving prison suffer from anxiety and depression; many are also diagnosed with personality disorders. We have found that while these things need to be monitored, the provision of stable and safe accommodation, a supportive social network, a routine and clear boundaries ameliorate the problems to a large extent, though it may take a considerable time for this to become apparent.

    The continued use of certain drugs (such as amphetamines and cannabis) and even the short-term use of some of the 'new psychoactive substances' (such as 'spice') can lead to symptoms of psychosis, which is harder to manage.

    Those diagnosed with psychotic illness will need expert mental health supervision; their behaviour can be unpredictable and disruptive. If they are on prescribed medication, this needs to be taken properly and closely monitored. Addicts tend to trade their meds and also to binge on them – and this has potentially serious consequences.

- Suicide risk and self-harm

Many, if not most, of the people we work with have used self-harm as a kind of self-medication. Some may also have attempted to take their own lives at some point.

Self-harm

Some people inflict injury on themselves as a way of externalising internal trauma or frustrations. Sometimes this is quite minor, but there are people who inflict maiming or life-threatening injuries on themselves. It should be understood as a coping strategy; we should work with self-harmers to find another – safer – outlet for their feelings.

Suicide

Significantly more prison-leavers attempt or complete suicide than the general population. In itself, leaving prison is a major and potentially traumatic life change. For the most part, we cannot know how someone is coping or feeling unless they choose to tell us – so suicide is not predictable. However, whether a person has attempted suicide in the past may indicate that they might try it again.

We ask questions directly about this in the initial interview.

Self-care and living skills

Not having good self-care and living skills is unlikely to be a factor in a person's reoffending; nevertheless, it is a very important area of consideration in rehabilitation and resettlement.

Self-care refers to things like the ability to prepare a meal, keep a reasonable standard of personal hygiene and manage any chronic health conditions; living skills include managing a budget, shopping effectively, opening a bank account and learning to drive. This area overlaps with other Strands, but taken together, we consider the things that reinforce a person's ability to live independently in the community.

Money and debt management

Most participants are carrying debt when they come to us. Sometimes this is a lot, but it mostly amounts to between a few hundred and a couple of thousand pounds, usually in the form of unpaid fines, rent or council tax, or mobile phone contracts. The amount is almost immaterial – it can seem an insurmountable obstacle for a person trying to put his life together. As soon as they have a 'settled' address, the letters start arriving from collection agencies; and this can be a real disincentive to getting a job and earning proper money. The person assumes that it will simply be taken from them – and it might, without intervention.

We divide this heading into two aspects:

- Historical debt

  Walk will link the participant up with an appropriate service, who will work with him to manage his situation and mediate with creditors, where necessary.

- Personal finances

  When participants first arrive, we rarely let them have access to their money. Generally, we keep their bank cards under lock and key, and only let them have access to them under supervision; this usually lasts for a few weeks. It might sound extreme, but relatively few even have bank accounts when they first arrive. Sometimes, they will have had their benefits paid into a friend's account – which is a risky thing to do.

  Being able to keep and manage your money through a bank account is quite a high-order skill.

Attitude, thinking and behaviour

This is one of the largest and most important areas we work within; it impinges upon every aspect of a person's life and is too big to discuss fully here. We divide it into five sub-headings:

- Relationships with statutory services

When someone first comes out of prison, often their most important relationship is with their probation officer. They will have licence conditions to comply with, and failure to do so can have them sent back to prison. Few released prisoners are happy about this, but the fact is that they were probably released halfway through their sentence, and so they are, in fact, still serving it.

Most probation officers are extremely busy and under considerable stress. At the time of writing, enforcement officers working with a CRC may have as many as *ninety* clients to supervise, so the quality of their attention is not always perfect. Moreover, for obvious reasons, most offenders have a cultural aversion to probation officers, but we want our participants to be courteous and compliant, and to do what is required of them, which is, of course, in everyone's interest.

The same applies to social workers, drug and alcohol support workers and medical professionals.

- Offending behaviour

There are many reasons why offenders stop offending, some of which are discussed in the earlier chapter 'Why People Stop Offending'. We want our projects to be part of that picture. There can be a fine line between equipping a person to break away from a troubled past and move into a better future, and enabling their problematic behaviour to continue.

Our aim is for participants to be able to identify and refrain from the problematic attitudes and thought processes that lead to offending. From a spiritual perspective, we would call this repentance.

- Thinking skills

Building good 'thinking skills' is one of the most important things we do at Walk. Thinking styles and patterns are at the back of a lot of offending; these include impulsivity, poor decision-making and cognitive distortions, where an offender will justify his actions on the grounds of a skewed logic or understanding of the world. These things affect a person's ability to relate to other people, to build healthy relationships, to participate in the community as a citizen and to respond well to emergencies.

In a very large part, these things are addressed indirectly through relationships, in the sometimes painful process of living and working together, but we also address them directly through one-to-one counselling and in the classroom.

- Citizenship

  We want our participants to go on from us to be active, pro-social citizens, in whatever context they find themselves. This is modelled through the relationships we have with them, but we also teach it explicitly.

- Emotional management

  Those of Walk's participants who have dropped out and sometimes reoffended, have often done so because they got angry or frustrated because they didn't think the programme was meeting their expectations. Quite often, this is because they met a woman. We have no problem with our lads meeting women as such, and it may be an ideal outcome in some cases. We love to go to weddings!

  Unfortunately, damaged people tend to attract other damaged people, and this is not a good foundation for a relationship. It has been well said that we are all looking for someone whose demons play well with ours. We address 'Building healthy relationships' explicitly; participants will only be able to build healthy relationships to the extent that they are managing their own issues.

  Other things addressed within emotional management are self-esteem, empathy and the ability to deal with boredom and loneliness.

Education, training and employment

One of Walk's primary aims is to get participants off benefits and into part-time work where possible within about six months, though it may take longer depending on each person's employability.

People who have been institutionalised may feel anxious about visiting the supermarket or crossing the road. The prospect of negotiating the benefits system, Jobcentre Plus and job interviews may be too much, so this is an area where support is needed.

Possibly they have come from a background where few people in their acquaintance had 'proper' employment, and they may have no cultural expectation of 'working for a living'. Or possibly, important developmental stages of their lives have been disrupted; they can learn the necessary skills to participate in the community, but this will take time, patience and a supportive environment.

- Literacy and numeracy
  While it's not the main priority, we will aim to give participants the opportunity to reach Level 2 in literacy and numeracy, where this is feasible. This is a requirement for registration on most work skills courses.

- Learning difficulties
  Where participants find it difficult to engage in learning activities because of some sensory, intellectual or physical impairment, we will seek to find them appropriate support.

- Work-readiness
  Much of the journey towards work-readiness happens 'on the job', but we also spend classroom time with participants. This gives us the opportunity to ask very specific questions about a person's ongoing level of need in particular areas and seek to address them. Work-readiness, it turns out, covers a lot more than the preparation for employment.

Spiritual growth

For Walk, spiritual growth is the fundamental Strand that underpins all the others, because it provides the context and the motivation for a participant to change his life. If a person desires 'to live godly in Christ Jesus' (2 Timothy 3:12), he will desist from offending, from taking drugs and from doing whatever other things were associated with his past behaviour. His relationships will be governed and articulated by love, and not by fear. Although this is never a linear path and there will inevitably be setbacks along the way, cultivating spiritual growth – or discipleship – is the key to a person living a new kind of life. We divide this Strand into two headings:

- Personal devotion and 'God-space'

  This is possibly the most important aspect of Christian discipleship. It is of little consequence whether a participant wants to follow a particular religious practice or expression – but it is vital that they develop their own relationship with God.

- Bible study

  We teach participants how to read and study the Bible for themselves, and also to explore their:

  o spiritual calling and gifting;

  o outward expression of faith; and

  o church participation.

These things are addressed specifically in worship and study sessions, starting with basics such as 'How do I pray?' and 'How do I approach the Bible?'. We work closely with a few churches from different denominations and seek to help participants to become active members of the congregations. Apart from the development of their faith, this helps provide a pro-social network.

Project monitoring

This detailed structure provides a strong framework for us to evaluate how each participant is progressing. We do this in three ways:

- We divide the Strands up in such a way that we can focus on how we deliver each aspect and, if necessary, which staff members are responsible for this.

- We can monitor each participant's level of engagement from week to week.

- We can readily identify participants' areas of outstanding need.

Each interaction with participants is recorded on a Contact Record, and these are reviewed with the participant every three months. At this meeting, we can discuss how he thinks he's doing and highlight any particular areas of concern or celebration; we can also assist in setting achievable goals.

Practical application – a community mentoring scheme

- How might you use this approach to set up and manage a different type of intervention?

Having developed an idea (refer to chapter 7, 'Realising Your Vision') that will address an identifiable area of need, look at the Pathways and determine which of them you will be able to address. Possibly, like Walk, you will adapt or interpret some of them – and you don't need to address them all.

You might address:

- Attitudes, thinking and behaviour

- Education, training and employment

Perhaps you feel unable to challenge 'offending behaviour' head-on (part of 'Attitudes, thinking and behaviour'), so your mentoring will concentrate on addressing things like developing a pro-social attitude, good decision-making and goal-setting, and emotional management. That looks like a feasible mission.

So, re-present those Pathway statements as your objectives. Perhaps you can formulate a mission statement around them that defines what you will do. Talk this over thoroughly with your team. Remember to consider the following:

- What are you trying to achieve?

- Why do you want to do this?

- Whom are you trying to reach?

- Who is going to run the project?

- Where will the project operate?

- How will the project operate?

Be aware of your local area and what the needs are. It's quite likely that the CRC will be interested in working with you, as may other agencies. Mentoring programmes can be accredited through the Mentoring and Befriending Foundation.[75] This will give you considerable traction with statutory agencies, but it is not a faith-based organisation, so beware of compromising any 'discipleship' aims you might have.

Possibly, in the future, you will want to expand your mentoring scheme to provide a drop-in centre as a base for your mentoring. If you were to do this, you would have to readdress your vision and mission statements, and ensure that your whole team was moving with you.

---

[75] www.mandbf.org (accessed 3rd August 2018).

Challenge

This chapter has described the Walk Project's operation is some detail. Each statement in the Strands has been developed to suit a particular need, and they provide an effective working model – but they are not set in stone. We are constantly revisiting and trying to improve the framework to make it more effective.

If you were operating a community mentoring scheme, such as the one described above:

- How would you go about selecting appropriate candidates?

- How would you ensure that your service was meeting their needs?

- How would you monitor its effectiveness over time?

10
Managing Property

One of the first things you encounter when you begin working with prisoners and ex-prisoners is the ongoing crisis in accommodation; in general, there are insufficient places for people to go when they leave prison. We have already mentioned that it is common for prisoners to be released to 'no fixed abode', or to be released into unsuitable or unstable circumstances. Prisons are under pressure not to make people homeless; sometimes, as we said earlier, they will find them one night in a bed and breakfast to get around this or supply them with a tent and a sleeping bag – both of which are obviously quite inappropriate.

Prisoners who present a higher risk of reoffending are sometimes accommodated in probation hostels (so-called 'approved premises'). These are reasonably safe[76] places – but when the time comes for them to leave, the same problem arises. And, of course, there are never enough places in hostels. In view of the scale of the problem, it is reasonable for churches and charities to want to get involved to address this need.

The first point to make here is that, while we as the Church have a role to play in supporting released prisoners and others who find themselves in need, it is the responsibility of the government and local authorities to ensure that there is suitable provision for the vulnerable people in our midst, and to have a strategic plan as to how this need will be met. For all the talk a few years ago of Big Society, and a genuine desire on the part of many to get involved in

---

[76] ... but not always. Crowson & Nelson, 2017.

social projects, it is not 'our job' to do things for which we are poorly equipped or resourced. Check your motivation for wanting to begin a project like this. You don't want to set off down a particular path and then realise that you have bitten off more than you can chew.

Charitable aims

Before you consider managing property, make sure that your constitution or your statement of charitable aims permits you to do this. Clarify this before you start; it may be necessary to set up a new charitable entity for the purpose.

What can the Church do?

The argument in this chapter is that, as part of a church-based group, you will manage accommodation in some respect for released prisoners as part of a more comprehensive resettlement or rehabilitation project, but there are several other reasons to manage property. For example, you might start a drop-in centre or a food or clothing bank, or a night-shelter,[77] or perhaps office facilities for your project.

There are many possibilities and opportunities; be responsive to the local situation but follow the vision that God has given you and the statement you have developed. As you meet people involved in the field, you will be told many times and in many ways what you should be doing, but don't be influenced too much by what other people's problems are. If someone is offering you a large, empty house 'for the ministry', it doesn't mean that you have to fill it with homeless ex-cons. Clarify your own vision and your objectives and follow them precisely. Always beware of 'mission-creep'; there are

---

[77] The Housing Justice Church and Community Night Shelter Network, 2017.

plenty of agencies who will send you inappropriate candidates if you allow them to. You can't fix the world's problems.

If your aim is primarily to provide accommodation, then it benefits you to be full most of the time, because this maximises your potential. If your aim is to provide a different service, such as Christian discipleship or a therapeutic intervention, you must be able to be selective about who you take, and your funding structure should reflect this. Can you survive if you are half full for a few months?

Acquiring property

How you go about acquiring property will depend on the economic situation where you are. In many areas of high social need, property prices and market rents are low; in other places the financial situation may be less favourable.

There are some Christian organisations set up to assist with this process. They purchase property and become 'the landlord'; they oversee all the maintenance and most of the property management functions. This is good – and it is good to work with another Christian organisation. It is definitely something to consider, but look at the deal carefully. These schemes often work out considerably more expensive than some alternatives, sometimes cripplingly so, and may lock you into a long-term contract that is hard to get out of. An arrangement like this, entered in good faith, might compromise the integrity of your project in the long term.

An alternative might be to find someone who either owns, or can acquire, property to let and will allow you to manage it, but who won't seek to maximise their financial return; a 'philanthropic landlord'. This is preferable, firstly because of the local connection. A local investor-landlord already has a strong interest in your project being a success. Secondly, and most importantly, a local person is more likely to share your vision. It is definitely preferable to work with landlords whose primary interest is not financial. If you manage the property well, they will gain on their investment over time, and also receive a modest rental income. You might think that this sounds quite unlikely, but this is not our experience, and currently four out of the five landlords we work with are on this kind of basis. This relationship should be governed by an appropriate contract that protects both parties, and since your landlord has a pecuniary interest, the extent to which they have any other role in your organisation must be carefully defined.

Finally, operating accommodation for vulnerable people is a massive commitment. It must be taken seriously: don't do this unless you are going to do it well.

Letting and subletting

Walk's model

This is not the only way to manage property, but it is what we have found to be workable, efficient and beneficial to everyone involved.

Typically, potential landlords in the process of acquiring a property contact Walk. In all cases – and they are quite diverse – the landlords share elements of Walk's vision and have a similar agenda; two of our landlords also work with other social housing charities. Walk agrees to manage the properties for them; in some cases this has involved carrying out extensive work to bring the properties up to the desired specification. Walk uses a standard contract with all the landlords; we are the tenant, but we also agree to arrange routine maintenance of the buildings and equipment because those skills are readily available to us.

Walk licences rooms within the properties to project participants. When a new man arrives at Walk we go through the Licence Agreement in detail with him. To avoid confusion, we are careful in our language to distinguish between our Licence Agreement and any licence they may have as part of their sentence. The Agreement covers almost all eventualities, because our accommodation is contingent upon the man engaging in the programme. The contract comes with a handbook, which gives detailed information about what is expected of participants. Sections include:

- Project aims and house rules

- Drugs and alcohol policy summary

- Code of conduct

- Disciplinary procedure

- Complaints procedure

- Instructions about electrical items

- Walk timetable

There are also various administration items associated with it that do not appear in the handbook; these include an End of Licence form, a room checklist and 'move-on' information.

Security

All Walk properties are covered by CCTV and, where appropriate, have exterior lighting; our shared houses have house leaders – participants who have been with the project for a considerable time and who are trusted. They oversee the day-to-day operation of things like cleaning rotas, shopping, etc, and are also the first point of support, identifying any developing problems early on. Part of the house leader's role is to be a spiritual 'anchor', and to ensure that everyone has the opportunity – and is encouraged – to participate in worship, personal devotions, etc, and that they attend church. The house leader also enforces the 10pm curfew: it is an important and demanding role.

All our properties are 'clean'. Our residents are subject to regular drug and alcohol testing and occasional room searches. Anyone bringing drugs or alcohol onto the premises will be asked to leave.

Planning housing

Your project will be different from Walk and you will develop your own distinct operating model, your own policies and procedures and your own relationships with landlords. You will need to develop your own policy framework and contracts.

Landlords

It may be that the limiting factor in any project is the availability of finance, but I'm going to assume that 'money is no object' up to a point. If what you are doing is 'of God', He will provide for you in it; if God isn't providing, you have to question seriously whether you are on the right track.

In most cases, it isn't necessary (or desirable) for the project itself to own much property. As discussed previously, it is better to work with landlords who share the vision for your project; however, it is unwise to strike deals with your friends or because people are fellow Christians. These arrangements have a habit of breaking down when people part company, and can lead to general difficulties and even allegations of fraud or corruption. Always be kind and compassionate, but always be professional, always be legal and always stick to the contract you have drawn up.

Your landlord's motivation is to serve God and the Church by investing a substantial amount of money in a capital asset, such as a house that you will manage. They stand to make a certain amount of money on the arrangement over time, and some of this will be from rent. How much this will be will depend on how full you are most of the time. This is an operational decision, but if you are under financial pressure to keep the house fully occupied, it will compromise your freedom of movement if, for example, you need to move somebody out. It is helpful if your rents are covered by Housing Benefit – which will limit the amount of rent your landlord is able to take. If your landlord has an operational role within your group, there may be (or appear to be) a conflict of interest.

Vision – build slowly

If your aim is to provide 'last resort' housing for people leaving prison who would otherwise be homeless, how are you going to do that? You may feel overwhelmed by the size of the problem but look at it rationally. Start small, grow slowly and concentrate on the quality of your service.

Consider these things:

• How will you keep your house safe?

Most people coming out of prison and who are likely to be of no fixed abode are either current or former drug users, or drinkers. It is likely that their offending is either directly or indirectly related to their drinking or drug taking. If your purpose is to help clients change their behaviour, you will have to keep your house free of alcohol and drugs, which means that you will need to make room checking and perhaps drug testing a condition of residency. Many organisations do not operate 'dry' houses, however. In that case, how would you maintain a safe environment?

Many homeless people have health or mental health-related problems. You must know if a resident is being prescribed medication, especially if this is opiate-based or susceptible to abuse.

Other problems may include victimisation and exploitation. Are you likely to be housing people with a history of violence alongside people who present as vulnerable?

Will you accommodate those convicted of sexual offences?

You must know if any of your clients present an elevated risk of suicide.

We recommend that accommodation is single sex, though we are aware that some projects provide mixed-sex accommodation within a shared house. Vulnerable women have rather different needs from vulnerable men, and a higher proportion of them will have been victims of sexual abuse or exploitation.

There is an especial need for projects that will support women leaving prison.

You may find yourself under moral pressure from various agencies to receive certain people they are having trouble housing. The bottom line in this is that you are responsible for the safe operation of your project, so you decide who lives in your house. You should have a clear admission procedure that includes some sort of risk assessment.

Your vision will also determine what, if anything, you are planning to do with people while they are with you. Are you only providing accommodation, or are you also going to offer a support programme, for example to get people into work or training? Are you going to signpost to other support services?

- Are you going to model or teach Christian discipleship?

This is a bit more problematic. Of course, our goal as Christians is to make disciples, so it's reasonable to offer to help people explore their faith. But what happens if non-Christians come to you? Or Muslims, or avowed atheists? Will they be welcome? If not, how will you present that?

All of this requires careful planning on the basis of your vision, and suitable personnel to be able to handle the day-to-day operation of the project.

You will find that your project has an optimum size, which has to do with how you engage with your client group and your community, your financial situation and who your staff are. Often the temptation is to expand to meet an apparent need, particularly if people offer you properties to manage and particularly if your income is related to the number of beds you can fill. Your focus must always be on the people you work with: all the other stuff, however pressing it may be, is peripheral to this. Don't expand faster than you are able to deliver your best service.

Funding for supported accommodation

At present, funding for those in supported accommodation comes through higher rates of Housing Benefit, administered by local councils. As part of the general reform to benefits, this arrangement will probably come to an end in April 2020 for 'short-term' provision (less than two years). The current proposal is that these schemes will no longer be funded through benefits, but from a ring-fenced funding pot held by local authorities for the purpose. It is not yet clear how additional support costs will be paid for, but our expectation is that the current model will be replaced by something roughly similar because the consequences of not doing so would be catastrophic for many providers of supported accommodation and their clients.

Support funding is granted on the basis of need, so if you make an application for it, you should be able to demonstrate what the client's need is and how you are going to address it. Some councils require regular and detailed reports on what support you are providing, but others are less stringent. The system has been somewhat open to abuse (or perhaps 'inefficiency' is a better term), in that some clients will regularly appear within the supported accommodation system, moving in and out of prison and from project to project, without appearing to make any substantial progress. We don't have to prove that any client has actually 'made progress', only that structured support is provided – and we may need to document this in detail (see chapter 9 on 'Strands'). Of course, if you succeed in moving someone out of support altogether, that's a bonus and the council will love you.

This funding is only available to those on Housing Benefit or with very low incomes, so when clients start to earn 'proper' money, they must come off the system and therefore move out of your house.

You should be aware that overpayments of support money, for example, if clients have moved into work or onto a lower level of support, will be reclaimed *from the client* and not directly from you – and that such an overpayment was probably triggered by your failure to inform the council quickly enough when your client moved on.

Challenge

If you live or serve God in a population centre of any size, you will be aware of the problems in the housing sector. This is visible at almost every level, from the lack of council-operated and other 'social' housing, to the provision of 'affordable' homes and the difficulty of even moderately well-paid people in living close to their employment in some cities.

As gospel-focused Christians, however, we must be concerned with the provision of appropriate housing for vulnerable people, including those who have been released from prison. All kinds of provision are necessary, from private lets to supported housing of various kinds and hostels for those in crisis and, as we shall see in a later chapter, women with children have particular needs in this respect.

Consider the following questions and seek the Lord as to how you might be able to help:

- Where are the housing pressure points in your locality?

  o Is this situation under active consideration by your local council?

  o Is there a local 'development plan'?

- What provision is there for people released from your local prisons?

- What is the nature of 'homelessness' in your community?

  o For example, are people sofa surfing, living in 'temporary' bed and breakfast accommodation, or sleeping rough?

  o Why are people homeless?

- What organisations are active in the provision of accommodation for vulnerable people?

- In your estimation, what does 'basic' accommodation look like?

  o What is a 'basic' level of space? Furnishing? Equipment?

  o Is this affordable by people on benefits? On minimum wage?

  o What level of amenities are there?

  o Is it close to shops and schools?

  o Is it close to public transport?

- How can you or your church be part of the solution?

Part 4

11
Assessing and Managing Risks and Needs

We looked in an earlier chapter at the models of offender management that there have been in recent decades, particularly the Risk-Need-Responsivity (RNR) model and more recent holistic approaches. We have also looked at how an offender's risk of reoffending can be estimated based on their history and their current 'criminogenic' needs. In this chapter I want to look at how you can apply these things practically in your project. First, let me reiterate the fundamental difference in approach between the way the criminal justice system treats those who have offended and how we ought to treat them in Christian ministry.

When a person goes before a court and is found guilty of a crime, the system will fall into place around them to try to prevent them from doing something like it again. In most cases, this intense scrutiny only lasts as long as the sentence imposed by the court, but in some circumstances, for example where Public Protection Arrangements are involved, or where there is Post-Sentence Supervision (PSS), it may last longer. Every decision made about the offender is taken on the basis of the risk they present of reoffending; this is based on computer-aided assessments and mediated by the experience of an offender manager. Whether or not the person is released from custody and into what circumstances, their level of supervision and any interventions they may be subject to post release are decided on the basis of risk – which is effectively the risk that they will be reconvicted of a similar offence.

We must be different from this and ask ourselves: 'How does God see this person?'

Imagine a man convicted of murder – we'll call him Joe. He's hypothetical, but there are plenty of people like him. He grooms a vulnerable young man before torturing him, killing him and dumping his body in a lake. He did it because he enjoyed the feeling of power it gave him. When talking to psychologists afterwards, he spins all sorts of half-convincing stories about his abusive upbringing, none of which are true. The assessment is that were he ever to be released from prison, he would probably do it again. Joe will spend a lot of time in 'maximum security' conditions and be handled with great caution. He is broadly compliant with the regime but does not fully engage in any courses or interventions. He maintains a quiet and superior demeanour, which is interpreted as arrogance. If he does start to change his attitude (which is what everyone wants, but no one expects), this will be regarded as a further attempt to manipulate, at least to begin with.

How does God see him? Is he an evil sinner, beyond redemption? His victim's family could be forgiven for thinking so. As could the police team who apprehended him.

The truth is that as well as 'people like me' and 'people like you', the sins of 'people like Joe' were carried by Jesus at Calvary. Joe is part of the world, and his sinfulness has found a particularly nasty expression. But God's grace is for him too. If he turns to trust Jesus Christ, he will be saved. The things that he has done do not disqualify him. I believe that God also sees more. Joe, like everyone else, is made in the image of God (Genesis 1:27). It's not just that Jesus' sacrifice throws a blanket of grace over the whole world so that 'whosoever will' may 'take the water of life freely' (Revelation

22:17, KJV), but that he is actively searching out the Joes of the world because He loves them and longs to see His character reflected in them. It brings Him especial glory and delight when people like this turn to Christ (Luke 15:7,10). It's vital that we keep a spiritual perspective and do not get drawn into condemnation.

This is not to say that someone like Joe does not have to pay the just penalty for the things he has done; of course he does, and must carry that for the rest of his life. Perhaps he will never be able to be released from prison; or perhaps in due course he will, but there is atonement for him in Christ. Nor is it down to us to 'forgive' him. We sometimes hear people say things like, 'I don't think Joe should be forgiven for what he did.' It is not for us to 'forgive' other people's sins in the sense of 'absolving' them. We can, and must, 'forgive those who trespass against us', but it is God's prerogative to forgive sin (Mark 2:7). This is an important distinction. This doesn't mean that we have to like everyone; and it certainly doesn't mean that we have to trust them. People like Joe must be treated with appropriate caution. But it does mean that as God works in us the grace to do it, we must demonstrate to them the love of Christ and rejoice with Him when they find salvation. Should they – after their release – find their way into our congregation or support project, we must give them the opportunity to grow in and explore their faith, and to live a 'good life'.

What risk?

When a prisoner is released, the main risk the authorities are attempting to mitigate is the risk that they will be reconvicted; implied in this is also the risk that they will cause harm to another victim. For us, working in the Christian charitable sector, and seeking to assist people in changing their lives for the better, there are risks too. In order, the risks we work with are these:

- The risk that our client will cause harm to other people.

- The risk that the person will harm himself or herself.

- The risk of harm to our staff, other participants or the project itself.

- The risk of recall or reconviction.

The safety of others and the integrity of the project (which has to be there to help the next man) is much more significant than the risk that the person will go back to prison. If he is in prison we know where he is and that he is reasonably safe; sometimes it appears that offenders are released too soon, and that their motivation to offend has not really been challenged.

Risk and needs assessment

In 1943, the psychologist Abraham Maslow identified different levels of need that human beings experience, and therefore different types of motivation that they have. Some people are motivated by very basic needs, such as the need for food or shelter; others are motivated by more refined needs, such as the need for friendship or fulfilment. He arranged these into a pyramid, from the most fundamental needs for shelter and food at the bottom, up to the 'higher' needs, for what he described as 'self-actualisation', where a person is able to realise their full potential, whatever that may be.

Then again, there are specific needs that individuals may have that tend to lead them into crime – such as a need for alcohol or heroin, or a need for proper employment. These crime-related, or 'criminogenic' needs are linked to the risk that an offender will reoffend. In the criminal justice system, this understanding is used to help assess the risk that an offender will be reconvicted in the future. It is measured in two elements:

- **The risk factors that do not change over time,** referred to as static risk factors, or sometimes actuarial risk factors, because they are used to calculate the statistical likelihood that an offender will reoffend. These include date of birth, previous convictions, age at first arrest, sex, employment history and relationship history.[78]

  Assessments based on these factors tend to be accurate predictors of whether a person will reoffend; they can also determine whether they are likely to present a risk to any particular people or groups – children, for example.

- **The risk factors that change over time.** These are known as dynamic risk factors or sometimes clinical factors because they respond to 'clinical' intervention or treatment. These include employment, cognitive abilities, drug and alcohol misuse, level of education, social networks, physical and mental health, and emotional management.[79]

  These are also known as criminogenic needs; the needs that a person has that are likely to lead them back into offending. They are not as clear an indication as the static factors, partly because these things will affect people in different ways, but they give support agencies a certain amount of leverage to be able to steer a person away from offending.

It is important to consider not just how risks can be managed and avoided, but how they can be mitigated or counteracted by 'protective' measures. A protective measure is like the antidote to a risk factor. If, for example, a person is at risk of offending because of his criminal associations, helping him to make new and different friends and to build a new 'pro-social' network will protect him.

We discussed these things in more detail in earlier chapters, which give some ideas as to how you might work with clients' needs. We believe that regardless of how troubled a person's past

---

[78] Kemshall, 2001.
[79] Arnold & Creighton, 2006.

might be, imparting to them the means to rise above it gives them at least the chance at a better life.

'Tom'

From our point of view, designing and operating a project intended to support those leaving prison is never as simple as arranging to provide for a person's physical needs.

Tom, a man in his forties, had been heavily abusing alcohol and other drugs for a long time; he also had some mental health problems. For the previous ten years, he had been going to prison several times a year for minor offences, calculated to put him in prison but not to cause any real harm.

He was released from prison to a Christian support project in a different city, which would provide accommodation, structure, supervision and spiritual direction. He was taken there by two volunteers from the prison chaplaincy, who picked him up from the prison gate and delivered him to the door.

After an interview, he excused himself to the toilet and absconded through a window. He subsequently attacked a police car and within three days was back in the prison he started from.

Six months later, exactly the same sequence of events was repeated, resulting in the mental health assessment he undoubtedly should have had in the first place.

Questions were later raised about whether an effective assessment had been carried out – but there had not been enough time for a thorough assessment in the few weeks of his sentence, nor were there many locations available to receive him. On previous occasions, he had been released to no fixed abode or to hostels, but always wound up back in prison.

What needs were the actors trying to fulfil?

The prison chaplaincy, probably by arrangement with the resettlement department, had a strong motivation to place Tom somewhere where he would be safe, find the support that he needed, and start to become more stable in his life. Their options were limited, however. Over the years, Tom had been in most of the available accommodation for released prisoners; none would take him now because his behaviour had proved difficult in the past.

The chaplaincy had links with several faith-based organisations that offered resettlement. This particular Christian support project, about forty miles away, offered certain advantages. They had space and were able to take Tom at short notice; their programme offered twenty-four-hour support and a safe and managed environment. However, although Tom acknowledged a Christian faith of sorts, the project operated an intense regime, and there was concern that Tom would find it intimidating.

Although the chaplaincy team were not privy to Tom's mental health diagnosis, he showed symptoms consistent with social anxiety. He appeared vulnerable and struggled with the prison environment – in spite of being such a frequent resident – and there was real concern that he would not settle well in the project. So, Tom was dispatched to his destination with some apprehension. It was not a great surprise that he returned quickly to prison.

On the second occasion, the circumstances were very similar. But this time, on his rearrest, he was referred for the psychiatric assessment he needed.

What needs was Tom trying to fulfil? What was motivating him? Why would he prefer to be back in prison than in a 'safe' place with the opportunity of moving on with his life?

One of the problems with Tom, and many people in similar circumstances, is that he does not actively seek a solution to his problems. He doesn't appear to be able to articulate his needs clearly, even to himself, and seems content to have other people make plans for him. However, given the opportunity to change, he 'votes with his feet'. He has a sense of purpose and an idea of what he wants – or at least, of what he doesn't want – but is so shy of personal interaction that he can't communicate it.

If we could perhaps sit him down in a quiet place with a cup of coffee and space to go and have a smoke, we might be able to get a 'snapshot' of his life and try to assess what his needs actually are, what risks he presents and what protective measures might be put in place. With his input (or at least, consent), we might be able to formulate a plan. This is likely to be a long process. Interventions in circumstances like these are only effective if the recipient freely embraces them.

Official agencies like the DWP, who arbitrate benefits these days, will want to see 'Tom' in the job market (it is likely that he would 'fail' a work capability assessment) but, in reality, he is a long way from being able to work. We have to start with the basics.

- First, *accommodation* is a serious problem, and without a safe and stable place to live, it will be hard to address any other issues.

  Tom knows how to survive on the streets or by sofa surfing. He may even feel safer in that environment than in a hostel or a shared house, especially since he is not confident around other people. He feels he has a measure of control.

  He might demonstrate this 'control' by offending again, being arrested and sent back to prison, where he can close his cell door.

- *Dependency.* Tom is alcohol-dependent. He will most likely steal from shops or people opportunistically; he may engage in street robbery (though this is unlikely). Depending on the amount he's drinking, a sudden withdrawal may lead to serious neurological damage and possibly death. Linked to this, therefore, is:

- *Physical and mental health.* If he's living rough, he may not be under the care of a GP or the community mental health team, though he may be able to access healthcare through a drug and alcohol drop-in service. This may be his only real source of support.

Whatever is going on in Tom's life is being driven by how he thinks and makes decisions; his attitude to himself and others, and his (compromised) sense that life is worth living. It seems likely that nearly everyone he has regular contact with is either in a similar position to himself or some kind of professional. There will be no substantial change to Tom's life unless the way he thinks changes. This will include his self-esteem, his ability to make decisions, his sense of purpose and his ability to form relationships that aren't based on an immediate need.

For Tom, those are the primary things keeping him in his unsatisfactory condition. If these things can be properly addressed and his situation stabilised, the next things to consider will be:

- Living skills and self-care: managing money, personal hygiene, managing his medication, shopping and eating healthily on a small budget.

- Work skills come a long way down the list. Ultimately, Tom will want to join the rest of society and become a net contributor to the community rather than a perpetual recipient, but this is not something that can be considered in the short term. If other aspects of his life can be stabilised, Tom may feel it helpful to undertake voluntary work. This will help him develop self-esteem, working skills and the beginnings of a positive social network.

All of this is going to take place as Tom begins to see himself as part of a community; a group of people who relate to each other in a positive way and can look out for each other. This is not a short process and while, with good and continuing support, we might expect to see rapid progress at first, it is not unreasonable to expect it to be several years before someone in Tom's position can live independently in the community.

The spiritual dimension

People in different churches, and with varying expressions of faith, see what is before them with very different eyes. There are some who are sceptical about the prospect of people being demon-possessed; others will go so far as to say that the whole of psychology and psychiatry are myths put about to 'explain away' the spiritual world. Both of these are nonsensical from a biblical perspective.

If a person gives over control of their life to another entity, whether it be heroin, alcohol or anything else, this is a spiritual matter. If you speak to a heroin addict, most of the time you are speaking to the addiction, not the person. We can talk sensibly about the psychology of addiction and psychoses induced by certain drugs, but often these lifestyles and the motivations that drive them have a life and a dynamic of their own. They are often demonic in nature. At Walk, we have deliverance ministry, as well as therapeutic counsellors and input from medical professionals.

Spiritual deliverance, as with any other intervention, can only be undertaken with the active consent of the person concerned; in fact, if it isn't based on repentance and a deliberate turning towards Christ, we are wasting our time (see, for example, Matthew 12:43-45). This ministry always needs to be carried out with care, and some people are so deep into the demonic that it seems to be only the demons that enable them to function at all. So, when the person turns to Christ it is often not without conflict.

Jesus tells His disciples to cast out demons and heal the sick (for example, in Matthew 10:8), but this is a long process; we will seldom see quick or dramatic results.

Managing risk and need

Whatever your particular project is set up to do, you must identify and manage the risks and needs presented by your participants.

Above, I gave a snapshot of Tom's life. As soon as a new client or participant joins your project, and preferably well before that, you should gain as accurate as possible a picture of where they are and how you can help them.

We do this in two stages.

1. A risk assessment

We request a risk assessment from the prison or supervising agency (probation or the CRC). This gives the static risk factors and is usually summarised in a nominal level of risk: Low, Medium or High. It may also give the probability of the candidate being reconvicted within a certain period of time, and an indication as to whether they present a risk to any particular group.

This is confidential data and is protected by law, so we need the candidate's written permission for it to be disclosed, which we submit with the request.

2. A needs assessment

At Walk, we assess need by means of a detailed interview, which we usually conduct under the auspices of the prison chaplaincy, sometimes with the chaplain present. We ask the candidate searching questions about their offending history, where they would be living if they were not in prison, their relationships, their physical and mental health (any diagnoses as well as the candidate's 'felt' symptoms; we also include our own observations where appropriate), any prescribed medication and any history of substance misuse, any debt, any history of self-injury and any history of attempted suicide.

We try to do this in a cordial and conversational way, and the process can be lengthy – possibly spread out over several sessions.

This needs assessment interview is based on the 'Strands' (see chapter 9) and forms a baseline for the matrix of information we keep on each client to enable us to monitor their progress and to help with things like development planning. All this information is stored securely and is only accessible by certain named members of staff.

Important

There is a danger for us that any risk assessment might become a means of labelling the candidate in some way. This must be avoided: we are not in the business of judging people by their past but of opening opportunities for a better future. However, it benefits no one if, like Tom, the man or woman returns to prison, perhaps making another victim, because they didn't get the right support.

Risk and faith

One of the criticisms of models of intervention based on risk, need and response is that they lead to a culture of risk aversion. Offenders attending the officially accredited courses are taught to identify risk and minimise it, as if a person can live 'crime-free' by being hyper-vigilant and avoiding tricky situations.

Churches are often like this too. 'Best practice' models for welcoming ex-offenders into congregations[80] in most of the main denominations look through the lens of 'safeguarding'. It is likely to leave you thinking – wrongly – that most ex-offenders are 'sex' offenders and that all ex-offenders are inherently dangerous. As we discussed previously, this is a fallacy in that it presupposes that the only 'offenders' present are the ones who have been convicted, sentenced and released and have told you about it.

In a support project, you have to deal with the reality of that situation and engage with all the statutory agencies on the basis of

---

[80] See for instance the Baptist Union (n.d.), though lately there have been signs of careful improvement, for example Diocese of Oxford, 2016.

thorough risk and needs assessments, but a church congregation is not the right place for this.

What about worship in church?

If a person is subject to public protection arrangements, they will arrive, as it were, 'in a package' from probation or the police; the situation will be closely managed. For the most part, however, if someone new joins your congregation, you have no idea who they are, and you won't until you build a relationship with them and begin to establish trust.

There are things that can be done in the pastoral management of a church to provide mutual accountability as part of the general discipleship programme, as well as an effective safeguarding policy. This will allow the whole congregation to grow together safely.

In the end, it comes down to trust – to faith, indeed. *Faith* and *risk* are inversely linked. When someone entrusts his life to God, it is a matter of faith. But he may also have an offending past – which is a matter of risk.

General risk management

In most congregations there will be people whose behaviour or attitude pose a cause for concern. They might actually be dangerous – and the dangers may not be what you expect. It might be the person doing the finances or driving the minibus. They may not be identified as 'offenders' and have never been convicted of anything as far as you know – but any safeguarding policy that applies to released prisoners must also apply to everyone else. Relationships within the church must have appropriate boundaries and everyone with any responsibility should hold themselves accountable.

Challenge

At the beginning of this chapter we tried to look at offenders in the way that God sees them and discussed the idea of 'forgiveness'.

- In the words of the Lord's Prayer, how can we forgive those who 'sin against us' (Matthew 6:12, NLT)?

- How can this be applied practically?

Those who present what we see as 'risky' behaviour can frighten us or leave us concerned for the welfare of the 'vulnerable'. One approach to managing this would be to restrict the freedom and behaviour of the person, and to be vigilant at all times, but it's better to address these risks with protective measures that reduce or remove the 'need' to offend. Heroin addiction, for example, can be addressed with detoxification and a series of interventions that teach the person to identify the things that might trigger them into relapse, but it is better to rehabilitate them to the extent that they no longer need the solace or escape that the drug provided.

- How can we make our church or our communities 'protective' communities?

For us, the spiritual answer to 'risk' is faith – or perhaps this can be expanded to 'faith, hope, [and] love' (1 Corinthians 13:13). As Christians, these are our ultimate resources and the source of our motivation and energy. This does not mean that we naïvely ignore the real dangers that certain people present, but that we are proactive in addressing them.

12

Safe Working

Staff

Your staff, paid or unpaid, are your most valuable asset. They underpin your project. It consists of their vision; it is realised by their expertise and dedication. Most likely, all your core team and most, if not all, of your other colleagues have lived and breathed your work for years, probably working long hours with little or no pay. They may have been prisoners themselves, or addicts or homeless, or they may have had professional experience in the criminal justice system somewhere. They are all brilliant! Nevertheless, it's worth going over some basic principles again. Volunteers speaking or behaving inappropriately, but with the best of intentions, have been a major headache to us at Walk and will be for you too.

People can be institutionalised in churches in much the same way as they can in prisons. Their thought, speech and behaviours tend to follow set patterns and they can find it hard to think 'outside the box' (or 'beyond the car park', as it were). They are easy to manipulate – and prisoners are experts in getting what they want.

Example 1: A prison wing

Jack and Terry are playing pool, while Jim, an officer, looks on. After a while, Terry goes away, and Jack offers Jim a game. Jim sees no harm in this. They play a few frames; Jim wins most of them.

Terry comes back and plays Jim; Jim wins again. They praise his 'mad skills'.

A few days later, the scene repeats, and the next time they play for a Mars bar. After a few weeks, they start playing for small bits of money, then for fifty quid. Then Jim starts to lose.

Now, Jack and Terry have Jim over a barrel and can make him do more or less whatever they want; if they report him, he'll lose his job. Before long he's carrying a phone into the prison.

Possibly, there's no malice in this to begin with, and Jack and Terry start off entertaining themselves to see how far Jim will go. Or maybe the original intention was malicious; never forget that there are some bad people in prison. Either way, the consequences are serious. A phone is a valuable and potentially dangerous commodity in a prison. Meanwhile, Jim's life is a mess; if he's caught, he could get five years. Time is no object to many prisoners; they will work on a vulnerable member of staff for months or maybe years.

Example 2: A prison chapel

Mary is a chaplaincy volunteer. She has been helping the chaplain to run Alpha on Saturday afternoons. At the end of a session, she is approached by Mr Smith, a prisoner in his forties, a kindly man who knows the Christian faith well. He apologises and says that it's his daughter's birthday on Monday and that he's missed the post. Would Mary mind dropping a card in the letter box for him? He shows her the card, which simply says, 'To Emily with love from Daddy', places it in the envelope and seals it in front of Mary.

What Mary doesn't know, because she's a chaplaincy visitor, is that Mr Smith is serving a long sentence for abusing his daughter. He has been forbidden from contacting her. He has cultivated a relationship with Mary over several weeks and it makes her feel important that he asks her to inspect the letter.

The right thing for Mary to have done would have been to make sure that the chaplain was present when Mr Smith produced his letter and, failing this, to have given it to the chaplain. Those working in prisons follow the rule 'nothing in: nothing out'. They should *never* carry anything out on behalf of a prisoner. In addition, Mr Smith's request should have been recorded in a security information report.

Sometimes attempts to manipulate are more direct than this; for example, an officer in a Category A prison was insidiously shown a photo of his daughter playing outside his home. But subtlety is the norm.

Most of the people we work with have been doing this all their lives. They are good at it. When they come to Christ, their lives begin to change. Their frame of reference changes and their basic motivation is different, but these behaviours are deeply ingrained. In the context of a community project, there is little need for people to enter the long process of 'operant conditioning' as Jack and Terry did with Jim, but ex-cons are generally adept at getting what they want. We need to be circumspect all the time. This is one of the reasons why it's prudent to have some ex-prisoners in your team. They are wise to this kind of thing and will call it out immediately.

Managing manipulation

Example 3: Sunday morning, church

'Good morning, how are you today?'
    'I feel awful.'
    'Oh dear. Do you want to talk about it?'
    'No.'
Have you ever had encounters with clients, colleagues or congregants that start along those lines? Most people simply say 'fine' to make you go away (which is also manipulative); more than this is either a request for prayer or an attempt to draw you into some sort of game. The person is attempting to make you feel sorry for them so that you will enter their little scheme, whatever it is. There will be some sort of payoff for them, probably at your

expense – even if it's only the satisfaction of having five minutes of your undivided attention.

This type of behaviour was documented by the psychologist Eric Byrne in the book *Games People Play*.[81] The most common type of psychological game, however, was described by one of Byrne's associates, Stephen Karpman, as the Drama Triangle.[82] We should make ourselves familiar with this.

A person who comes along with an obvious need – for housing or to stop drinking, for example – probably has a deeper need that is different and harder to fix. The behaviour they present, their request for help or support, is always being driven by the deeper motive; we must not allow ourselves to get drawn into a relationship that finishes up where we didn't want it to go, perhaps with people phoning in the middle of the night, or asking for money, or possibly more dangerous situations. Think of Jim or Mary in the examples above.

Discipline

We absolutely need to keep ourselves and each other safe in our work – and we are working with people who have proved themselves to be dangerous. We must be strongly disciplined, and there are two kinds of discipline:

- Discipline that comes from the outside – which will be derived from policies and procedures.

- Discipline that comes from the inside – from self-discipline informed by good training.

We'll look at these more closely in a little while, but first we consider roles.

---

[81] Byrne, 1964.
[82] Karpman, 1968.

Playing roles

When you meet with a client, you both begin to play a role. You will assume the role of a 'support worker'; the person you're talking to will assume the role of a 'client'. Another example: most people are baffled by the complexity of the benefits system, but in the Walk office, we have watched people who are barely functional in most aspects of life snap into gear when they get on the phone to the Jobcentre and play the role of a 'vulnerable adult'. They know which menu options to select before they've even heard them and exactly what to say to get what they want. They will even draw other people into the conversation to play the roles of 'case worker' or 'carer' as required. Later they resume their normal disposition. It's a game they play.

Whether staff are paid or voluntary, they are investing a considerable amount of their time and energy into the participant's support and welfare, and they do so without judgement. They are a source of stability and trust, and must avoid being sucked into clients' dark and chaotic worlds. It's vital that they keep a distance between themselves and the person they are working with.

So, when you meet a client you will put your 'support' hat on; the client will put their 'needy' hat on – or whichever role they are going to play that day. All clients do this to some extent and in some way. This is why, at Walk, we prefer to cast the people we work with as 'participants', who have agency, rather than as 'clients', who do not. Sometimes the language we use encourages people to adopt particular roles.

You have to keep in sight the journey this particular person is on: where they have come from and where they are hopefully going, and the fact that you are offering them a real opportunity to move on with life and to break out of the cycle of offence. Keep that fact in sight – it will anchor you.

The Drama Triangle

In certain personal interactions, especially where the relationship is 'staged' or constrained in some way (teacher–student; doctor–patient; support worker–client), people can slip between three roles, which are positions of relative power within the interaction:

- a Rescuer;

- a Victim; and

- an Oppressor or Persecutor.

They move between these positions as they try to gain a psychological advantage.

- The Rescuer believes that they have something to give; in fact, that they can 'fix it', whatever 'it' is.

- The Victim seems to lack something that maybe the Rescuer can give them. Sometimes people present as genuine 'Victims' with a legitimate need; sometimes they manufacture a need – the effect is much the same. They will draw the Rescuer to them.

- Persecutors always seek to control and want to create another Victim.

So, these are power positions within a relationship; roles that participants assume to gain an advantage.

Example 4: Probation office

John, a recently released prisoner, needs to be in a certain place at a certain time next week so that he can do some important 'business'. He's supposed to have a probation meeting then, but he knows that Jill, his offender manager, won't approve a change in the meeting time. So, he goes into the probation office in a blazing rage, fuming against everyone and everything (except Jill) and refusing to engage meaningfully with her. She naturally seeks to calm him down because there is work they need to do. After a while, apparently in response to her soothing, he calms down and becomes more compliant. Jill is pleased with this small result. When John asks her to change the meeting time the following week, she is open to the idea.

John enters as a Victim of some imaginary offence and invites Jill to become his Rescuer. Jill is happy to be the Rescuer because that suits her agenda, at least to begin with. After drawing her in, John becomes her Persecutor because he is manipulating her to get his own way, and she ends up as his Victim, though she may not even be aware of it.

In this Drama Triangle, the Rescuer, Jill, in intervening to 'help' someone in apparent distress, is acting out of a mixed motive. She is looking for a 'payoff' of her own, in this case to achieve a work result, or at least a quiet afternoon. The Rescuer is the most vulnerable position because it is deliberately unguarded.

The Rescuer is always after a payoff. In many cases, this might be taking the 'moral high ground' or possibly a sense of self-satisfaction. It feels good to rescue people!

The Victim, John, is using an appearance of 'hurt' or outrage as a kind of moral trap to get what he wants. This is the most devious position, as it draws the Rescuer in with a pretence. He is also looking for a payoff – the opportunity to advance his criminal career!

The Persecutor is the Victim's other mask. Persecutors can sometimes be aggressive, but not in this case: John stays in character and is very grateful to Jill for letting him get away with it! (Though if Jill had challenged his manipulation, he might have become aggressive.) The Victim uses the Rescuer's openness to turn her into a real-world victim.

In the context of a support project, if the Rescuer (most likely the person offering support) becomes the Victim, the client will be offering to rescue her. At this point, the client will be dictating the terms of the project:

> ... the Victim is not really as helpless as he seems, the Rescuer is not really helping, and the Persecutor does not really have a valid complaint.[83]

Most ex-prisoners are adept at turning situations to their advantage and assuming a phoney 'Victim' status; they've been doing it for years and might even believe it. We must not be naïve.

Sometimes, as in the example above, this game-playing is deliberate, at least by one of the participants, but it may also be subconscious, as the participants are drawn into the prescribed roles by their circumstances or by habitual behaviour. It can be very hard to break out of this; you will come across clients who have only ever known manipulative relationships, and bringing them to a place of mutual trust and respect will take time and much patience. Such manipulative behaviours must *always* be challenged – and this can be a hard thing to do. 'Clients' often resist becoming 'participants', where they must be active, responsible and accountable. Their default position will be to get you to enable and endorse their problematic behaviour, if they can.

We find that many volunteers find it hard to manage boundaries well and accept accountability structures. This leaves them open to manipulation. Also, if a person has difficulty managing their anger, if they are carrying hurts or traumas that they have not properly addressed, or if they struggle with a wide range of other problems, these things will make them vulnerable. They may also be vulnerable if they feel they want to 'help', or if they are acting out of a sense of obligation or religious duty. It will be easy for a manipulative person to blindside them.

---

[83] Steiner, 1979.

The real danger is not so much that the volunteer might get hurt (though this is possible), but that the client will steer the conversation and ultimately avoid having to address the things he is in the project to deal with.

People who have been effective chaplaincy volunteers in a prison can sometimes struggle when they come to work with the same or similar clients outside the gate. In prison, boundaries of all kinds are strictly imposed; all interactions take place in controlled environments and everyone is trained to avoid the kind of drip-feed conditioning that prisoners often use. Outside prison, the rules are different, and boundaries must be explicitly defined.

Boundaries

Boundaries can be *external* or *internal*. One way of telling if a person is institutionalised is by how well they can create appropriate internal boundaries or whether they have to rely on the imposition of external ones.

External boundaries

In a prison, these are pretty obvious. There are walls, fences, razor wire, cameras, locks, keys and uniformed staff who are capable of physical enforcement. Then there is the 'regime', the rigid routine, the protocols about when people eat and what they can wear, with whom they can associate and for how long. If you behave yourself, you get a TV: if you don't, it's taken away. If you still don't behave, *you* are taken away. There is also what is sometimes called 'dynamic security': the picture that staff build up over time of what is going on inside the prison – information gleaned from a variety of sources and pulled together – 'intelligence'. Then there are the unofficial boundaries; the pecking orders; who runs the rackets in tobacco, drugs and phones; who has friends on the outside; who the 'faces' are; who is vulnerable and who is a 'grass'. In prison, everybody knows their place. If they're not sure, they find out pretty soon.

Little of this is there on the outside or, where it is present, it is less visible. People have freedom; they have to *take* responsibility for themselves and *do* things. While some released prisoners acclimatise very well, others will not. Some long to go back to prison where they feel safe.

Your project needs some visible boundaries that everyone will adhere to. These may be external elements of security, such as cameras and locked offices, or a regime, such as a timetable and peer mentors, etc. But all this is driven by policy. You must have policies for everything, and everyone must work within them. Policies will control (for example):

- Tenancy agreements

- House rules

- Complaints and disciplinary procedures

- Timetable and programme

- Admission criteria and procedures

- Health and safety

- Risk assessments of various kinds

- How clients' progress is monitored

- How vulnerable people are kept safe

- How and when external agencies are contacted

- How data is protected, and confidentiality maintained

- Who is employed and how they are selected

- Contracts of employment and contracts for volunteers

- How the project is managed, and the roles of trustees, core staff, etc.

These are developed over time and should be revisited periodically, and unfortunately this involves a great deal of administrative paperwork that is not specifically client-facing. You are probably not very motivated to put all this in place – but you need it – and much of this material evolves as the project develops. While the core team may be perfectly clear about how a thing should be done, the ex-participant who has recently been appointed as a peer mentor may be less clear; and someone volunteering on the fringe of the project has very little idea. Policies should be summarised into participant and staff handbooks.

Everything may run smoothly for months or years without any specific written policies; but when something goes badly wrong, you need them. You may need to demonstrate that they are fit for purpose and have been followed. In fact, you should be referring to them constantly and modifying them where necessary. Policies are your tradecraft; they define your best practice and ensure the quality of your service.

Internal boundaries

Everyone has certain internal boundaries. If someone starts shouting close up in your face, you know that a boundary has been transgressed. Internal boundaries are to do with taste, decency, culture, manners, mutual respect and, ultimately, self-preservation. Our culture and the process of socialisation – our relationships with our family and friends when we are young – build them into us; they are personal expressions of our character. Some of these things remain hidden from sight; others are displayed openly, like a sign that says 'no callers'. They might range from the sort of language you are comfortable hearing or using and in what circumstances, to whether you drink alcohol or listen to Radio 1, and to whom you are prepared to go to bed with. We need to check our barriers frequently and prayerfully.

First, what is your personal motivation?

This can be quite a tough one to answer. I know what I would like it to be – but is that the truth? I think that all of us probably have a mixture of motives. If we place ourselves in the service of God, we place our personal boundaries with Him too. We see this in Scripture; for example, in the account in Acts 10, where Peter is instructed, through a vision of unclean food, to take the message of Christ to the Gentiles.

Peter, a Jew, would never eat anything that was unclean. He's hungry and dreaming of the food that was being prepared for him (verse 10). He has a vision of a large sheet full of animals, including 'unclean' ones, coming down from heaven, and the Holy Spirit prompts him to 'kill and eat' (verse 13). At first, he is resistant; his initial reaction is 'Not so, Lord! For I have never eaten anything common or unclean' (verse 14). When Cornelius' messengers arrive shortly afterwards, Peter is mulling this over and ready to listen to what they say. The fact that he invited them in and subsequently went with them shows Peter transgressing huge personal, cultural and religious boundaries.

Although Peter obviously struggled with this at first, it is significant that his first gut response is: 'Not so, Lord!' He knows who is showing him these things, and he knows that in the end, he will have to go with it. When you are a disciple, 'No, Lord' isn't an option.

Second, do you have past hurts or experiences that make you vulnerable?

Do you feel the need to try to 'fix' people who have been hurt in the same way you were? Are certain kinds of offender anathema to you because of your past? Are you open to flattery because you have delicate self-esteem? Are you a 'people pleaser'?

As far as the staff and volunteers in your project are concerned, personal boundaries should fill the gaps left by policies. On the one hand, these will be things like how you treat and communicate with people that you struggle to respect, how you handle disagreements, and having a respectful work style that doesn't impose your personal baggage on your colleagues. On the other hand, it may include things like work-life balance and how you manage your personal commitments. Is there, for example, going to be a conflict between your commitment to the project and your church or family responsibilities?

Part of the work you will do with released prisoners will be to teach them to develop appropriate personal boundaries themselves; this goes alongside building self-respect, healthy relationships and a positive social network. To do this effectively, you must model it in yourself and your team.

Welcoming released prisoners into church

Consider this. Bradley has been a heroin user since his teens. He is now in his late fifties and has been clean for two years – a major breakthrough in his life. He came out of prison about a year ago and has been worshipping as part of your small church for most of that time. He's friendly and funny and is growing in his faith – a popular member of the fellowship. About a month ago, he started using heroin again, at first small amounts that he thought he was handling, to help deal with an injury, but now he is back in the grip of addiction. His behaviour is spiralling out of control.

He knows the phone numbers and addresses of many congregation members and has been welcomed into many of their homes. Also, there are a couple of other guys in the church who have recently come off drugs and have been looking to Bradley for encouragement.

The solution for Bradley is that he needs a rapid intervention. He can register with Addaction[84] or whichever community drug agency operates locally, or he can refer himself to a Christian residential rehab project such as Betel;[85] failing that, he will inevitably be back in prison again soon. In that sense, the situation is likely to resolve itself, at least temporarily. In the meantime though, the chaos and hurt he is causing in the church, and in some people's lives, is considerable.

While we believe that we are saved by God's grace, and seek to extend a genuine welcome to everyone, regardless of who they are, we must also be realistic. If Bradley has a bad day, he is capable of creating mayhem. This is not because he's a 'bad person' or that he isn't 'saved', but because the choices he has been making have consequences.

It's tempting to want to place all released prisoners into a separate 'ex-cons' church; such things do exist, but this is not the answer. That will only create another ghetto within a Church that already has too many obscure subdivisions. Another temptation that might look like a solution would be to place all ex-offenders in your midst under some kind of special arrangement.

Best practice

If Bradley were a 'high risk' offender, he would be under 'public protection arrangements'. For him to be allowed to attend a church at all, the church would need to demonstrate that it had 'safeguarding' procedures in place. Bradley would only be allowed to attend subject to these arrangements and regular communication between the church leaders and a police risk assessor for the Public Protection Unit (PPU). This will be for the protection of the other churchgoers and possibly also for the man himself.

---

[84] https://www.addaction.org.uk/ (accessed 6th August 2018).
[85] http://www.betel.uk/ (accessed 6th August 2018).

In most cases, and where no such arrangements are in place, we don't need to be so extreme (after all, we are endeavouring to see the person as God sees him, not as the probation service sees him) but we do need good boundaries.

- There should be a firm safeguarding policy with a designated person responsible for those who might be 'vulnerable' within the congregation. In this case, a 'vulnerable' person is anyone whose address or phone number Bradley knows; in other circumstances, Bradley himself might be 'vulnerable'.

If you are devising policy, it's safe to consider everyone 'vulnerable' in some respects. Such policies must be applied even-handedly across the whole congregation and not levelled only at ex-offenders or any other minority group.

- It is helpful to have a small team of trained people who will specifically welcome released prisoners to the church. This group will manage the visitors within the congregation and perhaps offer 'signposting' to local services, should they need it. When things started to go wrong for Bradley, they would have picked it up quickly and been able to point him in the right direction for help.

Be aware of the support groups in your area; the drug and alcohol groups, the rough sleepers' team, the street pastors or chaplains, the bereavement counsellors, the food banks and the mental health and domestic violence support groups, etc.

Dealing with people in full addiction is always difficult. There are few specialist places that will handle a supervised detox, and most clinical rehabilitation units need a referral from a doctor with a guarantee of funding. Most of the Christian groups like Betel or Teen Challenge will do a rapid 'cold turkey' withdrawal – and not everyone is prepared to go through this.

- Any new person who enters your church for the first time should be treated in much the same way. We must welcome all visitors with the love of God and also with wisdom. For example, if an unknown man walks into your building before a meeting, he should be greeted by a man and not by a young woman.

- Having come out of prison doesn't mean that a person is necessarily dangerous, but it does mean that they probably need help.

You might consider setting up small accountability groups (remember prayer triplets?) where people can pray together, read the Scriptures and generally check in with each other. There can be no compulsion about this, of course, and it might be hard for some people to manage for various reasons, but it's a good way to create a context for people to grow in their faith and be able to look out for each other.

> Let each of you look out not only for his own interests, but
> also for the interests of others.
> *Philippians 2:4*

This kind of thing should be a routine part of discipleship within the church, and if situations like Bradley's arise that cause concern, they are more likely to be identified compassionately and dealt with at an early stage.

Safeguarding in the church

'Safeguarding' has become a big issue across the Church in recent times, as more truth emerges from year to year about abuse of various kinds, alleged or proven to have taken place. Most churches now have safeguarding policies and safeguarding officers, and regional and national structures to back these up. This shows an awareness of a problem. Furthermore, at best, these policies use inclusive language and acknowledge that 'all people are vulnerable in one way or another and promise to care for and supervise'[86] those known to have been a risk in the past. Some policy statements,[87] however, taken at face value, appear to allow little room for those who have offended in any way or at any time to be welcomed back into the community of believers. In all this there is a danger that a culture of 'safeguarding' will make us defensive against one another, rather than allowing us to 'love … fervently' (1 Peter 1:22). Furthermore, in our efforts to minimise the risk of those 'known to have harmed … in the past',[88] we can be blind to those who have the potential to cause harm now.

We will look further at how 'safeguarding' works in practice in the chapter on working with high-risk offenders. Here, I want to look at some ways in which we can make 'safeguarding' work, to strengthen and edify the body of Christ.

A theological statement

Everyone in Christ, without exception, is an ex-offender.

> … all have sinned and fall short of the glory of God.
> *Romans 3:23*

We could elaborate on this and see what Jesus says about adultery and murder in the Sermon on the Mount (Matthew 5:21-30). We approach God with humility, knowing that without His grace and Jesus' cleansing blood, we would all be entirely lost. In John 8:1-11, the religious leaders and Pharisees brought to Jesus a woman who had been caught in the act of adultery. Her guilt was

---

[86] The Archbishops' Council, 2006.

[87] 'If we become aware of someone within our congregation known to have harmed children or adults in the past, we will inform the Synod Safeguarding Officer and co-operate with them and the relevant statutory authorities to put in place a plan to minimise the risk of harm to children and adults', URC Communication Office, 2015, p4.

[88] URC Communication Office, 2015.

not in doubt, and they were about to execute summary justice on her by stoning her to death. She was a sinner, after all.

Jesus challenged them: 'He who is without sin among you, let him throw a stone at her first' (John 8:7). As students of the Jewish Law, they understood that no one among them dared stand as her judge, and Jesus forgave her and told her to repent – 'go and sin no more' (John 8:11).

It is not our prerogative to condemn or to forgive anyone for what they have done in their lives (except to forgive those who offend against us personally), but to 'love one another fervently with a pure heart' (1 Peter 1:22). So, how do we do that while protecting those who are vulnerable in our midst? We need to take another look at ourselves and each other.

Who presents a risk?

Certain people have been convicted of offences. If they are referred to you by a prison chaplain, or if they pluck up the courage to tell you that they've been in prison, then you know about it. Sometimes, as we mentioned above, where someone is under public protection supervision, the police or probation service will want to talk to you and check your safeguarding procedures, but this will only apply to a small number of individuals who present specific risks. But what if people don't tell you? Or what if they haven't even been caught yet?

You can only identify a few of the people who present a risk of harm, and if you single out released prisoners who come to you looking for support as presenting a particular risk, you will push them away.

Whereas some released prisoners certainly have the potential to cause harm in church congregations, such as in the example of Bradley above, in reality, this is quite an unusual situation. More likely sources of threat will be financial misfeasance by the treasurer, other manipulative people entering the church with undisclosed agendas, or sexual misconduct, often by a member of the leadership. By and large, a man or woman who arrives, admits to past offences and asks for support is likely to be relatively safe, though they will need to be loved and supported wisely.

Who is vulnerable?

The Church of England statement that 'all people are vulnerable in one way or another'[89] has it exactly right. We come to Christ, who is our Saviour, because we all need saving. Among us, there are certain people who will present with particular vulnerabilities because they don't have a voice, or they are young or old, or disabled or marginalised in some way. And, as I hope I have demonstrated so far in this book, people coming out of prison are also vulnerable.

We should support one another safely to the degree each of us needs supporting. We do this by keeping accountability at the heart of our fellowship. What this looks like in practice will vary widely depending on the size, age range, style and type of the congregation, but you may find Neil Cole's book, *Cultivating a Life for God*[90] to be a useful resource in this respect.

Challenge

I want to pick up two thoughts here: 'boundaries' and 'accountability'.

Psychologically healthy people are able to set appropriate boundaries in their relationships, but many things can compromise our ability to do this – in particular where people have suffered hurt or trauma in the past, and this has not been effectively addressed. If we are working with or ministering to those whose boundaries

---

[89] Church House Publishing (2006). The policy has since been updated (2017) and lost the Archbishops' Foreword, whence the quotation.
[90] Cole, 1999.

are compromised, we must be confident of our own boundaries or we will be open to manipulation.

Look at the examples earlier in this chapter and consider the following:

- How can you protect yourself from manipulation?

- Can you identify any personal boundaries?

These may also be reflected by policy statements within your organisation.

There is no merit in trying to 'push' your own boundaries! You must work and worship in ways and places where you feel safe.

- Are you familiar with your church's safeguarding policy?

- Is it fit for its purpose?

Perhaps a working party within your church should work through it critically and suggest any revisions that are needed,

- How does accountability work in the local congregation?

Explore further

Cole, N (1999), *Cultivating a Life For God: Multiplying Disciples Through Life Transformation Groups* (St Charles, IL: Church Smart Resources).

Byrne, E (1964), *Games People Play: The psychology of human relationships* (New York: Grove Press).

13

Good Communication

Everything we do as Christians is about relationship. Jesus condensed the Old Testament teaching into two commands: *love God; love your neighbour.* These two relationships define us: how we walk with God and how we walk with each other. In passages like the Good Samaritan (Luke 10:25-37), Jesus doesn't appear to distinguish between 'our Christian brothers and sisters' and 'everyone else'. In this parable, the 'neighbour' to the man who had been beaten and robbed was not a religious type but a 'Samaritan', who went out of his way to help him. Jesus picked a Samaritan for His illustration, because it was the very last person His Jewish audience would consider 'neighbourly'.

So, we are to love God and, equally, to love our 'neighbours', who are not whom we expect.

Love, in this sense, is to be articulated in words and actions, and it only makes sense if the other person receives it. This is true of all relationships; they consist of words and actions. Love only exists inasmuch as it is communicated. We might feel affection or compassion towards a person, or their company might be pleasant to us, but unless we communicate that, we are on our own with it. It remains a feeling.

The first point, then, is that our words and actions must agree with each other. They must be coherent. If I say I'm going to do something and then don't do it, this will not engender trust.

This starts with your closest colleagues.

Communication within the team

Write the vision
And make it plain on tablets,
That he may run who reads it.
Habakkuk 2:2

As we have previously discussed at some length, your core group has come together around a common goal. Write it down. Express the goal, talk about it and debate it until you have a very clear sense of what you are going to do.

Within your group, individual members will also have their own interests, which might be slightly different. Talk about these: where are the areas of overlap? What things are different?

Within Walk, the core team came together around the statement:

> Equipping released prisoners to develop tools for a new life through fellowship and unity in Christ.

However, members of the core team are also passionate about other things, such as building men's ministry, evangelism, or developing training materials (of which this book is an example). These may not contradict the vision, but nor are they the core activity of the Project. Make sure that you communicate clearly what is and what is *not* your project, and that other interests are subordinated to your main purpose.

Related to this, team members also have different strengths and weaknesses. The key roles that people naturally fall into (which later become their job descriptions) will reflect this. There will probably be a point in the early stages when 'everybody does everything'. But this isn't sustainable in the long term: you will tread on each other's toes and cause irritations and disagreements; after a period of time, as things become clearer, distinct roles emerge by negotiation.

How are you going to get the best out of yourselves and each other?

Boundaries are very important here. Over time, you work out job descriptions for yourselves: areas of responsibility and development. You might have two team members with particular aptitude for working with participants. Maybe one focuses on developing their work skills; the other focuses on living skills and interpersonal relationships. These might have some overlap, but are distinct and have scope for development. This enables your core team to have ownership of what they do; to develop their own portfolios within the project. Nobody is empire-building or pursuing their own agendas; they are integrated parts of the whole.

This comes about through clear communication; through mutually agreeing the vision in the first place, and then developing within it. Job descriptions are explicit; they are first discussed and then written down. *Writing things down* gives much better clarity than relying on speech alone, when people can mishear, misunderstand, misremember or misconstrue your words.

In a previous chapter, we discussed how policy documents define boundaries. Policies should describe the operation of the project and, once in place, should also define its limits.

Day-to-day communication is best carried out, or at least reinforced, by email. If you've had an informal conversation and agreed something, confirm it by email. This provides a permanent dated record of what was said. Remember to include everyone in the 'To' or 'Cc' line who needs to be there; all interested parties. Use your own dedicated email boxes and not generic ones like 'Gmail'.

It's a good idea to have a 'staff only' area in your office. In this type of project, participants will need access to you much of the time – but many discussions are confidential, sometimes highly so. So, have a private space for meetings. Also, you need space for relaxation.

Encourage openness within the team, including people who are not from the core group, while preserving appropriate boundaries. It's important not to develop a 'them and us' mentality with project participants.

Effective communication reduces the chances of misunderstandings and conflicts among team members, keeps everybody 'on the vision' and makes it less likely that people will go off on wild goose chases, or feel peeved at being left out of a decision loop they should have been in. Good communication within your staff also makes manipulation by clients less likely.

Communication with other agencies

There seems to be a tendency everywhere for people to sit in their groove, do their thing, and not notice what the rest of the world is doing. You see it in the Church a lot; the church down the road puts on an evangelists' conference and tells the people who are immediately part of their group via social media, but neglects to tell the other churches in town. A prison ministry group puts on a conference, but only invites its immediate partners.

Recently, I was meeting with a probation officer who had no idea what Walk was, or what we were doing, despite the fact that we have been working with her office and several of her colleagues for four years.

You would think it obvious that we would want to network as widely as possible among those who share an interest in our area of work. We want to know who we can usefully work with and also who to avoid. Your group will not be able to help every vulnerable person you meet, but it is likely that someone in your area will have exactly what that person needs. We have to be aware of our strengths and weaknesses, and also who might be able to offer the services that we cannot.

In the present political and economic situation, there is no such thing as 'too much help'. People die from overdose, from alcohol withdrawal, from hypothermia, from taking the wrong combinations of substances and from suicide. We absolutely must be aware of who our partner agencies are and how to move clients effectively to the places where they can receive appropriate support.

A common forum for this to take place may be through a local prison's resettlement or integrated substance misuse team. If it doesn't exist, suggest it.

If we are going to work more or less together with other agencies, we are required to handle clients' personal information with respect, consistent with data protection law.[91] In brief, this guarantees that client-confidential information (which is anything by which a client can be identified) and certain other information must be protected. When we begin to work with a new client, we can ask them directly for the information we need and they are free to supply it or not, but if we seek information from another agency, we must have each client's explicit (ie written) permission. Under the 2018 Regulation, this consent must be kept on record. Likewise, you are not permitted to disclose any information about a client without their permission.

Communicating with clients

The apostle Paul famously wrote that he could be 'all things to all men' (1 Corinthians 9:22). He was equally at home talking to religious Jews, Roman governors, Greek politicians, imprisoned slaves and Philippian jailers. If we are going to slip between church, prison and street settings, we must be able to do this too. This is not to say that we become cultural chameleons – I don't believe that Paul did – but that we are able to listen to people and understand where they are coming from, and speak to them in language that doesn't alienate them.

---

[91] At the time of writing, the EU General Data Protection Regulation 2018 is about to supersede the Data Protection Act 1988, ICO, 2017.

It might be extremely obvious to us that clients have to change; it might be clear to a person we are working with that they need to change too, because what they have now doesn't work well. But if we haven't made the effort to understand them, it can come across as disrespectful: 'Who are you to tell me I have to change?!' The implication in our words might be that we want them to change into something more like us.

The truth is that we must all change into something more like Christ – we are all on a journey of change. We must speak in ways that our listeners understand and that don't alienate them.

What does it mean to communicate effectively?

Communication is 'the imparting or exchanging of information'.[92] It derives from a Latin word meaning 'to share', which implies that all the parties involved have an active role. If you are speaking and no one is listening, or the listeners are unable to understand, then you are not communicating. Effective communication takes place only when the listener clearly understands what the speaker is saying.

By its nature, the relationship between a client and a support worker is not equally balanced, as there is a differential of power; the support worker holds more power than the client and is seeking to empower the client to embrace change in certain aspects of their life. Language is about power; having the ability to communicate clearly is a powerful thing, but it can easily be used to manipulate. If we seek to engender trust, we must be careful how we speak. This is not to say that the client is power*less*, and in the end, if they are dissatisfied, they will simply leave.

The support worker must be confident, to put the client at ease; the client must feel able to be straightforward; the supporter must

---

[92] Oxford University Press, 2017.

be able to listen carefully and respond in a positive and productive way.

Appropriate methods of communication

While most of your interactions will probably be face-to-face and one-to-one, you might find yourself in a small group with participants. This can happen in a wide variety of contexts, most obviously a therapy group, course or intervention of some kind, but it could be with a few people in a car, or in a workplace, or sharing a burger. We can teach life skills and other things explicitly, but people sometimes learn them best through practical situations, far from the training room. Your life, your language, your attitude and your behaviour are under scrutiny. You are modelling Christian living; you are an ambassador of Christ. How you respond in different situations reflects on Him.

You might also communicate with participants via phone or text but use these wisely. SMS text is good for communicating small pieces of data to one or a few people – for example, a change in the time of a meeting. But it is very rarely a substitute for a conversation.

Be very circumspect with social media. A well-edited Facebook feed can be a really effective way to keep people in touch with your project, but it needs to be moderated. It can be easy for someone with a grudge to air their dirty laundry there and that can be damaging. You may want to celebrate the successes of your participants, but there will be some who won't want their picture shared online. In fact, licence conditions may disallow certain people from using social media.

Certainly, social media is not the place to share advice, guidance or ministry, and your project's page is not the place for your personal or theological views or opinions.

Social media and the internet in general are powerful and therefore dangerous. There is a lack of accountability and little or no quality control. If someone has it in for you because they think you failed them (it will happen!), they can take you apart through your website or Facebook page relatively easily. So, don't give hostages to fortune:

- Have a media policy that defines what is and is not acceptable.

- Have a person whose job it is to edit and moderate online content.

- Be aware of what you can and cannot show.

We strongly advise that participants have access to only basic phones when they first arrive with you. Most of your participants will not be very wise with social media. Smartphones and tablets can be used for all kinds of wonderful things, but mostly they serve as portals back into your participants' old lives. In the end, effective communication of your message creates a desire to respond positively. This is equally true if you are reading a story, delivering a report or mentoring a client.

People have different learning styles, different ways in which they feel comfortable gaining information. Some people do this best through *images*: they like to watch something demonstrated, maybe through a video. Some people like to *listen*: they will retain a lot of what you say to them. Others need to be *active*: they like to role play and build models. Others can *work things out* if you give them the building blocks: they will like to develop their own processes. Some learn best in groups, interacting with others; others like to go away and do it on their own. These styles will overlap to some extent. Women and girls tend to learn better by listening and in groups; men and boys often prefer to go and do things.

Many ex-prisoners' experiences of formal education were unpleasant. At least in part, this will have been because their learning style wasn't properly addressed; also, their attention span is likely to be limited to a few minutes. So while we need to understand as far as possible how people learn best, and cater for their needs, we must not underestimate people who may not have a conventionally good vocabulary or much formal education. Make your group sessions as lively and interactive as possible and use a range of learning resources if you can. Make sure that everybody is being catered for.

There is a tendency to want participants to undertake accredited courses, and they will almost certainly need to do some if you're looking at building work skills, literacy, numeracy, etc. But in terms of 'life skills' and some of the 'soft skills' they need, like citizenship and decision-making, our experience is that it is more effective to address these informally. It is more important that the person understands the importance of sequential thinking or of relating well to their neighbours than it is for them to own a certificate in these things. These are better approached through flexible and informal processes, whereas accredited programmes will tie you down to assessment criteria and the production of portfolios, etc.

Through all this, your aim in communication is to build trust and respect.

Positive language

Say what you mean; mean what you say. If you have nothing to say, say nothing.

We should be positive wherever possible. We always try to 'speak life' into situations. We use our language to bless and not to curse. Negative language may inhibit the participant from talking freely and may trigger resistance. It might sound politically correct, but it's important to use positive, empowering and edifying vocabulary. Where you need to admonish, criticise or 'speak the truth', always be courteous, specific and loving, and – as far as it lies within your power – try to provide a face-saving way out of difficult situations:

- Make sure your comments are focused on the matter in hand, and relevant.

- If someone needs to be challenged, do it immediately if possible. This is much more effective than comments given some time after the event.

- Make sure you are understood.

- Ask open questions – ones that require an answer other than 'yes' or 'no'. Try using 'Where?', 'What?', 'Why?', etc.

Barriers to communication

Polite British people rarely say exactly what they mean. This can be a problem.

I remember watching a leader from a local church explaining to a homeless man who had come into the church's coffee shop what his options were. He was being quite pleasant, but he was obviously busy – someone had summoned him to talk with the fellow. He explained the local rough-sleepers' scheme that had recently been set up, and the Salvation Army's clothing bank. I think the visitor was simply wishing that someone would offer him a cup of coffee because he was cold. The two men appeared to occupy completely different spaces. The church man came over as patronising and a bit dismissive, although this obviously wasn't his intention. He would be mortified to think that that was how he was perceived, but this was carried through in his body language. The visitor sat at a table, while the church man stood, leaning on the chair opposite, literally looking down on him.

Either party can easily create barriers to communication, which might include the following:

Indirect and imprecise language

Using *indirect language* can complicate things and leave the listener unsure of what you mean, and might undermine trust and respect. You use euphemisms because you think that people might be offended by what you say or because you feel embarrassed to say it

– and this demonstrates a lack of trust. If you speak euphemistically to people who are used to speaking directly, you will probably leave them confused, and you might cause the very offence you were trying to avoid.

Loaded words carry an implied moral judgement. You can use certain words and phrases without realising that you are causing offence. For example, referring to someone as a 'prostitute' is quite derogatory. The word carries a moral weight and an implied judgement. Some people prefer 'sex worker', but this isn't always right either, since it implies that the person has made a career choice like a factory worker or a retail worker. A better, neutral phrase might be 'those involved in prostitution'. This is a bit cumbersome, but is accurate and implies no judgement.

Similarly, we avoid using the term 'ex-offender' because it can be a difficult label to live down – and the only way you can stop being an ex-offender is either by reoffending or by dying. Not everyone coming out of prison is an offender. They may have been remanded in custody and then acquitted, or they may have suffered a miscarriage of justice. We prefer 'released prisoner' because it is simply descriptive and doesn't make any assumptions.

It can be very hard or near impossible to get this right all the time – 'addict', 'alcoholic', 'asylum seeker', 'homosexual' – even the current use of the term 'black'; the linguistic culture changes all the time.

This is not mere political correctness. If we want those we work with to engage with us, we must use language that demonstrates respect for them and a degree of empathy. If we get it wrong (which sometimes we will), the person may respond unexpectedly, or misunderstand or misconstrue what we are saying and be left feeling defensive or angry. We may not even realise that certain words or phrases we use are 'loaded' – indeed, it has more to do with the context in which a word or phrase is used rather than the language itself.

Before meeting a client or participant, you should think carefully about what you intend to say and choose your words accordingly. It's best not to meet if you're feeling angry or annoyed with the person, unless the matter is urgent, in which case make sure there's another reliable person there.

Pay attention to the words you are using and watch the expressions and body language of the person you are talking to. If they look defensive, hostile, puzzled or confused, rephrase what you are saying in clearer or more neutral terms.

It is not useful to ask things like, 'Do you understand?' or 'Do you get it?' Most likely, they'll just smile and nod.

Body language

Be calm and confident; don't invade the other person's space. Body language helps us pick up visual clues from people's reactions to what we are saying to them. Presenting yourself as defensive, hostile, antagonistic or fearful will create anxiety on the part of the listener or make you open to manipulation. Being aware of body language as both speakers and listeners can help us to diffuse the tension surrounding difficult conversations.

How can we control the conversational space without being aggressive?

Not controlling the space may diminish our confidence; it may mean that we can't say the things we want to say in the way we want to say them, and there might also be security or health and safety issues. Consider three scenarios:

- Meeting a potential candidate in a prison prior to his release.

- Meeting a non-compliant participant in a shared house.

- Meeting a participant for a check-in session at the office.

In general, when meeting clients or project participants, it is best not to be alone; meet the person with a colleague wherever possible. The examples below are typical of activities within Walk.

1. Meeting in prison

Environment

At Walk, we try to visit candidates in prison a few weeks before they are released. We might meet them a couple of times, depending on their need, the available time and the logistics involved. The purpose of the meeting is to get to know them a little and explore 'what they want'. If it turns out that they are only looking for a safe place to land when they come out, we are less likely to accept them than if they embrace the ethos of the Project. This is a conversation best had a few weeks before release.

By its nature, meeting in prison is hard to control. You may not know who is going to be there ahead of time, and you can't easily abort the meeting if things aren't going well. We try to arrange the meeting in the prison chaplaincy; there is often an empty office or meeting room that can be made available. This is generally a calm and relatively pleasant environment conducive to a constructive chat – and there is usually coffee and biscuits! Often, we can conduct the meeting one-to-one; sometimes the chaplain will be present, sometimes not.

Alternatively, we can arrange a 'legal' visit – which will be more constrained (ie no biscuits). On occasions, we have met potential candidates on wings (prison wings usually have a group room of some kind), and even once or twice in the Segregation Unit. Once we met a candidate who was considered to be 'high risk' and he came accompanied by two senior officers, who both sat in. That was far from ideal and effectively reduced the interview to a 'box-ticking' exercise.

Behaviour

In this kind of meeting, typically, you are in the room before the person arrives. As he (we'll use the masculine here) arrives, come out of your seat with a smile and greet him in the middle of the space with a handshake. It's also polite to greet any officer or member of staff who comes in with him. It can diffuse tension to some extent if you make them part of the conversation rather than having them sit or stand there passively, though they may be resistant to this.

I usually start by saying, 'Hi, it's great to meet you. Thanks for coming across. I'm Steve from Walk.' Then I'll ask how he is, how he heard about us, what he wants from this meeting and what his wishes are for the future. (This often comes down to: I want to go somewhere safe when I get out; I want to do it differently this time.) I might do a little spiel about Walk, but I'm more interested in hearing what he has to say. I want to understand what makes him tick.

Most of the content of the meeting will be filled with the Needs Assessment interview, which is based on a big, detailed questionnaire. We do want answers to everything, but not necessarily there and then – some of the questions are intrusive – and sometimes we can glean an answer from something he said elsewhere. Sometimes a person's offence or their circumstances mean that some of our questions are inappropriate, so we improvise. I try to conduct it as conversationally as possible. The main things I want initially are:

- What's his offence and what's his licence going to be like? (We don't necessarily need to know all the detail straight away.)

- Is he on maintenance medication, such as methadone, and has he been using drugs inside?

- Is he in a relationship and will that affect his stability when he gets out?

- What's his mental health like? (Apart from his answers, we can observe his state of anxiety, rationality and mood control.)

- What other medication is he on?

- Is he a suicide risk?

Everything else can wait for a second meeting or maybe until he arrives, if we accept him. Provided we get the basic details, we can keep the tone of the conversation quite light.

We can learn a lot from his general demeanour. Does he appear confident and friendly, or is he nervous? Does he make eye contact, or is he evasive? Is he alert? Is he 'wired' or does he appear subdued? Are his pupils 'pinned' or dilated? This might be down to any meds he has taken, or he might be 'on' something, or it might indicate a mental health condition.

It's important that the candidate feels as relaxed as possible, which might be hard for him because a lot is at stake. It's important to be friendly and personable without breaking professional distance.

2. Meeting in a supported house

Environment

In this case, you are meeting the client in his home, his personal space – and possibly you are not the person he wants to see right now. In the context of a project like Walk, this should be a relatively safe thing to do; even if the participant is not complying, and might be angry and evasive. The ethos of the house will be conducive to a frank conversation that will often resolve things, and there is a house leader on hand. If the house is less closely managed than this, it may not be as safe. You should have a 'lone working' policy, which sets out where and under what circumstances it is acceptable or advisable to be alone with a client. You'll meet in one of the shared areas of the house, probably the living room.

Note: You should never be alone with a person of the opposite sex.

Behaviour

Possibly he is waiting for you and possibly he's aggressive. If he's drunk or under the influence of a drug, it will be pointless for you to have the meeting, so tell him to see you in the office the following day and begin a disciplinary procedure. If he threatens or offers violence, leave immediately and start a disciplinary procedure. If he has assaulted someone, call the police.

If he's angry or tense, you need to diffuse that before you can talk, by being calm, patient and insistent. Offering him a cup of coffee will possibly break the tension. You can't let an angry person 'win' by being angry, especially if his 'anger' is an attempt to manipulate (in this context, it probably is). This is 'your' project and he's in 'your' house; he agreed to abide by 'your' rules, and he will have to do that. The priorities here are the physical safety of everyone concerned, the integrity of the project and whatever the issue might be, in that order.

In general, meetings in and visits to houses almost always go smoothly; if someone is up to no good, they will most likely be keeping it quiet. However, it is advantageous for one of the people doing the visiting to have enough 'physical presence' to discourage aggressive behaviour.

3. Meeting at the office

Environment

Here, you can control the environment, either in the main office or the meeting room. The room should have a door that closes securely and a window to allow observation. It should be reasonably soundproof. It's a good idea to arrange the seating with the client facing away from the window.

It's best to set the room up with the chairs at a right angle to each other, maybe with a small table between them or in front as the focus. Allow enough space for both participants to feel comfortable. If a third person is present, seating should be roughly triangular. This feels comfortable and is non-confrontational; it allows participants to look at or past each other (to observe the other person's facial expressions and body language) without either turning their heads away or facing each other directly.

Rooms used for counselling or private meetings should feel welcoming, with neutral colours and soft furnishings or curtains to soften the acoustics. Consider framed prints, maybe some verses of Scripture on the wall, and a pot plant or two. Natural light is good and use lamps softly – for example, shaded table lamps or spots bounced off the walls (strip lights and blue-white LEDs can make you feel a bit edgy before you start).

If you are meeting a client at the office, ensure that there is someone else on the premises.

'Active listening' skills

One of the most common mistakes we can make is confusing hearing with listening. Hearing is passive; listening is active. Active listening requires the listener to hear the words and identify the feelings associated with them. We should be able to understand the client from his point of view – in other words, to empathise.

Active listening is intelligent. There are broadly two skill sets associated with it. Non-verbal skills, which are the things we do while listening, provide the speaker with helpful and encouraging feedback. Verbal skills are the way we use our own language to encourage the other person to speak. We should use both.

Non-verbal listening skills

Maintaining eye contact is the most important way of showing your full attention to a speaker. Lack of eye contact may be interpreted as disinterest, disapproval or embarrassment. Making eye contact with the speaker focuses your attention, reduces the chance of distraction, and gives helpful feedback to the speaker.

You can also use non-verbal prompts to show your engagement and to invite the speaker to continue speaking. Affirmative head-nodding, appropriate facial gestures and the use of silence are all helpful ways to show that you are really listening. Silences can also be helpful to allow the speaker time to reflect on what they have just said. We might have to work hard to feel comfortable with silence; for many of us, our first instinct is to fill every space up with words, either to rescue the other person or to take away our own discomfort.

We can give unhelpful non-verbal signals, if we're not careful. Gazing into the distance, playing with pens or phones, or shuffling papers, etc will be distracting.

Being relaxed will usually encourage the other person to relax too. When you show openness and receptivity, the other person is likely to talk freely and be less defensive.

Verbal listening skills

While you're listening, the other person might 'dry up'. The temptation is to launch into a little story of your own – 'I remember when I' – but this won't be helpful. Instead, use brief verbal prompts to help the speaker continue. For example, these techniques encourage understanding:

- Encourage: 'Tell me some more'; 'You were saying earlier'; 'Could you explain that more fully?'

- Acknowledge: 'I understand'; 'I see'; 'That sounds really important to you.'

- Check: 'You seem really angry'; 'Am I right in thinking that you said … ?' But don't 'inform' what the other person is saying. He must be using his own words.

- Clarify: 'I'm not sure I understand'; 'Did you say this happened once or twice?' Also, try paraphrasing what the speaker has said back to them in slightly different words: 'So you mean to say that ...'

- Affirm: 'I appreciate that you have been so open with me.'

- Empathise: 'I can understand why you are worried by this'; 'I think this situation has been very difficult for you and you are getting impatient.'

- Ask open-ended questions: 'Can you tell me more about that'; 'How do you feel about it now?'; 'I'm wondering what your options are here.'

- Reflect: 'I can hear the anger in your voice'; 'You seem very happy about that.'

- Summarise: 'So there seem to be several things that are important to you.'

These phrases can become 'active listening' clichés – so beware of sounding like a robot: 'I feel your pain.' Do you really? There are certain common habits of conversation that will inhibit good communication:

- Interrupting the speaker. Allow the speaker to complete their thought before responding.

- Talking too much. Talking is easier than listening intently to someone else, but you are not necessarily there to talk, especially ...

- ... talking about yourself: this is irrelevant.

- Advising, diagnosing or criticising. You're not qualified to do this (unless it is a project-related matter – or unless you are actually qualified). Especially, don't answer with Scripture!

- 'Thinking ahead' about what you will say. If you're trying to think of a wise answer or some good advice, you've stopped 'actively' listening to the other person.

- Ignoring or denying the other person's feelings.

- Pretending you have understood them if really you haven't. Ask sensible and sensitive questions if you missed something.

Other blocks to listening

- Comparing. While someone is talking, you are thinking things like: 'I wouldn't have done that', or 'in my experience this is what happens …' This stops you hearing what the other person is saying.

- Mind-reading or looking for hidden meanings. This suggests that you don't trust what the other person is saying because you think they are covering up what they want or think, so you are trying to guess what they mean by 'reading between their words' rather than listening to what they actually say.

  This is a problem if you are talking to someone who you think is probably trying to manipulate you, perhaps because of your previous experience with them. A man convicted of a historic sexual assault once expressed great frustration at his offender manager's unwillingness to listen to what he was saying.

- Rehearsing. You don't have time to listen properly because you are mentally practising what you are going to say next.

- Derailing by suddenly changing the subject because you are feeling bored or uncomfortable. You can also 'derail' by making a joke to avoid the discomfort or anxiety you might feel if you really listened to the other person.

  Sometimes clients will share things that are hard to listen to; they might even do this deliberately to shock or unsettle you, but don't be fazed and don't judge. It's important to understand that everyone – including you – has the potential to do awful things if the right buttons are pressed, and all of us have 'sinned and fall[en] short of the glory of God' (Romans 3:23). A client's story is an essential part of who they are; they have the right to share it without judgement being made or offence taken.

- Being ironic. Most people don't understand irony. They will think that you're being sarcastic or 'taking the mick'. You can rapidly lose someone's trust and respect without even realising it. Use words simply at their face value.

- Patronising. We patronise someone when we treat them as if they are inferior or less intelligent. This can be subtle.

    We might effect an emotional response that we don't really feel; we might pretend to understand a person's situation when we don't and cannot (especially since we are not really listening to them!). Or we might allow ourselves to come across as smug or superior in some way, as if 'we have all the answers', or as if the person we are speaking to doesn't quite measure up. Any of these things will kill any relationship stone dead because they stem from a basic lack of respect. Just because a person has done some stupid things doesn't make them stupid. Who hasn't?

Again: do not be afraid of silence

The speaker will be silent at times. They may need time to absorb what they have heard or said, they may be testing you or they may just not feel like talking. It does not necessarily mean they don't want to be with you. Allow some silences, or the client may feel pressured and you will disempower them.

The church setting

This chapter has been written with the context of a community-based project in mind, but most of the points are equally relevant in a church setting, although there may be differences in how they are applied. I want to focus on two things here.

Using 'spiritual' language

When a person becomes a Christian and joins a local church community, they will begin to adopt the language and mannerisms of the church, possibly without fully understanding what they mean. It can happen alarmingly quickly because they want to sound as if they belong. It can be a particular problem for 'cultural' Christians, who have been brought up in the Faith, to communicate with people who haven't. It doesn't matter how theological, or articulate, or witty, or topical our speech is, if the people we are talking to don't understand it, we have wasted our breath.

I remember being quite shocked when I first started volunteering in a prison chaplaincy, at just how few points of contact there were between me and the people I was trying to talk to. In the end, if we are sincere and use plain language, and we allow the Holy Spirit to work, He will communicate on our behalf, but we still must pay attention to this.

This isn't a thing that only applies to people coming out of prison; it is quite likely to be true of most of the people in our communities. As 'Christian culture' drains out of our society, we are left with a generation to whom the Church appears irrelevant and who, for the most part, have no idea what we are talking about.

Of course, the gospel – the Good News about Jesus Christ – is just as powerful as it always was. But we must take care to communicate it clearly. Beware, though, there has been a tendency among some churches to dilute the message, to make it more palatable or more acceptable. We must never do this, but we must speak in language that ordinary people understand.

Patronising

You will remember the example of the church leader 'talking down' to the homeless man. This betrays an un-Christlike attitude. We might patronise people in other denominations because they lack our distinctive characteristics, language or 'revelation', or because they disagree with us politically. We have patronised our 'young people' so that they left the church at the first opportunity.

There is a kind of elitism among many Christians. Too often we struggle to accept people for who they are, because they dress, speak and behave differently from us. We assume that we are culturally, if not morally, superior. It isn't often a deliberate thing, but it is a thing nonetheless.

So, when a man who has been in Christ for half a dozen years, and out of prison for five, begins to gain a profile in Christian ministry, local church leaders struggle to accept him. They perceive him as a threat; he isn't 'one of us'. They may be waiting for his 'inevitable' fall (and if he slips up, they are merciless!). Of course, God uses him anyway, and the world at large responds readily to him because he speaks their language.

In this book, we've said a lot about *boundaries*, assessing risk and accountability. This is all good practice. We must have good boundaries; we must understand risk and we absolutely must hold ourselves and one another accountable. But at the same time, we should see each other as God sees us.

> Do not judge according to appearance, but judge with righteous judgment.
> *John 7:24*

When we speak to people who have come out of prison, who perhaps have a very different experience of life from most of us, and who might struggle to understand much of what we say, we must be absolutely straight. We must say what we mean, and respect that the people we are speaking to are adults of sound mind. And usually, they will tell us if they don't understand.

> Love must be completely sincere. Hate what is evil, hold on
> to what is good. Love one another warmly as Christians,
> and be eager to show respect for one another.
> *Romans 12:9-10 (GNT)*

Challenge

> Even though I am free of the demands and expectations of
> everyone, I have voluntarily become a servant to any and
> all in order to reach a wide range of people: religious,
> nonreligious, meticulous moralists, loose-living
> immoralists, the defeated, the demoralized – whoever. I
> didn't take on their way of life. I kept my bearings in Christ
> – but I entered their world and tried to experience things
> from their point of view. I've become just about every sort
> of servant there is in my attempts to lead those I meet into
> a God-saved life. I did all this because of the Message. I
> didn't just want to talk about it; I wanted to be *in* on it!
> *1 Corinthians 9:19-23 (*The Message*)*

The apostle Paul is the epitome of the Christian communicator,
as he explains in this passage. He makes himself the message and
lives it out as fully as he can. He says something similar in his second
letter to the Corinthians:

> You are our epistle written in our hearts, known and read
> by all men; clearly you are an epistle of Christ, ministered
> by us, written not with ink but by the Spirit of the living
> God, not on tablets of stone but on tablets of flesh, that is,
> of the heart.
> *2 Corinthians 3:2-3*

The psalmist of the sons of Korah declared that his tongue was
'the pen of a ready writer' (Psalm 45:1). The Bible has a lot to say
about making messages clear – indeed it is the Word of God that
imposes order on the primordial chaos and brings light out of
darkness (Genesis 1:2-5; John 1:1-5). If we are presenting Christ to
prisoners and ex-prisoners, we must also model the message we
bring.

As individuals:

- How can we make our message clear?

As organisations:

- What challenges do we face in communicating clearly with other organisations?

14

Working with Those in Dependency and Addiction

A very large proportion of the people coming out of prison have a history of alcohol or drug abuse. They may have continued using drugs inside and may leave prison on a prescription for a replacement drug like methadone or Subutex®. They may also be prescribed a cocktail of other meds that they may or may not need. Some of the mental health problems that prisoners suffer from are the result of prolonged drug taking, so coming off drugs may reduce and eventually remove the need for antidepressants and antipsychotics. On the other hand, long-term drug or alcohol use may sometimes disguise an underlying or undiagnosed mental health condition.

Almost all prisoners also smoke tobacco addictively and, while this isn't necessarily a behavioural issue, it definitely has long-term health implications. At the time of writing, UK prisons are phasing in a general 'no smoking' policy, which should affect this.

When we think of 'dependency', we normally think of this kind of 'substance dependency', where a person is in the grip of an addiction to a chemical substance of some kind. We understand that these things are often very damaging to the individuals concerned, to their families and to the wider community. We are familiar with the idea of *rehabilitation* to help people break free of these dependencies, and of *resettlement*, the longer process of supporting the person in rebuilding their life after addiction. But people can also be dependent on, or 'addicted to', many things apart from alcohol, illegal drugs or tobacco. For instance, they may behave compulsively regarding food, sex, pornography, exercise, relationships, working, gambling or computer games. Even religion or 'spirituality' can be a problem. These things appear to have little in common with substance dependency, but, as we discuss below, a common process is at work.

What harm do drugs do?

There has been a debate for many years over whether some or all drugs should be legal. Tobacco and alcohol are legal to buy, possess and consume, in spite of being very harmful. A 2010 survey showed that alcohol is more harmful than other drugs by a considerable margin. While it is less harmful than heroin and crack cocaine to the individual user, it is much more disruptive to others.[93] There are arguments and political pressures to decriminalise the use of at least some drugs that are currently illegal, primarily because this would enable their use and effects to be controlled more effectively.

It is certainly the case that a lot of the harm in drugs like heroin and cocaine is caused precisely by their illegality. These drugs are only accessible by breaking laws, and this supports large-scale criminal activity across the world; the global trade in cocaine and opiates is worth about $153bn.[94] Heroin addicts are likely to commit a range of offences in order to obtain their drug, from shop thefts to domestic burglaries and violent assaults. And having 'scored' their illegal drug, there is no quality control. What they take will certainly have been 'cut' at several points in its journey across the world, possibly with something dangerous in itself. Then, sometimes a particularly 'pure' batch will slip through, and this can lead to users overdosing accidentally. Recently, heroin has been cut

[93] Nutt, King & Phillips, 2010.
[94] Global Research News, 2017.

with a synthetic opiate called Fentanyl,[95] which is particularly dangerous.

Most psychoactive substances are dangerous to take.[96] There is growing evidence that the long-term use of amphetamines and some forms of cannabis leads to psychosis; it also seems likely (though there is little hard evidence as yet) that the new synthetic drugs, which are relatively cheap and easy to manufacture (and were legally available until May 2016), cause more serious neurological or psychological harm in much smaller quantities.[97]

Injecting drugs (several types of drug are taken intravenously) may cause damage to blood vessels, resulting in the loss of limbs through thromboses, stroke and cardiac arrest; there is also a significant risk of contracting blood-borne diseases like hepatitis C and HIV. Some drugs are smoked, in which case they will probably be combined with tobacco; the health risks of smoking are serious and well known. In addition, as with alcohol, ingesting drugs over extended periods of time may cause damage to the liver and other organs.

Apart from these harms caused to the individual, the illegal drugs industry puts tremendous strain on the criminal justice system (the estimated annual cost of drug-related crime in the UK is £13.9bn) and, in addition to the impact of tobacco and alcohol, onto the health service (the estimated annual cost of drug misuse to the NHS is £488m).[98]

What do we mean by 'addiction'?

We speak quite loosely of being 'addicted' to things, but what do we mean by this? Is 'addictiveness' a property of the drug or

95 McKenzie & Daeid, 2017.
96 Center for Substance Abuse Treatment, Substance Abuse and Mental Health Services Administration (SAMHSA), 2005.
97 Walton, 2014; Scharff, 2014.
98 National Treatment Agency for Substance Misuse, 2012.

substance, or is it something happening within the person? If so, is that a physical or psychological thing? Or is it spiritual? Or are there elements of all these things? Are substances like heroin and activities like gambling addictive in the same way?

The *Diagnostic and Statistical Manual of Mental Disorders* (DSM),[99] a tool used by medical and mental health professionals to identify and diagnose mental health problems, refers to 'substance-related and addictive disorders'. It lists ten distinct categories of problematic substances; it also mentions 'behavioural addictions', but only includes gambling in this category. Other behavioural addictions (like 'sex addiction' and 'exercise addiction') are mentioned but not formally defined. In these cases, it may be more accurate to talk about problematic or compulsive behaviours than addictions. The DSM identifies the characteristics of addiction as follows:

- The individual's use of the substance is out of control.

- The individual shows tolerance, withdrawal, increased use over time, and a preoccupation with obtaining, using or recovering from the effects of the drug.

- The individual gives up other interests and activities in favour of use, and continues to use in spite of obvious harms.

Let's look at what these points mean in real life.

Tolerance to a drug means that over time and with repeated use, larger doses are required to achieve the initial effect and ultimately to maintain 'normality'. Hardened alcoholics consume amounts of alcohol that social drinkers may find hard to imagine; similarly, heroin addicts might regularly use quantities that would have been a dangerous overdose early in their drug taking. It can be very dangerous for a drug user returning from prison, if their tolerance has dropped, to go out and 'score' the same amount that they were using before.

---

[99] Derived from American Psychiatric Association, 2013, pp484-485.

Withdrawal refers to symptoms of illness when a drug is stopped or reduced, for example the flu-like symptoms when the effects of heroin wear off, and the need for the same (or a similar) drug to relieve these symptoms. It is very uncomfortable for people coming off opiates, but however bad the person feels, it is unlikely to be life-threatening. The same cannot be said for alcohol: sudden withdrawal from large amounts of alcohol can lead to seizures, and it is not uncommon for people to die. Detoxification from alcohol must be medically supervised.

Preoccupation with using. Where someone is dependent, either on a drug or on an activity such as gambling, it can grow out of any reasonable proportion, so that relationships, employment and financial commitments become compromised. This is the aspect of addictive behaviour that is most problematic in terms of disrupted family relationships, financial hardship and criminal activity. Sometimes the distress caused by the addiction in turn feeds the addiction or can lead others to become addicted – for example, the child of a heroin-addicted mother, who in time starts using the drug to deal with their feelings of rejection, stress and social stigma.

Continued use despite obvious harms. One would think that, faced with the prospect of death from lung cancer or from a range of other terrible diseases, a smoker would simply stop. However bad withdrawal might get, a lingering death is much worse. But this understanding often fails to stop use; many addicts show signs of distorted reasoning, at least in the early stages as they seek to justify their behaviour to themselves, or to minimise its consequences. Serious disruption to life – relationship breakdown, debt, imprisonment, loss of livelihood and health, and ultimately death – often results from drug addiction.

In addition to these issues commensurate with addiction, long-term drug or alcohol users may suffer other life-limiting illnesses, including blood-borne viral infections, deep-vein thromboses from intravenous drug use, and severe liver disease. It is not unusual to meet long-term drug users who have lost limbs or have other medical complications. Recently, there have been reports of increased deaths among older drug users[100] as they suffer organ failure from prolonged use.

How addiction works

The first point to make is that people respond to drugs, as to other physical stimuli, differently. If two non-drinkers with the same weight and level of fitness consumed the same moderate amount of alcohol, one may appear and feel quite 'drunk' and the other notice no particular effect. The same is true of other drugs and in the way people respond to addictive behaviours, as well as to rehabilitation treatment. Ed Byrne[101] writes of using heroin every day for weeks before being aware of a physical dependency. He makes the point that heroin itself wasn't the problem so much as the process of 'addiction'. While we can always generalise and quote statistics, we have to keep in mind that individuals will respond differently, and some responses might be unpredictable.

The second point is that although there may be psychological and spiritual factors at work, and although drugs such as heroin have very definite physiological effects, the process of addiction is primarily *neurological*. It is to do with how the brain processes experiences, rewards and memories, and not so much with the properties of the substance itself.

Lying on a sofa, eating a bar of chocolate and watching *Star Trek* might make you feel good. Neurones in a very basic part of the brain, known as the 'reward centre', are triggered to release a neurotransmitter called dopamine. Your brain then creates a memory of this feeling of satisfaction. In a healthy person, this process reinforces things that are useful for survival, such as eating, having sex and interacting socially, or things that reduce our level of destructive stress, like watching *Star Trek*. We enjoy these things;

---

[100] Ross, 2017.
[101] Byrne & Sargent, 2014.

the activities are pleasurable and memorable, so we want to do them again.

Having an activity that you enjoy doing periodically because it makes you feel good or helps you relax isn't an addiction; however, some substances are particularly good at hijacking this reward system. Different drugs work in different ways, but the result is that they replace a person's natural desire to feel good with a desire for the drug, and addictive behaviours like gambling have much the same effect. The level of dopamine in the reward pathway is artificially boosted. Continued use eventually desensitises the system as the body naturally tries to bring itself back to equilibrium. The result is that the body produces less dopamine of its own, so there will be too little without the drug or activity to replace it. Everyday pleasures like chocolate and *Star Trek* will no longer work, and too little dopamine can lead to feelings of depression, anxiety, fatigue and an inability to concentrate; you 'need something to pick you up'.

Eventually, even the drug stops producing enough dopamine, and a bigger dose is needed. You build up tolerance to it.

In addition to this addictive cycle, drugs of abuse produce effects in themselves. Heroin, for example, mimics the effect of the brain's natural painkiller, serotonin, while amphetamines block the body's reabsorption of dopamine, further raising its level. This disruption of the brain's chemistry is why, in addition to the medical complications mentioned above, long-term addicts are also susceptible to a range of psychological disorders, ranging from increased anxiety to full-on psychosis.

Working with people in addiction

It is unhelpful to treat addictions simply as diseases. An addict is undoubtedly sick and needs treatment, but the key to recovery will be in their attitude and thinking.

A person who has cancer cannot decide one day that they no longer have cancer and stop suffering from it; this is not necessarily true of an alcoholic or a heroin addict. They may need medical assistance to detox and ongoing support to recover, but at the root of their recovery the addict has made a decision to change. In spite of the changes to their brain chemistry described above, some of which may be permanent, they have found the motivation to pursue a different outcome in their life.

It is crucial to recovery from addiction that the addict acts freely out of a sense of 'self-liberation'.[102] Where addicts are coerced or 'guilt-tripped' into quitting, their cessation is likely to be less complete or long-lasting than where they are self-motivated.

Also, it is rarely helpful to look at the addiction in isolation. Each individual is different, but it's unlikely that they set out with the intention of becoming an addict; they started doing whatever they do in response to something that was happening – or not happening – in their life. A person's addiction may be to do with issues of self-esteem, or a deep-seated trauma that they may not even be aware of; the drug use or problematic behaviour may be an outlet for feelings or impulses that are otherwise impossible to express, or it may be an attempt to self-medicate where the underlying issue is not clearly seen or understood. It can be very difficult for a person in the grip of an addiction to find the necessary motivation to move out of it. Any lack of self-esteem or other challenges that they were facing before they became addicted will only be worse now. Those supporting recovering addicts should be aware that – at some point – past traumas, as well as current challenges, will appear and will need to be addressed.

Practicalities

For most people, coming out of prison is a stressful transition and this in itself may be enough to trigger a lapse into drug use, so be

---

[102] Prochaska & DiClemente, 1986.

aware of what the risks are with each client. An addict's default behaviour under stress will be to 'score'; as soon as this happens, they are back where they started. It's not uncommon for former drug users coming out of prison to kill themselves with an overdose because, while their craving for the drug seems as strong as ever, their physical level of tolerance has reduced.

The same transition out of prison can be used in a beneficial way. The passage cited above from the DSM notes, 'Craving ... is more likely in an environment where the drug previously was obtained and used'.[103] Taking a motivated person out of their familiar environment, even though this might be stressful, can be a trigger to break or disrupt an addiction. It is in itself an act of repentence; the person is saying, 'I want to live a different life,' and verifying it with their actions. They are taking a step of faith. This process was demonstrated very effectively with US soldiers returning from Vietnam in the 1970s.[104] But the transition needs to be carefully managed if this is to work.

Even with the motivation of the client and the change of environment, the likelihood of successfully detoxing someone in an open house in the community is small, especially if there are other ex-addicts or active users in the environment. There is also a likelihood that any 'replacement therapy' drugs, like methadone or Subutex®, will be shared with the other house residents, or that at some point they will go and obtain street drugs. Addicts returning from prison need to be detoxed in a specialist closed unit. And (I reiterate) withdrawal from alcohol always requires medical supervision.

If you're working with substance abusers, you must have close accountability within your team; this may involve some sort of 'buddy' or peer mentoring arrangement. Adhere to your policies and observe boundaries; you cannot take an addict at their word (however much you may want to). You must also keep accurate,

---

[103] American Psychiatric Association, 2013.
[104] Gupta, 2015.

up-to-date records of everything you say and do, so that one person cannot easily be played against another.

You are supporting the client in their positive decision to change – they are driving the process. But they will not always be consistent in their thinking or behaviour. You must have a plan in place for when they lapse or, better, try to identify the changes in thinking and behaviour that occur before the lapse takes place, so that support can be provided. It's essential to keep a clear head and to confront evasion, denial and other manipulative behaviours that may occur. It is very easy to be drawn into the inevitable chaos that will result from a relapse.

Rehabilitation

Change is *necessary*. Change is *desirable*. Change is *possible*.

Most drug and alcohol rehabilitation uses a model of change put forward by James Prochaska and Carlo DiClemente in the early 1980s, known as the Transtheoretical Model.[105] Working with patients who were giving up smoking, they put forward five stages of change and pointed out that the stage a patient was at was a much better predictor of their success in quitting than either the severity of their addiction or any mental health diagnosis, because success is mainly to do with the addict's motivation and the extent to which they feel empowered to change, and less to do with their circumstances or their actual symptoms. The stages are:

- *Precontemplation* – where the individual is in their addiction or problematic behaviour; they are ignorant of any problems their behaviour causes and are not intending to take any action to change it.

- *Contemplation* – where the individual is beginning to see that their behaviour is problematic, or where a desire for 'change'

---

[105] Prochaska & DiClemente, 1983.

is a response to fear or dissatisfaction, or is instrumental in some ulterior motive.

- *Preparation* – where change is seen as beneficial and an individual may begin taking small steps towards it.

- *Action* – where change is seen as realistic and the individual takes specific action towards modifying their problem behaviour or acquiring new healthy behaviours.

- *Maintenance* – where change is an ongoing reality and an individual sustains it for at least six months, perhaps actively working to prevent relapse.

Some frameworks also add a sixth stage:

- *Termination* – where individuals have zero temptation and they are sure they will not return to their former behaviours.

This process appears to be linear, and we might expect a client who has moved from 'Precontemplation' into 'Contemplation' to move through the stages in a nice smooth sequence and, after a couple of years, maybe, to be living a life 'clean' and free from all temptation. This hardly ever happens. For most recovering addicts, 'Maintenance' continues for many years and 'Termination' never becomes a reality. It is not unknown for people to relapse into full addiction after decades of being clean.

Once a person begins to 'Contemplate' their behaviour and its possible consequences, even in the most self-serving way, they cannot go back to 'Precontemplation'. They can't unthink those thoughts (there is no such thing as a 'post-contemplator'). So, if they slip back into addiction for some reason, they are aware of what they are doing, even if they feel that they have no control over it and may even be in denial about it. So, while they can't go back to 'Precontemplation', at every other stage, the person can slip back and move forward again. It's a bit like a game of snakes and ladders.

Prochaska and DiClemente cite various studies showing that between 70 and 80 per cent of alcoholics, heroin addicts and smokers relapse within a year, but that most people do not give up trying. Eighty-four per cent of those who relapsed moved back to the 'Contemplation' stage. 'On average, self-changers make three serious revolutions through the stages of change before they exit into a life relatively free from [addiction]'.[106] Some people will never completely break free but become stuck at a particular stage.

So, if you are working to move released prisoners away from addictions to street drugs, alcohol or their replacement therapies, you must anticipate that this will not be a smooth journey. If you have access to a closed detox unit, this will make life considerably easier in that you can control the environment to eliminate the availability of drugs and reduce the general temptation, and also work to build the clients' own sense of purpose and motivation. It's also important to this process that clients have as much agency as possible within the process, so your intervention needs to be staged in the way that it is delivered and accessed, as clients are prepared to embrace life in the 'real world' again. Clients and those who work with them should speak openly about what challenges they face, how they are able to make progress, and the difficulties they are encountering.

For some people, the transition from prison to the outside world is drastic and traumatic. This can easily trigger their addiction, even if they had been clean for a while in prison. But if the transition is managed effectively, it can have the effect of disrupting an addiction, and perhaps refocusing the person in a positive way.

You must be aware of where each individual client has come from and what their issues have been. A blanket approach to addiction recovery is unlikely to be successful in the long term. You will need to support your participants through their own struggles.

---

106 Prochaska & DiClemente, 1986, p6.

We have previously mentioned the ideas of 'self-liberation' and 'agency'. People breaking free of addiction are moving *into* freedom as the constant demands of the addiction recede and become less urgent, but to come to that place, they must also move *in* freedom. In order to break free, the person should believe that they *are* free and that *they* are able to do it. As well as moving away from something, recovering addicts need an achievable goal to move towards.

Spiritual issues

I mentioned earlier that there was a 'spiritual' aspect to addiction. This is not to downplay the importance of psychology or the essential role played by brain chemistry, but we are whole people, made in the divine image, and not merely biochemical machines.

I want to make a couple of points. First: addiction is not a moral issue. The choices that people make while they are addicted certainly have moral implications – it is always wrong to steal from shops or to rob people, and there can be no justification for these things – but having a depleted level of a certain neurotransmitter does not make you a bad person or a 'sinner'; nor does attempting to self-medicate to cope with the consequences of some trauma, and nor, necessarily, does choosing to use a recreational drug such as alcohol. We have to be careful not to rush to judgement.

The word 'addicted' is defined by an etymological dictionary as:

> 'Delivered over' by judicial sentence (as a debtor to his creditors) … sense of 'dependent' (1560s) … [107]

The original idea is of somebody being *taken into captivity* and of *becoming dependent*, or more recently, of being 'devoted' to something. Another useful non-technical definition of addiction is:

---

[107] Harper, 2003–2017.

> The state of being enslaved to a habit, practice, or
> something that is a psychological or physical form of habit
> ... to such an extent that its cessation causes severe
> trauma.[108]

The key word here is 'enslaved'. At some point, whether consciously or not, somebody with an addiction has relinquished control over part of their life to another entity – and this is a spiritual matter. Paul writes to the Galatians:

> Stand fast therefore in the liberty by which Christ has made
> us free, and do not be entangled again with a yoke of
> bondage.
> *Galatians 5:1*

Christ makes us free from whatever forces or situations have previously enslaved us, but that freedom has to be claimed and lived as a conscious choice. 'Stand fast ...'

If a person allows themselves to slip back into addiction, they are being 'entangled again with a yoke of bondage' and not standing fast 'in the liberty by which Christ has made [them] free' – they're not serving the Lord, or being responsible to their family, their employer, etc. A clear decision to follow Christ is a decision to walk away from the addiction – and that decision must be reinforced by action carried out over a long period of time. For an addict of any dependency, that choice must always be a present and ongoing decision.

At Walk, we believe this is best addressed through active discipleship to Christ.

> Set your affection on things above, not on things on the
> earth.
> *Colossians 3:2 (KJV)*

---

[108] Dictionary.com, 2017.

Challenge

There are a number of Christian organisations who work with addicts to disciple them to Christ. The most long-standing of these are Teen Challenge[109] and Victory Outreach,[110] both of which trace their origins back to the work of Rev David Wilkerson in New York City in the 1950s and 60s, made famous by the book *The Cross and the Switchblade*.[111] Another well-established organisation working in the UK is Betel UK,[112] which originated in Spain.

Smaller UK-based organisations include The Carpenter's Arms,[113] based near Leicester.

Look at these organisations' websites, and also the Walk Ministries[114] website and answer the following questions:

- What do these projects have in common?

- Can you identify a feature that makes each one distinct?

If you are planning to operate or start a project, consider your own vision:

- How does your vision fit in with the existing organisations mentioned above?

---

[109] http://www.teenchallenge.org.uk/ (accessed 25th July 2018).
[110] http://victoryoutreach.org/; their UK base is in Manchester, http://vomanchester.org/ (accessed 25th July 2018).
[111] Wilkerson, 1963.
[112] http://www.betel.uk/ (accessed 25th July 2018).
[113] http://carpenters-arms.org/ (accessed 25th July 2018).
[114] http://walkministries.org.uk/

A brief internet search will reveal several other private and charitable organisations that operate community or residential rehabilitation facilities in the UK[115] and facilities within the NHS.[116]

- What can you learn from these?

Finally, from a local church perspective:

- How can you direct those who come to you looking for detox and rehabilitation?

---

[115] For example, BAC O'Connor https://www.bacandoconnor.co.uk/ (accessed 27th July 2018).

[116] For example, https://www.nhs.uk/Services/hospitals/Services/Service/DefaultView.aspx?id =235957 (accessed 27th July 2018).

15

Working with Sexual and Other High-Risk Offenders

In this chapter, we will discuss working with 'high-risk' offenders who are under Multi-Agency Public Protection Arrangements (MAPPA). We will look at what MAPPA means and who such arrangements apply to, and working with this group within a project supporting released prisoners in the community. Then we'll explore some issues specific to sex offenders, and, finally, we will discuss receiving high-risk offenders into church. Working with some MAPPA offenders will present complications for support projects and churches; sometimes significant restrictions will be placed on the individuals concerned that may affect where they can go, who they can associate with and what they can do. You will need to work together with the statutory agencies; in some cases, this will shape or dictate your response.

In all this, while safeguarding will be a major consideration, you must not lose sight of your fundamental aim to minister the fullness of the gospel to the people concerned. Sometimes there can seem to be tension between these things.

MAPPA

Multi-Agency Public Protection Arrangements allow for the supervision of high-risk offenders after they leave prison, by a Public Protection Unit (PPU) consisting of specialist prison, probation and police officers. This unit will assess and manage the risk presented by the individuals concerned, share information where necessary and organise supervision, which will often entail 'informal' visits at home by plain-clothes police officers.

Three groups of offenders come under MAPPA: Category 1, registered sex offenders; Category 2, violent offenders sentenced to imprisonment for twelve months or more, those detained under hospital orders and some other sex offenders who do not qualify for registration; and Category 3, other dangerous offenders who pose a risk of serious harm. All these need interventions beyond their normal licence supervision. Violent and sex offenders under MAPPA will also have to sign the Violent and Sex Offenders Register.

While some other groups of offenders may present a greater likelihood of reoffending, for example those identified as 'prolific offenders' and supervised by a police Integrated Offender Management (IOM) unit, those supervised under MAPPA present a greater risk of harm should they reoffend. While the likelihood of reoffending by these offenders is relatively low, great trauma to victims and significant disruption to communities is likely if they do, and therefore they need special supervision.

There are three levels of MAPPA, based on the level of coordination needed to manage each offender's risk effectively:

- **MAPPA-1: 'Ordinary management'**

These will be managed by probation in the same way as non-MAPPA offenders.

- **MAPPA-2: 'Active multi-agency management'**

These offenders' risk management plans require the active involvement of several agencies via regular multi-agency public protection meetings.

- **MAPPA-3: 'Active multi-agency management'**

Arrangements are like those for Level 2, but these cases also require the involvement of senior officers to authorise the use of special resources, such as police surveillance or specialised accommodation, where necessary.

Level 3 offenders (sometimes called the 'critical few') pose the highest level of risk to the public. It is very unlikely that someone in this category would be referred to a support project (for example, they would not be allowed to associate with other offenders), though it's not impossible that they will want to go to church, and this may be permitted after careful consideration.

Working with MAPPA offenders

People at the lower end of MAPPA-1 will not need any special arrangements. They will have a separate supervision plan parallel to their normal licence, and may need to report to a designated police officer from time to time and notify changes of circumstances, address, etc. If they begin an intimate relationship, the police risk assessor with the PPU may want to interview their partner and notify them of any risk. The MAPPA may run for longer than their licence; it isn't part of their sentence, but something which is imposed separately as a safeguarding measure.

MAPPA-2 is actively managed and therefore more imposing. Bringing someone in this category into your project or your congregation will only happen with the explicit permission of probation or the police. Bringing a person on MAPPA-2 into a project where they might have contact with other offenders, perhaps including former associates, is possible but will only happen with great circumspection and on the advice of the MAPPA agencies. It is worth noting, however, that MAPPA-2 offenders are often accommodated in probation hostels after their release from prison, where they will be with other offenders, but these facilities are carefully managed and supervised by probation.

In the case of sex offenders, the procedure is the same but the criteria may be different. Environmental factors, such as the proximity of schools, play areas and young families, will be a consideration, depending on the nature of the risk the person presents; they may be 'tagged' or denied access to the internet. The PPU is unlikely to approve putting a sex offender into a shared house.

Whose risk?

We use the term 'high-risk offender'. What do we mean by that? What risk and to whom? As we noted above, MAPPA covers a wide range of people, from those deemed 'extremely dangerous', such as terrorists or those associated with gang violence, to those who present an elevated risk in some respects or to particular people – for example, someone convicted of domestic violence.

Risk to the community

The risk to the community is the risk that the person will offend again in a similar manner, making further victims. Obviously, minimising this risk will be the first consideration. Whatever we plan to do with the person, we must keep this in mind; somebody on MAPPA is on it for a reason. A person with a history of violence, and perhaps connections into organised crime, requires circumspection. He might be fine while everything is going well, but how will he be when things go wrong? To state that he is a new creation in Christ (see 2 Corinthians 5:17) is absolutely true, but might be unhelpful if it enables him to 'play down' the risk that he knows he still presents, and it won't make his old friends go away. In working to resettle and rehabilitate high-risk offenders, we need to make certain that we are part of the solution and not a complication to an ongoing problem; we want to provide all those we support with the opportunity to grow in faith and in life; to '[increase] ... in favor with God and men' (Luke 2:52), but in doing this we must keep a sense of perspective.

It is quite possible to treat someone kindly and welcome them as part of the worshipping community, to work with them to address some of their ongoing problems and help them into work, while still observing boundaries as we previously discussed. Working safely with any offenders is at least as much about how we handle ourselves as about how we manage them.

While believing in change, we must also manage risks.

The MAPPA agencies will work hard to protect the public from those deemed to be dangerous. We might be tempted to take shortcuts with these measures, but we must not. If, for example, an offender has a Christian faith in which he wishes to grow, but because his offences have involved the grooming of vulnerable people, 'going to church' may be judged to be a risky thing for him to do. It would give him ready access to a pool of potential victims. The statutory agencies cannot deny him the freedom to practise his religion (though they may suspect that his conversion to Christianity is an excuse to place himself in proximity to potential victims), so written into his licence may be a clause that prevents him from attending any church more than once. He is able to practise his faith, but will have no opportunity to create more victims.

From the agencies' point of view, this is an elegant solution. They have met their legal and moral obligation to allow him to practise his faith, while protecting potential victims. But it presents a big pastoral problem to those wanting to minister to him.

The temptation for us would be to set aside the terms of his supervision and make some sort of compromise on the grounds that it's in his 'spiritual interests' (he is a very plausible person – of course, his modus operandi is to 'groom' victims – he appears harmless enough). To compromise his supervision regime, however well-intentioned, would be to undermine the integrity of everything that probation and the MAPPA agencies are trying to achieve with him. It would play directly into the likelihood of his creating a new victim and would certainly lead to him being 'breached' and recalled to prison. It would also guarantee that probation won't work with us in the future.

Sometimes these restrictions are inconvenient: they are supposed to be, but nevertheless we must work within them. Their purpose is to protect the public (and sometimes the offenders themselves) from harm.

Risk to the released prisoner

There are things you can do that will place the released prisoner at risk. Some of these are fairly obvious, such as making alcohol available, or allowing them to come into contact with a former associate or partner without properly recognising the dangers of this. But it might also be hazardous for his identity to become known; while the person might not have access to the internet, you should be aware of the possible consequences of allowing a photo of them to appear on your website or Facebook page. It could have the effect of retraumatising victims and it may indicate his current location. (Showing pictures of released prisoners on websites in general may not be advisable, and certainly should only be done with their permission.)

The locations of registered sex offenders are in the public domain through the Register, though the information would need to be specifically sought. It isn't the kind of thing that you would be wise to discuss openly, at church, for example.

There may be other factors that you have little control over, but that you should be aware of. A person convicted of a historic sexual offence might be required to undergo polygraph testing, which is quite intrusive, or to attend a sex offenders' treatment course, which will deliberately rake up uncomfortable memories and associations. These may counteract some of the work you are doing to resettle the person into the community after their imprisonment.

Be prepared for some emotional and possibly mental health fallout from these things.

Risk to your project

While by their nature, high-risk offenders present certain management challenges, most of these are undertaken by the MAPPA agencies. You are providing a structure and possibly accommodation within which the person can begin to build a new life. The long-term success of this, however, depends entirely upon the client's motivation and willingness to engage with your programme. In this, all the criteria for working with high-risk individuals are the same as they are for any other released prisoner, but they must be applied with added vigilance. Remember boundaries and always be aware of the potential for manipulation or false compliance: accountability is central.

We don't need to speculate about possible scenarios for disaster, but the potential outcome for your organisation in terms of loss of confidence, loss of credibility and perhaps actual harm to staff or other participants is serious.

Sexual offending

The term 'sex offender' is almost too broad to be useful; it denotes a wide range of offenders from those who present very little risk of ever offending again, right across to predatory individuals who repeatedly offend, and who present a real danger. In the public imagination though, all 'sex offenders' are tarred with the same brush and are subject to the same stigma. They are the modern-day lepers. This, as much as any behavioural or management challenges presented by some offenders, makes this a difficult field to work in.

Why are sex offenders treated differently?

Sex offenders are subject to similar risk, need and responsivity criteria as other offenders, but the nature of their offending – or the drive that leads to it – is widely believed to be innate and not changeable: once an offender, always an offender. In other words, there is a popular sense, sometimes reproduced by the statutory agencies, that sex offenders' responses will never be complete or genuine, in spite of the additional work done with them and the conditions to which they are subject. Once convicted, they will always be under suspicion.

Sexual offending, as opposed to other categories of offending, threatens to contaminate our most intimate relationships, and transgresses our most basic boundaries, such as those within families or at critical moments of children's development. Sex in itself is such an intimate thing. It is *ours*, deeply connected with our ideas of personhood and identity; to be raped is to be violated, to have one's integrity as a whole person compromised. Because these crimes are usually perpetrated by people we trust, they evoke deep revulsion.

There has been much research into the roots of sexual offending. Is the desire to offend in this way produced by some social malfunction? Is it a psychological problem? Or do some people have a biological or genetic predisposition for sexual 'deviance'? Until recently, there were no firm conclusions, though studies indicate a matrix of different factors. The current model of offender management tries to evaluate the risk of reoffending based on offenders' criminogenic needs, but the needs of sex offenders in this respect are categorically different from the needs of other types of offender. If you are intending to work with sex offenders – and this is a growing necessity[117] – you must have some understanding of the issues involved in order to respond appropriately, both to support them effectively and to protect those who might be vulnerable. Addressing and managing a person's addiction to heroin is one thing; addressing or managing their sexual attraction to children, for example, is quite another.

---

[117] Barrett, 2017.

The simple answer to the question at the head of this section is that sex offenders are treated differently because we fear them. Their offences threaten us and threaten our closest relationships; this is made worse by the suspicion that they are somehow different from us and not capable of change.

Here is the news: God loves sex offenders too, and so must we.

Competing theories

Sigmund Freud[118] described sexually deviant behaviours in terms of 'character disorders' formed in the development of a child that either could not be changed, or could only be changed with great difficulty. This idea is attractive because it seems to align with our experience; it is resilient, though it lacks any theoretical underpinning. More recently this idea has been finessed by the psychologist John W Money, with the idea of a 'love map',[119] a person's formative internal sexual blueprint developed in childhood and adolescence in relation to the people and circumstances that are significant to them. Again, it is an attractive idea, and one that offers some scope for helping people to understand their sexuality, but it is unclear how much actual 'science' is behind it.

Other researchers in the latter part of the twentieth century looked at the problem through different lenses, including Behavioural Theory, which is interested in the deviant behaviour itself, rather than any deeper psychological origin and biological theories, where deviant sexual preferences are produced by biological factors such as hormonal imbalances, or genetic predispositions to certain types of response. These see sex offenders as people who are medically 'ill' and able to be treated, rather than as those who are morally 'bad'. There has even been a (rather fatalistic) suggestion that sexual deviancy is a function of

---

[118] Freud, 1905/1953.
[119] Money, 1986.

'maleness',[120] in which case 'some sexually deviant behaviours are ... inevitable'.[121]

Perhaps all these have merit, but none of them gives an explanation. Each idea explains sexual offending from within a particular discipline, but offers a narrow and partial account at best. It wasn't until the first decade of the twenty-first century that Tony Ward[122] and his colleagues put forward an Integrated Theory of Sexual Offending, which considers the complex interaction of the many different factors shown to contribute to a person's sexual behaviour. This Integrated Theory draws together ideas from many distinct sources and considers a wide range of studies over a long period of time. It tries to avoid the narrow thinking and limited focus that have been prevalent in this field. Perhaps now, with the perspective of 100 years and more of research, we are coming to a useful understanding of the factors that contribute to sexual offending.

The 'Four Preconditions'

In this section we will consider one more theorist, whose ideas have been influential in the management of sex offenders in the last couple of decades. In the 1980s, the sociologist David Finkelhor devised a model of offending based on four preconditions[123] that must be met before offending takes place. It can be applied to offending generally, but he applied it particularly to those who offend sexually against children. His four preconditions are:[124]

---

[120] Wilson, 1987.

[121] Lanyon, 1991, p39.

[122] Ward & Beech, 2006.

[123] Finkelhor, 1986.

[124] This is a brief synopsis of his argument.

- The Thinking Stage. People don't generally do things 'by accident' but use some kind of premeditation, particularly when their actions involve offending against other people.

- Overcoming internal inhibitions. Most potential offenders have a sense that what they want to do is 'wrong' (though not everybody's moral compass points in quite the same direction); they rationalise the thing that they want to do and give themselves permission to do it. This involves some level of self-deception or cognitive distortion.

- Overcoming external inhibitions. They create the opportunity. Sex offenders will sometimes go to extraordinary lengths to put themselves in a position to assault their victim.

- Overcoming the victim's resistance. In some cases, this will involve a direct and violent assault; in other cases 'grooming' or some other form of manipulation. Up to this point, no offence has been committed, even though the person's behaviour might have been cause for great concern.

Finkelhor's model is quite useful, though not without its critics.[125] However, it has given rise to several widespread and rather dangerous assumptions,[126] including that:

- Offenders will have committed far more offences than those for which they have been convicted.

This runs against the evidence, which suggests that reoffending among sex offenders is significantly lower than for other categories of offender.[127]

---

[125] Ward & Hudson, 2001.

[126] FPP Ltd, 1999, p7.

[127] Grubin & Wingate, 1999; Hanson & Morton-Bourgon, 2004.

- The offender will try to deny all or some of the offence or say that it is 'out of character'.

- They will seek to lay the responsibility for the offence elsewhere.

- They will have built up an addictive cycle of behaviour.

- The offender will say: 'I won't do it again.'

- There is no cure, only control.

I emphasise that these are *assumptions*, and not based on any evidence or analysis of risk, and while some are made in the light of experience, it is clear that 'making assumptions' about anyone will get you into difficulties. It will misrepresent the person concerned, and it may leave you open to manipulation because you will also be 'in denial' to some extent (consider the Drama Triangle, discussed earlier). While we are not naïve about the nature of sexual offending, and have our 'safeguarding' policies to hand, we should always approach our clients with a non-judgemental attitude.

Cognitive distortion

The second of Finkelhor's Four Preconditions notes that 'overcoming internal inhibitions ... involves ... self-deception or cognitive distortion'. Cognitive distortions are the lies that offenders tell themselves to justify their offending and minimise their responsibility for its impact. While almost all offenders do this to some extent, cognitive distortions are especially significant among sex offenders. One prisoner serving on a Vulnerable Prisoner (VP) wing once commented to me: 'There are 190 people on this wing, and I'm the only guilty one!' People have the capacity to convince themselves that everything is OK.

A person who smokes may feel troubled by the fact that they like smoking and by the knowledge that it will almost certainly kill them. This is called cognitive dissonance – the discomfort caused by holding two contradictory opinions at the same time. The smoker's response to this might be to tell themselves that 'Uncle George smoked until he was 107 – it never did him any harm', or 'I can't possibly stop smoking while I'm going through such a stressful period in my life'. They are going through a process of making themselves feel better about smoking, a process called 'dissonance reduction'; these thoughts are examples of cognitive distortions.

A cognitive distortion is a thought process that removes responsibility from the individual and places it somewhere else: 'It was OK for Uncle George to smoke, so it's OK for me.' If the person then becomes ill, it will be 'Uncle George's fault' in some way. Everybody engages in these cognitive distortions to some extent – we all have our pet beliefs and prejudices. They are basically lies that we tell ourselves to:

- justify an action;

- rationalise something we may feel guilt for;

- externalise responsibility for an action;

- minimise the consequences of an action.

These lies can become deeply embedded. If much offending involves cognitive distortion at some level (for example: 'I am managing my addiction'), in sexual offending, it is front and central:

- I was drunk, and I let my daughter touch me. I feel so awful.

- I have a very low risk. Everybody says so.

- She wanted me to.

- It was a misunderstanding.

Mostly, this involves the denial of responsibility.

As we embark on this kind of work, we must be aware of our own prejudices and rationalisations. If we can't engage with the person sitting in front of us on the basis of their actual need (as opposed to what they say it is, or what we suppose it might be) we are unlikely to make any real progress.

Denial

It is understandable for offenders to be in denial about some aspects of their offending. In many cases, they have worked hard to justify their course of action and have a considerable investment in this. Their actions, and they themselves, may be widely spoken of in disgust, and they may have become pariahs in their former communities. What we are asking them to do is to express the same disgust for their actions and attitudes as others, while at the same time retaining psychological health and integrity. That is a hard thing to ask, but necessary. It's the process that all offenders – indeed, all repentant sinners – must embark upon in order to embrace genuine change.

Denial occurs at different levels. An offender may:

- Flatly deny that they committed the offence.

- Deny that what they did was wrong.

- Deny that they were responsible for it.

- Deny that what they did caused any real harm.

- Deny that they present an ongoing risk in the future.

These denials may seem quite plausible (at least to the person making them); they may even believe them, but we need to engage with our clients from the standpoint of truth. Like any other kind of addiction, a tendency to offend sexually needs to be managed, and in reality, no one has a zero probability of offending.

A person's walk with God is predicated on their honesty. It starts with repentance: 'all have sinned … ' (Romans 3:23); 'while we were still sinners …' (Romans 5:8); 'If we confess our sins …' (1 John 1:9). This doesn't mean that our understanding of our 'sin' is complete at any given time, and repentance is an ongoing process in which we deliberately surrender our lives to God. Offending works in much the same way. And offences always have sin somewhere behind them: unbelief, denial of the truth or self-preservation. But it does mean that – as far as I am able to understand – I seek to identify sin in my life and turn away from it. I don't 'sweep it under the carpet' and pretend that it doesn't really matter. 'Sin' is itself a kind of cognitive distortion – something you think you can get away with before God (see Genesis 3:4-6).

So as Christian ministries, we should be in a good place to work at breaking down these denials and distortions, because it's what we do (or should be doing) all the time.

A final thought on sex offenders

When I first started volunteering in an HMP chaplaincy, the chaplain shared that she had been working with an elderly man who had been convicted of sexually assaulting his daughter. He was duly released from prison after serving a substantial sentence, and within a week had taken his own life. At his funeral, his daughter confessed that she had made up the allegation.

Never 'assume'.

High-risk offenders in church

In some ways, having MAPPA offenders in your congregation makes life relatively simple because the boundaries are set and monitored by external agencies, and all you have to do is apply them.

A high-risk offender leaving prison will only be allowed to attend a church with the explicit permission and cooperation of the

PPU. In the first instance, the released prisoner will discuss the possibility of attending church with his offender manager. He might have a church in mind, or they may explore possibilities in the local area. The efficiency and effectiveness of this varies widely from place to place. Some offender managers will be keen for their clients to attend; others less so.

'Gordon', towards the end of the two-and-a-half-year licence period of a five-year sentence for a sexual offence against a child, was consistently blocked from attending any church he suggested as a possibility. In the end he stopped trying; he will try again after his licence is complete and – he hopes – most of his restrictions have been lifted and he can move to a different location. He will be on the Register for life, however.

On the other hand, 'Timothy', convicted of a similar offence and part-way through his licence in a different town, was so withdrawn in his probation hostel, and suffering from depression and anxiety, that his offender manager contacted a local Christian support group to ask if they could help find a suitable church for him.

Contracts

Some churches welcome released prisoners into their midst on the basis of a contract or 'attendance agreement' to ensure good behaviour and accountability. In my view, there are practical and theological problems with using contracts in this way; however, in some cases, they may be necessary. It is possible that if an offender is deemed to be high risk, the statutory agencies might insist upon this type of arrangement.

Problems with contracts

The first problem with an attendance contract in church, in its own terms, is that it seeks to circumscribe how the Holy Spirit will move in a person's life. By definition, it is applying boundaries to the grace of God. The church is not a club with rules: 'if anyone is in Christ, he is a new creation' (2 Corinthians 5:17) ... and a member of Christ's body, a living stone in His holy temple (see 1 Peter 2:4-6). Paul urged the Corinthian church to excommunicate a man in 1 Corinthians 5 for unrepentant sexual sin. This was to protect the witness of Christ and so that the man's spirit might be saved (verse 5). But it appears that the man was subsequently forgiven and welcomed back, presumably having learned his lesson (compare 1 Corinthians 5:1-5 with 2 Corinthians 2:3-11).

The second problem is that participation in the Church is by covenant. Ultimately, this is Christ's covenant with us, sealed in His blood, but there is also a covenant that we hold with one another and members of a local congregation. In some churches this might be an explicit thing as we welcome people into membership in some way, and this might involve the new member endorsing a constitution or statement of faith. To apply a separate contract on top of that is to say, 'We don't trust you.' While there might be an obvious reason for saying that, it surely invalidates the covenant for both parties. It's like saying, 'You can be here, but you're not really one of us.'

The third problem is purely practical. Former prisoners are very used to rules and explicit boundaries. They like them because they can circumvent them. When your contracted church attender is walking in repentance, there is no problem; he will observe his boundaries. Should he 'backslide' in his Christian walk, he will be inclined to slip between his restrictions – probably without actually breaching his contract. In spite of what we noted above about assumptions, sex offenders, should they lapse into offending, are likely to be devious. In these cases, applying a contract to a person's church attendance may have the paradoxical effect of enabling the very thing it is trying to prevent.

However, it is likely that the statutory agencies will insist on high-risk offenders who attend church to be subject to a contract of some kind. You must be wise and vigilant in applying it.

Here are some real-life examples of high-risk offenders attending churches. As usual, identities have been protected.

'James', a man convicted of offences involving 'extreme violence', was released from prison on MAPPA-3. He lived in a flat in a small village not far from the coast, where he was closely supervised. He had a part-time job but was unable to associate with or contact anyone he knew from his former life. He had come to faith in Christ in prison, through another prisoner who had now also been released, but he was not allowed to contact him either.

He remained in contact with one of the prison chaplains, who was able to direct him to a suitable church a few miles from where he was living. It wasn't a simple matter for him to attend church; with the support of the chaplain, he had to approach his offender manager, then police officers from the PPU had to speak to the pastor of the church and satisfy themselves that it would be safe. He would not be allowed to speak of his past or of the fact that he had been in prison; the pastoral team would be aware of his situation, but no one else.

At one point, a couple of volunteers delegated by the prison chaplain met him at church for the service – one of them had been invited to preach. She testified of their prior relationship with James and of how he came to faith, without at any time mentioning that this was in prison – it was a fair achievement.

After a time, James' MAPPA level was reduced, and he was allowed rather more freedom and was able at last to meet up with the friend who had led him to Christ; he has now moved into that area and into a different church under much less direct supervision. Nevertheless, when he started a romantic relationship, his girlfriend was interviewed at length by the police. MAPPA will be part of James' life for a number of years yet.

'Gerald' was released on MAPPA-2. He had also become a Christian in prison, participating in the chapel programme and at one time working as chapel orderly. He had demonstrated a significant and sustained change in his attitude and behaviour.

He relocated to another town at his own request, because under MAPPA he was not allowed to go to any of the places where he had offended, or to contact any of his former associates or victims. One of the chaplains arranged to link him with a suitable church where he would be able to develop his faith – but this had to be handled with delicacy.

Before Gerald's release date, the chaplain contacted the church's pastor and his offender manager. A meeting was arranged between Gerald's offender manager, a police officer from the PPU and the pastor. At this meeting, the church satisfied the police and Gerald's offender manager that it would be a safe environment for him and that the conditions of his licence would be upheld.

Apart from a couple of individuals, the congregation did not know who Gerald was, or what his circumstances were; they just knew him as a chap who joined them for worship and sometimes made the coffee.

A suitable member of the congregation was appointed to be Gerald's 'buddy', to pick him up before and drop him off after services, to share a coffee with him and generally to befriend him. Gerald attended worship, where he was introduced simply as 'Gerald'. The only people to know much about him were the pastor and his buddy. Within these constraints, Gerald was able to participate in church life, though his ability to attend evening activities etc was slightly restricted by his curfew. As time went on, the restrictions on him lessened.

Meetings between the MAPPA team and the safeguarding officer continued, but reduced in regularity, at some point being replaced by a periodic phone call.

'Joe' was released on MAPPA-2 to a probation hostel. He had come to Christ in childhood, but his faith had lapsed. He had recommitted himself to Christ just before he was sent to prison for a historic sexual offence.

Chaplains in 'sex offender' prisons face a continual challenge to find suitable congregations in which to place men such as Joe after they are released.

Many sex offenders are older men, and many profess a more traditional Christian faith, but it may be that the church has been the context of their offending in the past – and this is a particular problem. We believe that living as a disciple of Jesus Christ as part of the community of His Church is a large part of the answer to the challenge of reintegrating these men into the community, but it must be done carefully, with a structure of accountability around the person. The safeguarding measures required by MAPPA help to supply this, where they are delivered in a sensitive way.

Because of the circumstances of his offence and the fact that it happened twenty-plus years ago, Joe was not considered to present a very high risk within the community, though some restrictions were in place on his actions and movements. However, the trauma of his substantial prison term left him with some physical and mental health difficulties.

He was supported by a community chaplaincy team close to where he was living. It proved difficult, at first, to link him with a church that would welcome him, partly because of his shyness and his reluctance to undertake the necessary 'full disclosure' of his offence to a group of people he didn't know very well, and partly because of his same-sex orientation.

Joe's fear was that, having discussed the possibilities for attending church with his offender manager, he would turn up at the church with a big 'sex offender' label on his head, and that everyone would know everything about him. While the reality of the situation was quite different, it was a big disincentive for him to go to church in the first place.

Eventually a suitable church was found and agreed with the PPU. A 'buddy' from the church, who was connected with the community chaplaincy team, picked Joe up for church and dropped him off again after services, and for some midweek meetings. This particular church has a generally older membership, some of whom know a bit about Joe's background and circumstances and are able to support him, as he sometimes struggles with his mental health and with the terms of his licence. They were delighted to discover that Joe had been a chef in his previous life and could make use of his culinary skills in the church kitchen from time to time. In all this, Joe has seen the Lord move powerfully in his life since his release from prison.

Challenge

At the time of writing, I have been approached twice in the past month by offender managers from different areas asking whether I could help them find a church for a released prisoner with a sexual conviction. They had been unable to find any church willing to engage with them.

Many churches have a cultural antipathy towards those identified as offenders, and this is much more so where a person is identified as 'high-risk' or external agencies are involved, and especially where the offending has been sexual in nature.

This chapter has attempted to demystify this area to some extent. There are some difficulties and constraints for those who seek to support 'high risk' individuals, and this is particularly true where the person is also 'needy' in other respects.

A 'through the gate' approach will often be beneficial, so that churches or support groups can be part of the picture for the prisoner as he approaches release (though this may not always be feasible – high-risk offenders are often located in prisons some distance from home and assigned a place in a probation hostel on release. It is hard to maintain contact).

- If you have a 'sex offender' prison in your area,[128] contact the chaplaincy department and ask if you can volunteer. This will enable you to establish a relationship with the prison and get to know some of the prisoners a little. From this, the next step would be to:

- Ask how your church would be able to provide support for the men as they are released. This will make the chaplain's day, though it will undoubtedly involve conversations with the police and probation services.

---

[128] Currently the following establishments are designated for sex offenders: HM prisons Albany, Usk, Bure, Whatton, Ashfield, Stafford, Rye Hill and Littlehey. However, there may also be significant populations of sex offenders in other prisons for operational reasons.

16
Working with Women

We began this book by thinking about a woman being released from prison with tragic consequences, but almost everything we have written since then has been slanted towards working with men. But obviously, we can't discuss the subject of working with released prisoners seriously without considering the needs and vulnerabilities of women as they leave prison, and treating them as a distinct group. Women are different from men in terms of the offences they tend to commit and in terms of the support they need on release. While there are areas of overlap, the critical differences are that many women have the principal responsibility for childcare, and also, for a significant proportion, their offending has been linked to abusive or exploitative relationships. Because of this, women need different and more focused support from men in order to resettle successfully into their communities.

In addition to the original seven Pathways to reduce reoffending discussed previously (see the Chapter on 'Strands'), another two are identified specifically for women in the criminal justice system:

- Pathway 8: 'Abuse'. A range of supportive interventions should be available to women who disclose abuse or domestic violence.

- Pathway 9: 'Prostitution'. Women should be given every support if they ask for help to build a new life away from prostitution.

In this chapter, we will examine some of the issues related to supporting women who are released from prison. We will look at some 'best practice' ideas and, finally, as before, look at issues around welcoming released women into church congregations.

Engagement with the criminal justice system at any level ought to highlight particular areas of need and trigger interventions where necessary. However, historically, female-orientated services have been overlooked, perhaps because women represent such a minority within the criminal justice system. Also, because of the stigma associated with things such as prostitution, drug use and domestic violence, women have often been a low priority when it comes to allocating ever-dwindling local authority funds.

In 2007 Baroness Corsten drew attention to this in 'The Corsten Report', written in response to a spate of deaths in custody at HMP Styal. Her second chapter is titled: 'Men and Women; Equal Outcomes Require Different Approaches'.[129] She notes that the issues have been well known for many years; research has been carried out and reports written, revealing, for example, that:

> offending is less common among girls and women than among boys and men and that women offenders often have complex multiple needs, linked to drug and substance misuse and poor mental health. A significant proportion of women in prison are the mothers and sole carers of dependent children.[130]

It has not been a priority for government to address these issues, and much of the positive response to the report has been eclipsed since 2013, behind the Transforming Rehabilitation agenda.

I take issue slightly with the idea that 'equal outcomes require different approaches'; as we have discussed elsewhere, recent studies in desistance have shown that taking a holistic approach to released prisoners, treating them as the whole people they are, is more effective than merely attempting to manage their risk. This is true for both men and women, and we must embrace it if we are to

---

[129] Corston, 2007.
[130] Criminal Justice Joint Inspection, 2011.

help them make categorical and permanent changes to their lives. But, Corsten's point is well made, in that one size of support does not fit all. If we are going to work with women, we need to understand the specific issues they face and be able to provide them with properly focused support in overcoming these things.

Some facts and figures

Experiences of domestic and sexual violence are significantly more common among women offenders than among the general female population. While one in four women in the UK will experience domestic violence in her lifetime, the proportion of women offenders who have experienced abuse of this type is much greater. Estimates vary, but research by the Social Exclusion Unit in the first decade of this century found that around half of all female prisoners have suffered domestic violence and one-third have experienced sexual abuse.[131]

A Joint Inspection of the 'women's estate' and the subsequent 'Themed Inspection Report: Equal but Different?', carried out in 2011 by Her Majesty's Chief Inspectors of Probation, the Crown Prosecution Service and Prisons, made the following observation:

> In nearly three-quarters of all the cases and reports examined, the woman involved was seen as vulnerable in some way. Most of these women were, or had been, a victim of domestic abuse … Some were subject to sexual exploitation. There were concerns about self-harm in around one-third of all cases and of suicide in around one-quarter of the cases. They were therefore a very needy group of offenders who clearly required both careful monitoring and active input during supervision.[132]

[131] Norman & Brown, 2011.
[132] Criminal Justice Joint Inspection, 2011.

Russell Webster blogs:

> The charity Women in Prison reports that 79% of the women who use their services have experienced domestic violence and/or sexual abuse.[133]

The danger is that these women are released back into the same abusive situations they came from.

The Prison Reform Trust estimates that 31 per cent of female prisoners, as opposed to 24 per cent of males, have had contact with the care system,[134] compared with about 1 per cent of the population as a whole. In 2010, rates of self-harm were four times higher among female prisoners than males (29 per cent of female prisoners self-harmed compared with 7 per cent of males);[135] the figure for 2016 is 21 per cent, but this proportionate fall is due to a corresponding sharp rise in self-harm among male prisoners.[136] Approximately two-thirds of women in prison have dependent children under the age of eighteen years,[137] which becomes a factor in the provision of suitable housing.

So, while the challenges facing men leaving prison also affect released women, many women also have other needs and struggle to cope without targeted help. More women in prison than men have mental health diagnoses: 25 per cent as opposed to 15 per cent of men.[138] Corsten also reported that social exclusion is common: 'Many [women] lead or are coerced into chaotic lifestyles and have complex multiple problems.'[139] In a recent report by The Griffins Society highlighting the particular plight of street sex workers on their release from prison, Hazel Renouf writes:

---

[133] Webster, 2017b.

[134] Prison Reform Trust, 2016.

[135] NOMS Women and Equalities Group, 2012.

[136] Prison Reform Trust, 2016.

[137] NOMS Women and Equalities Group, 2012.

[138] Prison Reform Trust, Bromley Briefing, autumn 2017.

[139] Corston, 2007.

> My casework knowledge has shown me that leaving prison is clearly a challenging process for women. For street sex-working women in particular, these challenges are exacerbated by the complexity of their needs.[140]

A chaplain in a women's prison once shared with me a conversation she had had with a former prisoner who had phoned the prison chaplaincy in desperation. Having got clean from drugs in prison, she was sitting in the dark, frightened to go out because her dealer was parked in the street outside, waiting for her. The chaplain shared the frustration and sense of powerlessness experienced by many prison staff about the inevitability of women like this returning to custody so quickly.

Our response

We would do well at this point to take a step back from the immediacy of these challenges and remember who we are and what we are seeking to achieve as the people of God, and look once again at Jesus' declared manifesto at the beginning of His ministry:

> The Spirit of the Lord is upon Me,
> Because He has anointed Me
> To preach the gospel to the poor;
> He has sent Me to heal the brokenhearted,
> To proclaim liberty to the captives
> And recovery of sight to the blind,
> To set at liberty those who are oppressed …
> *Luke 4:18*

This is also our mandate as we reach out to those who are most vulnerable – and we must keep it close to our hearts. It's so easy to become swamped by the magnitude of problems faced by those we are trying to support, and influenced by whatever socio-political responses to them are currently in vogue, but in order to be

---

[140] Renouf, 2016.

effective we must keep our focus tight. The response we offer is first a response to the love and grace of God that we have experienced in our own lives – to love God first, and then our neighbour.

The first thing we are offering is hope. This isn't just the hope of a life free from abuse, addiction, debt or imprisonment, much as those things are important, but the hope of salvation; of a changed spiritual identity that gives the opportunity for these women to be the people they were made to be – the people they fundamentally want to be – in a context far greater than this world. '[God works] exceedingly abundantly above all that we ask or think' (Ephesians 3:20) – and this applies whether they believe in God or not. God doesn't change (Malachi 3:6) and His love is universal. This is the gospel – the Good News. Jesus takes upon Himself all the isolation, victimhood, hurt, sickness and brokenness that has been suffered by these women. He replaces their hopelessness with hope, and it is in the strength of this that we can 'heal the brokenhearted', 'proclaim liberty to the captives' and 'set at liberty those who are oppressed'.

We keep the gospel – the Good News about Jesus – front and centre of our response.

Working with women

Be non-judgemental

If you are creating a project to support vulnerable women, it is critically important not to make assumptions about the people you are working with. It is essential to work *with* them and not just provide a service *for* them. It's helpful if the people who have most contact with participants 'look like them' and to some extent have common experiences with them. While this isn't always possible or strictly necessary, it makes a big difference. There is always a danger that we make assumptions about clients as they walk through the door, and this perception of judgement – whether it's real or imagined – is one of the things that will keep potential participants away from projects where they might find valuable assistance. First impressions are important. Remember that, despite the statistics cited above, not all women coming out of prison:

- have been abused;

- have been addicted to drugs or alcohol;

- have been involved in prostitution or been trafficked;

- have low educational achievements;

- are inadequate parents.

So, avoid patronising, and don't assume that because a thing is statistically true that it's necessarily true of the person you are talking to at the moment. As always, you must treat each person on her individual merits, which means taking time to listen to her. You know that she needs to change her life; she knows that too (though she might not have the language to express it clearly), but always treat her with respect. This person's life might be deeply dysfunctional and generally a mess, but it is her life. Her experiences may be traumatic, hard to deal with and shocking to you, but they are her experiences and constitute her story. 'Change' may be essential but be careful what you say.

Your role is to support the person you are working with as she moves from her place of vulnerability to where she can be strong enough to take an active role in the community, and accept her …

> … adult role responsibilities according to her capabilities
> … , [her] perceptions of acceptance by the community
> despite what is often a stigmatizing status, and … sense of
> self-esteem or self-efficacy.[141]

---

[141] Cobbina, 2009.

In all of this, there is no guarantee that just because a service is offered, potential participants will take it up.

Types of project

There are many models of good practice that we can learn from; you shouldn't think that because you can't do everything that you can't do anything. Managing accommodation, for example, is more resource intensive than operating a mentoring scheme. Offering a 'safe place' as a drop-in, where visitors can be signposted to relevant services over a welcoming cup of coffee, might be relatively easy to do from church premises.

Mentoring

A mentor provides help for clients to build their self-esteem and confidence, and will be able to offer practical and emotional support. The aim of mentoring is to help the service users to develop their independence and decision-making, to improve their motivation and to work towards building a better and more satisfying quality of life. Mentoring is commonly defined as:

> ... a one-to-one, non-judgmental relationship in which an individual voluntarily gives time to support and encourage another. This is typically developed at a time of transition in the mentee's life, and lasts for a significant and sustained period of time.[142]

A mentor will come alongside the mentee, meet with her regularly to build up a level of trust, and usually help to guide her towards meeting an agreed goal. This might be, for example, to live free of drugs for a period of time, or to gain a particular qualification or find employment. Mentoring should be a long-term relationship – both parties must give a serious commitment to make the arrangement work. Mentors must be 'peers', in the sense that

---

[142] National Council for Voluntary Organisations (NCVO), 2017.

they have no legal duty of care: they are not offender managers, teachers, social workers or police officers. A client shouldn't be in the position of facing a sanction if they miss a meeting! While mentors don't necessarily have to be of a similar age or social background to the mentee (sometimes different life experience can give valuable perspective to a situation), it is usually helpful if they are. The DrugScope report, 'The Challenge of Change', makes the following observation:

> Effective mentoring often depends on matching service users with 'real' peers, i.e. those with similar histories and experiences. The gender of peers is important too, as is the provision of appropriate training and support to work with this highly vulnerable group.[143]

Mentoring can be beneficial to anybody who is willing to engage with the process. It is likely to be most effective where clients are ready to act on the conviction that they need to make changes to the way they think and act, and where their motivation is strong; a mentor may help them when their resolution falters.

Women's centres

In the last five years or so, women's community centres have been established in several cities around the UK. These provide a kind of one-stop shop for all kinds of help and assistance, advice and guidance, and a 'safe place' for those who attend. Sometimes these are set up with the active involvement of probation or a CRC, with the express purpose of reducing the risk of their clients' reoffending; others might be run by consortia of third-sector groups. All aim to provide non-threatening access to essential services.

The joint inspectors comment that:

---

[143] Holly & Lousley, 2014.

women's community centres are a useful resource which enable women ... to access a range of services offering practical support and help in a conducive and non-threatening environment. The services on offer ... typically include advice and guidance on a range of issues of concern to women, including employment, finance, benefits, debt, housing, childcare, health and substance misuse.[144]

For example, a community centre for adult women might offer support to women who have low self-esteem or need some new options and a fresh perspective, working alongside other local services. They might offer a timetable of classes and workshops ranging from basic skills to drop-in sessions from other agencies, including Citizens Advice and the local community mental health team.

Accommodation

According to Corston, 'for women [leaving prison], stable accommodation is ... the most significant resettlement need'.[145] It is a basic human necessity – almost the most basic. Without proper accommodation, it is difficult to address anything else, and its lack can itself be a driver for offending. A homeless woman may offend out of desperation to have a roof over her head, albeit in a police station or prison.[146] At the time of writing, access to suitable housing for women leaving prison is in crisis in several parts of the country; as with male prisoners, there have even been reports of tents and sleeping bags being handed out to women as they leave the prison gate.[147]

Women who have offended are sometimes deprioritised by local authorities for housing, on the grounds that they have made themselves 'intentionally homeless'.[148] This varies from region to

---

144 Criminal Justice Joint Inspection, 2011.

145 Corston, 2007.

146 Beresford, Earle & Litchfield, 2016.

147 Pells, 2016; Bentham, 2017.

148 Earle, 2016.

region but is most prevalent in the south-east, where social housing stock is under the greatest pressure. Sometimes women are offered accommodation outside their existing communities, sometimes a considerable distance away. While this may be beneficial to those who are fleeing abusive relationships or want to make a 'fresh start', they will face increased challenges establishing themselves without the support of family, friends and any services they may have linked with.

> Housing is a critical factor for women who wish to exit prostitution. A safe and secure home of their own helps women develop a stable lifestyle, seek employment, and have their children back.[149]

Writing specifically about street sex workers released from prison, Hazel Renouf makes the following recommendation:

> Street sex-working women need access to safe and supported housing on the day they are released from prison ...[150]

... along with access to good quality, appropriate and long-term therapeutic support.

While there is need for shared supported houses and managed locations where women can safely detox, in general the Prison Reform Trust's[151] recommendation to housing providers is that women leaving prison should be accommodated in self-contained flats in single-sex units. Clients with, or hoping to regain the care of, children need sufficient space for this to be realistic (ie more than one bedroom). There should be ready access to health and other services that they need to facilitate reintegration into the community. There should also be good security lighting, controlled entry and CCTV coverage of lobbies, entrances, etc.

---

[149] Holly & Lousley, 2014.

[150] Renouf, 2016.

[151] Beresford, Earle & Litchfield, 2016.

Challenge

As in the previous chapter, 'through the gate' working is likely to be more effective than linking vulnerable women up with churches and support groups post release, when the situation is more pressured. Since many women serve relatively short sentences in (more or less) local prisons, it is likely to be achievable. This will help to ensure that people are being offered the right support when they are released, and also that the whole process of release and resettlement is smoother than it might otherwise be. However, women-only support groups are few and far between.

- Where are your local women's prisons?[152]

- Who are the key staff that you should liaise with?

If you're intending to work with vulnerable women, you need a clearly stated mission to avoid becoming swamped by the level of need and fall into 'mission creep'. Understand what you are going to do, and do it well.

Consider the following:

- What support is already available for women who come out of prison in your area?

What can you add to this?

---

[152] Currently, UK women's establishments are: HM prisons Askham Grange, Bronzefield, Downview, Drake Hall, East Sutton Park, Eastwood Park, Foston Hall, Holloway, Low Newton, New Hall, Peterborough, Send and Styal.

17

Coping with Success and Failure

Defining success and failure

There's a temptation to congratulate ourselves when those we support do well and to beat ourselves, or each other, up if they 'fail'. But this is fundamentally wrong; we can't 'fix' anyone. People change when and as much as they want to change. God opens the door, brings healing and a new frame of reference, and our role is to be effective porters, to assist.

As we work with our participants, we see them growing and learning new things about themselves. We can celebrate small changes and little, positive steps, even if the person leaves and maybe returns to prison. Maybe they'll do better next time.

We once worked with a troubled young man who managed about five weeks with Walk, and then transferred to another project, where he went another few weeks before reoffending and going back to prison. Two months or so doesn't look great – it doesn't flatter your statistics – but then that was the longest he had been out of custody since he was fifteen.

Others have only lasted a night or two; still others have returned for the second or third time: 'I want to do it right this time.'

It isn't always clear exactly what constitutes 'success' and 'failure'. Projects need well-defined criteria to operate – but people stubbornly refuse to fit into boxes.

Funding bodies, including local councils, always need to see some kind of structure before they will give support, and may require detailed feedback on what support is being provided and to whom. This is a good thing in that it gives us accountability and a useful measure of quality control, but there is always the danger that it will take our focus away from the actual people we are working with and create a box-ticking exercise. You must keep your focus sharp; a drive for 'performance' may paradoxically compromise good pastoral care.

Unfortunately, we are working with people who have complex needs and minds of their own.

If a person with a long history of drug use and offending has stayed away from drugs and out of trouble for two years, he will probably have been helped by a lot of people, but in the end, he changed his behaviour because at a deep level he changed his mind. Various people will have helped him: a CRC worker or offender manager; an IOM officer; a drugs counsellor or the staff in a rehab; a mentor; or perhaps it was a group of friends, a study group at church, or his mother; or maybe he met the right girl.

There is always a danger that while providing all the help we provide – safe accommodation, employment and training opportunities, help with dependency and thinking skills – we can unintentionally validate and enable offenders to stay as they are; that we feed a 'dependency culture', or that they make only a superficial change. Remember that most offenders are expert blaggers and fundamentally lazy. They will stay as they are, if we let them.

Challenge

If a person you have been working with has messed up and gone back to prison, you will feel pretty bad about it.

Firstly:

- It's not your fault. He or she offended, not you.

Secondly:

- What lessons can you learn from this experience as an organisation?

    You probably didn't do anything that caused the person to reoffend, but there will definitely be some things that you could have done differently. With your colleagues, ask yourselves the following questions:

    o   Are your policies appropriate?

    o   Were they followed?

    o   Did the client understand the boundaries placed around them?

    o   Was your project able to address their needs?

    o   Did the client have needs that were not identified?

    o   How can you address these things in the future?

Thirdly:

- What can you learn from this experience as an individual?

    There is a tendency to take things personally, but don't – unless you were actually complicit in the offending.

    o   Were you manipulated or conditioned? (Probably, yes. Most likely, this offence has been brewing for weeks and no one spotted it because the client was very plausible.)

    o   Did you follow reporting procedures, etc?

    o   Were you appropriately supported by your colleagues/supervisor/ line manager?

It's important that you are able to debrief as a team and learn what you can, but if we believe that people fail because we let them down, it will impact our motivation. This is a dangerous tendency; if you try to take personal responsibility for your clients' decisions and behaviours, you will be open to manipulation, but you'll probably burn out through overwork before this happens.

If a client has moved on from you and is now living independently and crime free:

- Good job. Well done, him or her.

- Now you need to ask all the same questions.

That client changed because they 'saw the light' and was able to take advantage of opportunities. They might have done this *in spite of you*.

If we believe that our clients' success is down to our intervention, again we are making ourselves open to manipulation.

The truth is that sometimes offenders simply need more prison time. Next time round, they might be ready.

Appendix: What Can I Do ...?

Get to know your local prison chaplaincies

Maybe you could join an organisation such as Prison Fellowship that supports the work of prison chaplaincies and the men and women they serve. This can open up all kinds of ministry opportunities. Be aware, though, that some organisations that support prisoners inside don't support released prisoners outside.

If you are a church leader or worship leader, many chaplains (but not all!) would love to invite you into the prison, or for you to invite them to speak to your congregation.

Pray

Praying is the most important thing you can do to support any ministry among serving and released prisoners. Many organisations release prayer bulletins to subscribers, or to friends on social media – that would be a great way to start.

The chaplaincy team at your local prison will be able to give you more precise advice; if you want to support their work with serving prisoners and their families, contact Prison Fellowship.[153]

Support financially

You may not be able or feel any particular leading of God to work with people coming out of prison, but please do what you can to support those working in the charitable sector who do.

---

[153] https://www.prisonfellowship.org.uk/ (accessed 3rd August 2018).

It's unwise to give gifts or loans of money directly to individual people who are recently released. They will almost certainly be in some difficulty, but it will be far more effective to support them through a specialist charitable organisation. It's likely that any money you give to individuals will be spent on drink or drugs, or otherwise sunk into their chaotic life. If you want to help immediately, buy them a meal or a bag of groceries.

Welcome released prisoners into worship

If you are in a local church, especially if you are part of the leadership team, be aware of the 100,000 or more men and women coming out of prison each year, who have often not been served well by churches. A substantial number of these have a Christian faith that they would like to pursue and explore.

Have an effective and loving procedure in place to ensure the safety of the whole congregation; hold one another accountable. Don't be judgemental, never make assumptions and don't single particular individuals out. Never respond out of fear. Managing risks is necessary, but also consider that this is the opposite of moving by faith. Extend a warm welcome, but remember to love wisely, and that it might be necessary to communicate with external agencies such as the police or probation service (whose job it is to manage risks).

Welcome released prisoners into the heart of the church, as you would any other newcomer. Expect to see them grow spiritually and to have much to offer.

Community chaplaincy

Local community chaplaincy organisations may be able to offer a range of salaried and voluntary roles to experienced and/or qualified candidates. They may also be open to providing support to you if you have something slightly unusual to offer – creative writing or therapeutic dance, for example – or if you have a burgeoning project that you are trying to launch.

Community chaplaincies epitomise cross-cultural and 'multifaith' working, and usually have close links with the NPS and local CRCs. This means that they can sometimes be highly pressured and 'dynamic' environments.[154]

Set up a project

Community projects to support released prisoners of all kinds are much needed in the present economic and social climate. There are many things that you could do, either as a church acting alone or – more effectively – as a group of churches pooling resources. The text of this book contains a lot of detailed advice about how to go about this, but here is a bare-bones summary.

Scope the local area

Find out what support is already available in your area and get to know the people who are running it.

- Can you support their work?

- Can you provide a service that is currently in short supply?

The situation at present is that any good-quality service you provide will be helpful and much in demand, but it's best not to 'reinvent the wheel' if a good service already exists.

---

[154] More information and a map of the regional community chaplaincy groups is available at: http://www.communitychaplaincy.org.uk/ (accessed 6th August 2018).

Types of project

Here are some well-tested ideas for potential projects, but God may give you something different, of course; a fresh approach. Most of these could be operated out of existing church premises:

- A drop-in centre for coffee and the signposting of other services; add to this:

- Breakfast, clothing bank, a link to food bank, mentoring, debt counselling;

- Christian discipleship, Alpha, relationship guidance;

- One-to-one therapeutic counselling by appropriately qualified staff;

- Hosting sessions by NHS community healthcare, community mental health, Jobcentre staff, etc;

- Community chaplaincy service.

You may consider operating this as a gender-specific 'women's centre', though the need is general.

Another route to provide support might be to work with local colleges and employers to provide skills training and work placements for released prisoners.

Other potential projects that require some capital investment include:

- Providing emergency or short-term hostel accommodation for those released from prison. This is a really essential service, but a high-risk one, since it will be difficult to keep the premises free of drink and drugs, and therefore safe.

- This, plus life skills input and workshop sessions by other community organisations, such as community detox or debt counselling.

- A structured resettlement and reintegration programme, along the lines of the Walk Project, that provides good quality medium-term accommodation as the basis for a holistic support package covering everything from detox and basic living skills to routes into permanent employment.

Organisation structure

Getting the structure right is essential.

Different organisations will approach some of these things differently, but this is a summary of some of the things we have learned in the first few years of operating Walk:

- Projects like this need visionary leadership 'from the front'. In our experience, however many well-qualified people you have in a committee, you need a strong leader. Committees give good advice (sometimes), but hopeless leadership.

- Know what your legal status is; be a registered charity; if you're very small, operate under Charity Commission guidelines.

- Hold your visionary leader accountable! You need a strong team around them, plus a board of trustees who will ask difficult questions.

- Be careful about recruiting 'volunteers'; allow God to send you the right people.

- You should have some ex-prisoners in key positions – certainly managing participants. This is very important.

- Clarify your 'vision' and your mission at an early stage. Protect them.

- Define your boundaries and observe them.

- Be financially transparent. If possible, be financially independent.

- Model discipleship; have personal integrity.

- Don't expand your project beyond a manageable size.

- Aim for resilience in your organisation. What happens if your visionary leader is compromised?

People will accuse you of all kinds of things – 'running a criminal enterprise', financial irregularity, exploitation of vulnerable people, etc. Be proud of what you do and show it to those who need to know, but avoid giving 'hostages to fortune'. If there are any skeletons in your cupboard, they will come out at the most inconvenient moment.

> [Be] blameless and harmless, children of God without fault
> in the midst of a crooked and perverse generation, among
> whom you shine as lights in the world …
> *Philippians 2:15*

Finances

Consider all available sources of funding, but beware that it often comes with strings. Don't pursue funding at the expense of your vision, or at the expense of your core operation. Believe that God provides.

At the time of writing, there is concern among some small charities who are funded or part-funded through Probation as part of Transforming Rehabilitation. This funding model is inefficient at best and at worst leads to the charities effectively subsidising probation services. This should be avoided.

Aim to be self-funding through separate business ventures that feed resources into the project. This can be hard to achieve, but it will secure your future. It may also provide a route into work for at least some of your participants.

Employ released prisoners

If you are an employer, consider employing released prisoners where appropriate.

For many ex-prisoners, the prospect of 'having a job' is both liberating and intimidating. They often expect to be rejected by employers, and sometimes this is the case – though more employers are willing to consider them than in the past. The government has provided guidance[155] as to how this can be done. Our experience is that many prisoners have little or no work history or ethic, and need good leadership and mentoring in the workplace; however, where this is done well, and those concerned are given a sense that they can 'move ahead' and learn new skills, they are likely to make rapid progress and be well motivated.

As in other scenarios, 'safeguarding' is a consideration and some disclosure will be necessary – though check the law around disclosure because it isn't as simple as it seems.

The website cited above allows you to register your interest. From Walk, we have placed participants with our own building company, a local skip hire business, a garage, two furniture restoration businesses and several Christian organisations, including the YMCA and Cross Rhythms radio.

---

[155] https://www.gov.uk/government/publications/unlock-opportunity-employer-information-pack-and-case-studies/employing-prisoners-and-ex-offenders (accessed 16th August 2018).

Recommended Reading

There is very little literature on working with released prisoners in the community and nothing that I'm aware of from a Christian perspective.

If you only read one thing:

Russell Webster's blog (http://www.russellwebster.com/). This is astonishingly wide-ranging and updated several times a week. It is very useful at the moment as the political and policy framework around prison, probation, benefits – and everything, really – changes from month to month.

General reading

Tony Ward and Shadd Maruna: *Rehabilitation*, first published in 2007. This traces the evolution in criminological thought from 'Nothing Works' through 'Risk, Need and Responsivity' to the Good Lives Model. The new edition (2018) is quite expensive, but the first edition is still available in Amazon Marketplace.

Apart from that ...

I've included a comprehensive References section that should give you a good heads-up on most aspects of the subject. Many of the works cited are available online, so you can use that to springboard your own reading.

References

American Psychiatric Association (2013). *Diagnostic and Statistical Manual of Mental Disorders (5th ed DSM-5)*. Washington DC. Retrieved 6th September 2017

Andrews, D A, & Bonta, J (1994). *The Psychology of Criminal Conduct* (1 ed). New Jersey, Cincinnati, OH: Anderson Publishing Co

Arnold, H, & Creighton, S (2006). *Parole Board Hearings, Law and Practice*. London: Legal Action Group

Baptist Union (n.d.). *When a Known Offender is Present*. Retrieved 6th May 2017, from Baptists Together: http://www.baptist.org.uk/Groups/220817/When_a_Known .aspx

Barnardo's (2015). *Children Affected by Parental Imprisonment*. Retrieved 14th January 2016, from Barnardo's: http://www.barnardos.org.uk/what_we_do/our_work/childr en_of_prisoners.htm

Barrett, D (30th April 2015). *Number of convicted sex offenders in jail reaches record high*. Retrieved from Daily Telegraph: http://www.telegraph.co.uk/news/uknews/crime/11573580/ Number-of-convicted-sex-offenders-in-jail-reaches-record-high.html

Bartol, C R, & Bartol, A M (15th May 2014). *Psychology and Law: Research and Practice*. Los Angeles, CA, USA: Sage Publications, Inc

BBC (23rd June 2015). *Offending rates among children in care investigated.* Retrieved the BBC:
http://www.bbc.co.uk/news/uk-33221247

Bentham, M (21st November 2017). *Women who leave prison 'face life of abuse and homelessness' due to housing shortage, watchdog warns.* Retrieved from Evening Standard:
https://www.standard.co.uk/news/london/women-who-leave-prison-face-life-of-abuse-and-homelessness-due-to-housing-shortage-watchdog-warns-a3696936.html

Beresford, S, Earle, J, & Litchfield, Z (2016). *Home Truths: Housing for Women in the Criminal Justice System.* London: Prison Reform Trust

Blades, R, Hart, D, Lee, J, & Willmott, N (2011). *Care – A Stepping Stone to Custody?* Cambridge: Prison Reform Trust

Byrne, E (1964). *Games People Play: The Psychology of Human Relationships.* New York: Grove Press

Byrne, E, & Sargent, J F (16th February 2014). *5 Unexpected Things I Learned from Being a Heroin Addict.* Retrieved from Cracked:
http://www.cracked.com/personal-experiences-1306-5-unexpected-things-i-learned-from-being-heroin-addict.html

Center for Substance Abuse Treatment, Substance Abuse and Mental Health Services Administration (SAMHSA) (March 2005). Treatment Improvement Protocol (TIP) Series 42. *TIP 42: Substance Abuse Treatment for Persons with Co-Occurring Disorders*

Church House Publishing (2006), 'Promoting a safe church: Policy for safeguarding adults in the Church of England'.

Clewett, N, & Glover, J (2009). *Supporting Prisoners' Families: How Barnardo's Works to Improve Outcomes for Children with a Parent in Prison.* London: Barnardo's

Cobbina, J E (2009). *From Prison to Home: Women's Pathways out of Crime.* Rockville, MD: National Criminal Justice Referral Service (NCJRS)

Cole, N (1999). *Cultivating a Life For God: Multiplying Disciples Through Life Transformation Groups.* St Charles, IL: Church Smart Resources

Community Chaplaincy Association (August 2011). *Positioning Paper.* Retrieved 28th April 2018, from Community Chaplaincy Association:
https://www.communitychaplaincy.org.uk/importance-faith

Community Chaplaincy Association (n.d.). *Community Chaplaincy Association.* Retrieved 28th April 2018, from Community Chaplaincy Association:
http://www.communitychaplaincy.org.uk

Corston, B (2007). *The Corston Report: A Report by Baroness Jean Corston of a Review of Women with Particular Vulnerabilities in the Criminal Justice System.* London: Home Office

Criminal Justice Joint Inspection (2011). *Thematic Inspection Report: Equal but Different? An Inspection of the Use of Alternatives to Custody for Women Offenders.* London: HMI Probation, HMCPSI and HMI Prisons.

Crisis (2012). *Research Briefing: Young, Hidden and Homeless.* Crisis.

Crowson, I, & Nelson, S (7th August 2017). *Derby hostel cordoned off as police launch murder investigation - how it happened.* Retrieved from Derby Telegraph:
http://www.derbytelegraph.co.uk/news/derby-news/derby-hostel-cordoned-after-stabbing-287532

Dictionary.com 2017 (23rd June 2017). Retrieved from Dictionary.com Unabridged:
http://www.dictionary.com/browse/addiction

Diocese of Oxford (2016). *The Inclusion of Ex-Offenders in the Christian Community.* Retrieved 6th May 2017, from Diocese of Oxford: https://www.oxford.anglican.org/mission-ministry/faith-in-action/criminal-justice/the-inclusion-of-ex-offenders-within-the-christian-community/

Dominey, J, & Lowson, E (2017). *Community Chaplaincy and Desistance: Seeing a New Future.* Cambridge: University of Cambridge. Retrieved 30th April 2018, from https://www.ccgsj.crim.cam.ac.uk/pdf/SeeingNewFuture

Earle, J (23rd September 2016). *No Home, No Chance: Lack Of Housing Stops Women From Turning Their Lives Around On Release From Prison.* Retrieved from Huffington Post: http://www.huffingtonpost.co.uk/jenny-earle/women-leaving-prison_b_12136830.html

Finkelhor, D (1986). *A Sourcebook on Child Sexual Abuse.* Beverley Hills, CA: Sage.

FPP Ltd (1999). *Working with Sex Offenders: A Practitioner's Portfolio.* Birmingham: Forensic Psychology Practice Limited.

Freud, S (1905/1953). 'Three Essays on the Theory of Sexuality'. In *The Complete Psychological Works of Sigmund Freud* (Standard ed, Vol 7). London: Hogarth Press.

Gardner, T (4th February 2005). *Prisoner is found dead in cell.* Retrieved 11th January 2016, from Yorkshire Evening Post: http://www.yorkshireeveningpost.co.uk/news/latest-news/top-stories/prisoner-is-found-dead-in-cell-1-2278608

Global Research News (17th April 2017). *Cocaine, Heroin, Cannabis, Ecstasy: How Big is the Global Drug Trade?* Retrieved from *Global Research News*: http://www.globalresearch.ca/cocaine-heroin-cannabis-ecstasy-how-big-is-the-global-drug-trade/5381210

Goldblatt, P, & Lewis, C (1998). *Reducing Reoffending: An Assessment of Research Evidence on Ways of Dealing with Offending Behaviour.* London: Home Office.

Grubin, D, & Wingate, S (1999). 'Sexual Offence Recidivism: Prediction versus Understanding'. *Criminal Behaviour and Mental Health, 6*, pp349–359. Retrieved from The Lantern Project: Supporting Victims of Child Abuse: http://www.lanternproject.org.uk/library/research-about-sex-offenders/managing-sex-offenders/sexual-offence-recidivism/

Gumbel, N (2001). *Questions of Life.* Eastbourne: Kingsway Publications.

Gupta, S (23rd December 2015). *Vietnam, heroin and the lesson of disrupting any addiction.* Retrieved 30th June 2017, from Cable News Network (International Edition): http://edition.cnn.com/2015/12/21/health/vietnam-heroin-disrupting-addiction/index.html

H M Prison Service (1993). *Prison Service Annual Report and Accounts, April 1992 – March 1993.* London: HMSO.

Hanson, R, & Morton-Bourgon, K (2004). *Predictors of Sexual Recidivism: An Updated Meta-Analysis.* Toronto: Public Works and Government Services Canada.

Harper, D (2003–2017). Retrieved from Online Etymology Dictionary: http://www.etymonline.com/index.php?allowed_in_frame=0&search=addicted

Harper, G, & Chitty, C (2005). *The Impact of Correction on Reoffending – A Review of 'What Works'.* London: Home Office Research, Development and Statistics Directorate.

Harpin, L (22nd August 2015). *Tories break pledge to increase spending on mental health services.* Retrieved from The Mirror:

http://www.mirror.co.uk/news/uk-news/tories-break-pledge-increase-spending-6301666

Holly, J, & Lousley, G (2014). The challenge of change: improving services for women involved in prostitution and substance use. *Advances in Dual Diagnosis, 7*, pp80–89. Retrieved from: https://doi.org/10.1108/ADD-02-2014-0005

Hombs, M E (2011). *Modern Homelessness: A Reference Handbook*. Santa Barbara, CA: ABC-CLIO.

Howard, M (1993). *Prison Works*. Retrieved 3rd February 2016, from www.michaelhoward.org: http://www.michaelhoward.org/Prison_Works.doc

ICO (2017). *Guide to the General Data Protection Regulation (GDPR)*. London: Information Commissioner's Office.

Institute for Criminal Policy Research (ICPR) (15th January 2016). *Highest to Lowest – Prison Population Rate (Europe)*. Retrieved from International Centre for Prison Studies: http://www.prisonstudies.org/highest-to-lowest/ prison_population_ rate?field_region_taxonomy_tid=14

Jones, Owen (2017). *England and Wales have highest imprisonment rate in western Europe* from The Guardian, 14th March 2017, retrieved 23rd August 2018: https://www.theguardian.com/society/2017/mar/14/england -and-wales-has-highest-imprisonment-rate-in-western-europe

Karpman, S (1968). 'Fairy tales and script drama analysis'. *Transactional Analysis Bulletin, 26*, pp39–43. Retrieved 21st April 2017.

Kemshall, H (2001). Risk Assessment and Management of Known Sexual Offenders: A review of current issues. *Police Research Series, 140*.

Lanyon, R I (1991). 'Theories of sex offending'. In C R Hollin, & K Howells, *Clinical Approaches to Sex Offenders and the Victims* (pp35–54). Chichester: John Wiley & Sons.

Lloyds Bank Foundation, England and Wales (2016). *Commissioning in Crisis. How current contracting and procurement processes threaten the survival of small charities.* London: Lloyds Bank Foundation for England & Wales. Retrieved 1st May 2018, from: https://www.lloydsbankfoundation.org.uk/Commissioning%20in%20Crisis%202016%20Full%20Report.pdf

Mann, R E (2000). 'Managing resistance and rebellion in relapse prevention intervention'. In Laws, D R, Hudson, S M, & Ward T, *Remaking relapse prevention with sex offenders: A sourcebook* (pp187–200). Thousand Oaks, CA: Sage Publications.

Martinson, R (1974). 'What works? Questions and answers about prison reform'. *The Public Interest, Spring, 1975* (35), pp22-54.

McGuire, J (1995). 'What Works: Reducing Reoffending. Guidelines from Resarch and Practice'. Chichester: John Wiley.

McKenzie, C, & Daeid, N N (14th August 2017). *War on Fentanyl: the drug that killed Prince is linked to 60 deaths in the UK since 2016.* Retrieved from The Independent: http://www.independent.co.uk/life-style/health-and-families/fentany-drug-linked-to-60-deaths-uk-since-2016-opioids-a7884231.html

McNeill, F, & Weaver, B (2010). *Changing Lives? Desistance Research and Offender Management.* Glasgow: Scottish Centre for Crime and Justice Research.

Ministry of Justice (2009). *Reducing re-offending: supporting families, creating better futures - A Framework for improving the local delivery of support for the families of offenders.* London: Ministry of Justice, Department for Children, Schools and Families. Retrieved 14th January 2016, from:

http://dera.ioe.ac.uk/207/7/reducing-reoffending-supporting-families_Redacted.pdf

Ministry of Justice (2012). *Certified Prisoner Accommodation. PSI 17/2012*. Ministry of Justice.

Ministry of Justice (2013a). *Gender Differences in Substance Misuse and Mental Health Amongst Prisoners*. London: Ministry of Justice.

Ministry of Justice. (2013b). *NOMS Annual Report 2012/13: Management Information Addendum*. London: Ministry of Justice.

Ministry of Justice (2013d). *Story of the Prison Population: 1993–2012, England and Wales*. London: Ministry of Justice.

Ministry of Justice (2014a). Offender Rehabilitation Act 2014. Retrieved 9th February 2016, from http://services.parliament.uk/bills/2013-14/offenderrehabilitation.html

Ministry of Justice (2014b). *Costs per place and costs per prisoner by individual prison, NOMS annual report and accounts 2013-14: Management information addendum*. London: Ministry of Justice.

Ministry of Justice (2015a). *Offender Management Statistics Quarterly: October to December 2014*. London: Ministry of Justice.

Ministry of Justice (2015b). *Proven Reoffending Statistics: July 2012 to June 2013*. London: Ministry of Justice.

Ministry of Justice (26th July 2018). *Offender Management Statistics Bulletin, England and Wales*. Retrieved 20th August 2018, from GOV.UK: https://assets.publishing.service.gov.uk/government/uploads/system/uploads/attachment_data/file/729211/OMSQ-2018-Q1.pdf

Money, J W (1986). *Lovemaps: Clinical Concepts of Sexual/Erotic Health and Pathology, Paraphilia, and Gender Transposition in Childhood, Adolescence, and Maturity*. New York: Irvington.

Murray, J, & Farrington, D P (2008). 'The effects of parental imprisonment on children'. In M Tonry, *Crime and Justice: A Review of Research* (Vol 37, pp133–296). Chicago, IL: University of Chicago Press.

National Audit Office (2010). *Managing Offenders on Short Custodial Sentences.* London: The Stationery Office.

National Council for Voluntary Organisations (NCVO) (3rd February 2017). *Mentoring and Befriending.* Retrieved from www.mandbf.org: https://www.mandbf.org.uk/faqs/#c481

National Treatment Agency for Substance Misuse (2nd November 2012). *Why Invest? How Drug Treatment and Recovery Services Work for Individuals, Communities and Society.* Retrieved from Public Health England: http://webarchive.nationalarchives.gov.uk/20140727020135/http://www.nta.nhs.uk/uploads/whyinvest2final.pdf

NOMS Women and Equalities Group (2012). *A Distinct Approach: A Guide to Working with Women Offenders.* London: MOJ.

Norman, N, & Brown, J (2011). *Supporting Women Offenders Who Have Experienced Domestic and Sexual Violence.* London: Women's Aid Federation of England.

Nutt, D J, King, L A, & Phillips, L D (1st November 2010). 'Drug harms in the UK: a multicriteria decision analysis'. The Lancet, *376* (9752), pp1558–1565. doi: http://dx.doi.org/10.1016/S0140-6736(10)61462-6

Owers, A (2007). *The Mental Health of Prisoners: A Thematic Review of the Care and Support of Prisoners with Mental Health Needs.* London: HM Inspectorate of Prisons.

Oxford University Press (2017). *Communication.* Retrieved from English Oxford Living Dictionaries: https://en.oxforddictionaries.com

Pells, R (13th April 2016). *HMP Bronzefield: Women given tents instead of accommodation when leaving London prison, inspection reveals.* Retrieved from The Independent: http://www.independent.co.uk/news/uk/home-news/hmp-bronzefield-women-given-tents-instead-of-accommodation-when-leaving-london-prison-inspection-a6981926.html

Pocklington, D (7th May 2014). *Safeguarding in the Church.* Retrieved from Law and Religion UK: http://www.lawandreligionuk.com/2014/05/07/safeguarding-in-the-church/

Prison Reform Trust (2014). *Bromley Briefings Prison Factfile, Autumn 2014.* London: Prison Reform Trust.

Prison Reform Trust (2016). *Bromley Briefings Prison Factfile.* London: Prison Reform Trust. Retrieved from: http://www.thebromleytrust.org.uk/files/2016factfile.pdf

Prison Reform Trust (2017). *Prison: the facts: Bromley Briefings Summer 2017.* London: Prison Reform Trust. Retrieved from: https://www.bl.uk/britishlibrary/~/media/bl/global/social-welfare/pdfs/non-secure/p/r/i/prison-the-facts-bromley-briefings-summer-17.pdf

Prochaska, J O, & DiClemente, C C (1st June 1983). Stages and processes of self-change of smoking: toward an integrative model of change. *Journal of Consulting and Clinical Psychology, 50* (3), pp390–395. Retrieved 30th June 2017.

Prochaska, J O, & DiClemente, C C (1986). 'Toward a comprehensive model of change'. In W R Miller, & N Heather, *Treating Addictive Behaviors* (pp3–27). New York: Plenum Press.

Renouf, H (2016). *Resettlement experiences of street sex-working women on release from prison.* London: The Griffins Society.

Research and Statistics (2016). *Statistics for Mission, 2016*. London: The Church of England, Research and Statistics. Retrieved 7th July 2018, from: https://www.churchofengland.org/sites/default/files/2017-10/2016statisticsformission.pdf

Robinson, S (5th May 2015). *Mental health spending cuts forecast*. Retrieved from the BBC: http://www.bbc.co.uk/news/health-32596748

Rose, D (24th June 2017). *The scandal of the sex crime 'cure' hubs*. Retrieved from The Mail Online: http://www.dailymail.co.uk/news/article-4635876/Scandal-100million-sex-crime-cure-hubs.html

Ross, J (16th August 2017). *Experts think this is why Scotland has the highest drug-related death rate in the EU*. Retrieved from Buzz Feed News: https://www.buzzfeed.com/jamieross/this-is-why-experts-think-scotland-has-the-highest-drug?utm_term=.imDe7ZWLEV#.vjyxjLlq28

Sarre, R (1st April 2001). 'Beyond "What Works?", A 25 year jubilee retrospective of Robert Martinson.' *History of Crime, Policing and Punishment Conference*. Canberra: Australian Institute of Criminology, 34 (1), pp38–46.

Savage, M (February 3rd 2018). *Private probation firms fail to cut rates of reoffending*. Retrieved from The Observer: https://www.theguardian.com/society/2018/feb/03/private-firms-fail-cut-rates-reoffending-low-medium-risk-offenders

Scharff, C (27th May 2014). *Synthetic drug danger: 'Spice': synthetic marijuana, 'spice', poses a real threat*. Retrieved from Psychology Today: https://www.psychologytoday.com/blog/ending-addiction-good/201405/synthetic-drug-danger-spice

St Mungo's (20th June 2013). *St Mungo's says 'No More' to rising rough sleeping*. Retrieved from St Mungo's:

http://www.mungos.org/press_office/1622_st-mungo-s-says-no-more-to-rising-rough-sleeping

Steiner, C (1979). *Healing Alcoholism*. New York: Grove Press.

The Archbishops' Council (2006). *Promoting a Safe Church. Policy for Safeguarding Adults in the Church of England*. London: Church House Publishing.

The Guardian (21st January 2004). *Victims of despair: The 101 inmates who took their lives*. Retrieved 1st November 2016, from The Guardian: http://www.theguardian.com/uk/2004/jan/21/prisonsandprobation.ukcrime3

The Housing Justice Church and Community Night Shelter Network (2017). *The Housing Justice Church and Community Night Shelter Impact Report 2017*. London: Housing Justice.

The Methodist Church (2010). *Methodist Safeguarding Policy*. Retrieved 3rd February 2017, from The Methodist Church in Britain: http://www.methodist.org.uk/ministers-and-office-holders/safeguarding/methodist-safeguarding-policy

Unlock (20th October 2017). *Differences Between Unspent and Spent Convictions*. Retrieved from theInformationHub Knowledge Base: http://hub.unlock.org.uk/knowledgebase/differences-unspent-spent-convictions/

URC Communication Office (June 2015). *Sample Safeguarding Policy*. London: United Reformed Church Communication Office.

Walton, A G (28th August 2014). *Pharma and Healthcare*. Retrieved from Forbes: https://www.forbes.com/sites/alicegwalton/2014/08/28/6-reasons-synthetic-marijuana-spice-k2-is-so-toxic-to-the-brain/#46fc7b0573b1

Ward, T S (August 2003). 'The treatment of sex offenders: Risk management and good lives'. *Professional Psychology Research and Practice 34*, pp353–360.

Ward, T, & Beech, A (2006). 'An integrated theory of sexual offending'. *Aggression and Violent Behavior, 11*, pp44–63.

Ward, T, & Brown, M (September 2004). 'The good lives model and conceptual issues in offender rehabilitation'. *Psychology, Crime & Law, 10* (3), pp243–257.

Ward, T, & Hudson, S M (2001). 'Finkelhor's precondition model of child sexual abuse: A critique'. *Psychology, Crime & Law, 7* (1-4), pp291–307. Retrieved 4th July 2017, from: http://dx.doi.org/10.1080/10683160108401799

Ward, T, & Maruna, S (2007). *Rehabilitation: Beyond the Risk Paradigm.* London: Routledge. doi:10.4324/9780203962176

Ward, T, & Stewart, C A (2003). 'The treatment of sex offenders: Risk management and good lives'. *Professional Psychology: Research and Practice, 34* (4), pp353-360.

Webster, C, & Kingston, S (2014). *Poverty and Crime Review.* Leeds: Joseph Rowntree Foundation.

Webster, R (8th August 2017). *Peterborough Prison PbR scheme cuts reoffending by 9%.* Retrieved from Russell Webster: http://www.russellwebster.com/peterborough-prison-pbr-final/

Webster, R (7th October 2017). *The payment by results drug recovery pilots failed.* Retrieved from Russell Webster: http://www.russellwebster.com/final-drug-pbr-report/

Webster, R (11th December 2017). *Most women in prison victims of domestic abuse.* Retrieved from Russell Webster: http://www.russellwebster.com/prtwipda/

Webster, R (28th July 2018). *More details on the future of probation.* Retrieved 28th July 2018, from Russell Webster: http://www.russellwebster.com/probconsultation/

Wilkerson, D (1963). *The Cross and the Switchblade.* Grand Rapids, MI: Chosen Books.

Williams, K, Poyser, J, & Hopkins, K (2012). *Accommodation, Homelessness and Reoffending Prisoners: Results from the Surveying Prisoner Crime Reduction (SPCR) survey.* London: Ministry of Justice.

Willis, G M, & Ward, T (2010). 'Risk management versus the Good Lives Model: The construction of better lives and the reduction of harm'. In M Herzog-Evans, *Transnational Criminology Manual: Volume 3* (pp763–781). Amsterdam: Wolf Legal Publishers.

Wilson, G D (1987). 'An ethological approach to sexual deviation'. In G D Wilson, *Variant Sexuality: Research and Theory.* Baltimore, OH: Johns Hopkins University Press.

Glossary of Terms

Breach	An offender who 'breaches' his or her licence conditions, or the terms of a PSS order may be sent back to prison.
Counselling, Assessment, Referral, Advice and Throughcare (CARAT)	Part of drug treatment programme in prisons, mediating between specialist care (such as drug rehabilitation programmes and external Drugs Intervention Teams) and drug abusers.
Category (Cat)	The security rating of prisoners: Cat A require the most secure conditions, Cat D the least.
Cognitive Behavioural Therapy (CBT)	CBT is a talking therapy that can help sufferers manage their problems by changing the way they think and behave. It's most commonly used to treat anxiety and depression, but can be useful for other mental and physical health problems.
Chaplaincy	The department in the prison concerned mainly with spiritual welfare.
Community Chaplaincy Association (CCA)	The umbrella organisation coordinating the work of local community chaplaincies.
Community Rehabilitation Company (CRC)	Regional companies who will be responsible for supervising low-medium risk offenders on their release.
Criminogenic needs	A person's needs that increase their risk of committing crime; 'dynamic' risk factors.
Desistance	When offenders cease offending. Desistance Theory is a holistic approach to understanding why this happens.

Determinate (Fixed-Term) Sentence	A prison sentence with a fixed duration and release date.
Dopamine	Dopamine is a neurotransmitter that helps control the brain's reward and pleasure centres.
Drama Triangle	A type of transactional analysis that provides a means to analyse and understand communication between individuals.
DSM	The *Diagnostic and Statistical Manual of Mental Disorders* a handbook used by medical professionals in the diagnosis of mental illness.
DWP	Department for Work and Pensions
Extended Determinate Sentence (EDS)	A new type of fixed-term prison sentence that partially replaced IPP sentences from the end of 2012.
Employment and Support Allowance (ESA)	Sickness and disability benefit that lets claimants work a certain number of hours a week.
Good Lives Matter (GLM)	A model of rehabilitation proposed by Tony Ward and others at the beginning of the twenty-first century.
HMP	'Her Majesty's Prison' in the name of an institution, as in HMP Wandsworth.
HMPS	Her Majesty's Prison Service, the arm of HMPPS that runs state sector prisons in England and Wales.
Her Majesty's Prison and Probation Service (HMPPS)	(This replaces the National Offender Management Service – NOMS.) The body set up by the government to coordinate the work of prisons and probation.
HMRC	Her Majesty's Revenue and Customs. The government agency that administers taxation within the UK.

Incentives and Earned Privileges (IEP)	A system of sanctions and rewards used for behavioural support in prisons with three levels: Basic, Standard and Enhanced.
Integrated Offender Manager (IOM)	A department of the police responsible for managing the sentences and reducing the reoffending of certain prolific offenders.
Intervention	An action taken to counteract the effects of an illness or detrimental lifestyle.
Indeterminate Sentence for Public Protection (IPP Sentence)	Indeterminate sentence for Public Protection (until November 2012, now partially replaced by EDS). A version of a life sentence given to repeat serious offenders.
Licence	The period of supervision after a prisoner is released.
Life Sentence	An indeterminate prison sentence imposed for murder and certain other serious offences. It consists of the minimum term or tariff that the prisoner will serve before being considered for release. Any release will be on a licence that lasts for life, during which the offender can be recalled.
Mission (statement)	The practical outworking of your vision statement; what activities you will undertake to fulfil your vision.
Multi-Agency Public Protection Arrangements (MAPPA)	Serious violent or sex offenders are subject to MAPPA restrictions as well as their normal licence conditions. These will restrict where they can go and who they can meet, and will be reviewed from time to time.
National Probation Service (NPS)	New configuration of the probation service as of mid-2015 with responsibility for supervising higher-risk and long-sentence prisoners in the community after release.
National Offender Management Service (NOMS)	The organisation founded in 2004 to coordinate the work of the prison and probation services, superseded in 2017 by HMPPS.
New psychoactive substances (NPS)	Synthetic cannabinoids, formerly known as 'legal highs', such as 'mamba' and 'spice'.

Open prison	A Cat D prison where some offenders are able to leave the establishment to work or visit outside.
Opiate	A drug with a narcotic effect similar to opium, such as heroin. This includes the codeine in popular medicines such as co-codamol.
Parole Board	Committee of experts and lay members who decide whether a prisoner is ready for release.
Pathways	The nine areas of criminogenic needs identified by the National Offender Management Service (NOMS).
Payment by Results (PbR)	A controversial funding method where private and charitable sector agencies are paid according to a measure of the efficacy of their work.
PF	Prison Fellowship. An international Christian charity that coordinates prayer for prisoners and their families and the work of volunteers within many prisons.
Post Sentence Supervision (PSS)	Under the new probation arrangements, offenders leaving prison on sentences of less than twenty-four months will complete Post Sentence Supervision for up to a year after release.
Public Protection Unit (PPU)	The police unit within MAPPA that ensures offenders are managed safely.
RNR model	The Risk, Need and Response model of managing offending behaviour based on detailed ongoing risk assessments.
Recall	An offender on licence can be recalled to prison if they are suspected of involvement in a crime.
Rehabilitation	The process of restoring someone to health or normal life through training and therapy after imprisonment or addiction.
Resettlement	The wider process of reintegrating former prisoners into normal life.
Resilience	Psychological resilience is the ability of an individual to cope with adverse conditions without suffering trauma.
Restricted status	The women's equivalent of a Cat A prisoner.

Risk	1. Risk of harm to self or others. 2. Risk of reoffending. These are usually calculated by considering a number of risk factors, some of which are unchanging (static risk factors) and some of which can be changed by changing the person's circumstances (dynamic or clinical risk factors). See *Criminogenic needs*.
Release on Temporary Licence (RoTL)	Prisoners nearing release are allowed out for limited periods to work, etc.
Serotonin	A neurotransmitter involved in the transmission of nerve impulses, key to mood regulation; pain perception; gastrointestinal function, including perception of hunger and satiety; and other physical functions.
SIBs	Social Impact Bonds. Part of a model of Payment by Results pioneered in Peterborough by St Giles Trust.
Strands	The model for monitoring performance within Walk.
Tariff	The minimum term served by an indeterminate sentence prisoner.
Transforming Rehabilitation (TR)	The government's new programme to change the way prisoners are handled on their release, involving changes to the probation service and the supervision arrangements for ex-offenders.
Universal Credit (UC)	A new benefit system designed to replace several existing benefits, including ESA and Jobseeker's Allowance (JSA).
Vision (statement)	The statement of an organisation's core beliefs and purpose.
Vulnerable Prisoner (VP)	A prisoner who is accommodated on a specialist VP wing for their own safety. They might be sex-offenders, police informers or have some other distinct vulnerability, or they might be in debt to other prisoners.

| Whole-life tariff | A life sentence with no parole. |
| Young Offender Institution (YOI) | Prison for male inmates aged eighteen to twenty-two. |